Essential Retro

The vintage technology guide

Sputnik
Books

ESSENTIAL RETRO: The vintage technology guide

 For information write to Sputnik Books, P.O. Box 69010, Calgary, Alberta, Canada T2Y 4T9.

http://www.essentialretro.com

2nd Sputnik Books ed.
ISBN 0-9736838-1-3

Printed and bound in the USA and UK at Lightning Source, a Division of Ingram Industries Inc.

To Gita & Paul,
who suffered with great dignity
through countless boring tales of old gadgetry
and are my daily reminders
of all that is good in this world.

Any sufficiently advanced technology
is indistinguishable from magic.

Arthur C. Clarke

Contents

Treasures From a Golden Age

We live in an age of wonder. Each new year welcomes thousands of innovative devices that are smaller, faster and more beautiful than anything before. It is easy to get caught up in an endless quest for the ultimate new gadget, but don't forget that many brilliant old machines are hidden away in attics and garages throughout the world – forgotten movie cameras lie on dusty shelves beside obsolete computers and classic mechanical toys, all crying out to be rediscovered and brought back to life.

That's what this book is about – rediscovery. It's not a catalogue for collectors or a price guide for eBay sellers. The goal is to introduce you to as many vintage (or classically styled) gadgets as I can sanely cram into a couple of hundred pages. Treat this as an opportunity to revive the styles and technology of bygone eras, and to discover an earlier age of elegant mechanics and hand-drawn design.

It's hard to tell which of today's gizmos will become the design icons of our era, but it's easy to pick out beautiful and definitive devices from the past. And – best of all – yesterday's technology often sells for an infinitesimal fraction of what it cost new. So, rather than spending $1000 on a brand new camcorder, risk $50 on a mint-condition Super 8 camera. Or invest in a vacuum tube amplifier instead of the latest digital surround-sound wonder box with its baffling remote control. Your digital watch has stopped running? Go mechanical and you'll never worry about dead batteries again.

We take the breathtaking pace of technological change almost for granted. Just don't forget that most new equipment supplants something from an older generation – a new Xbox 360 videogame console might replace a classic Super Nintendo Entertainment System, and so on. Eventually, older machines find their way to garage sales and flea markets, where they often sell for a handful of spare change.

I've tried to list sources for the gear I mention, but many old items – like the beautiful wooden Gfeller Trub telephone and Audio Technica's brilliant Sound Burger portable record player – are almost impossible to find at sane prices. The Internet is partially to blame, since interesting old devices often gain cult status on forums and Blogs. And, once a gadget becomes widely known, it frequently becomes the focus of aggressive bidding on auction sites like eBay. The solution is to get your hands on machines that make you wonder why no one has discovered them yet. Rest assured that the masses will follow.

One book can't possibly cover every must-have piece of technology from the past few decades. You'll quickly discover that each chapter of *Essential Retro* provides only the mere tip of an iceberg. Rather than mindlessly cataloguing everything, I picked and chose things that caught my eye and imagination. Hopefully, some of these wonderful machines will capture your heart like they did mine, and you'll find yourself collecting and using magnificent contraptions from years past.

Many well-made mechanical devices are reliable and simple enough that anyone can maintain and repair them.

Mechanical Retro Things

Categorizing retro gadgetry is often a challenge, especially when looking at the world of mechanical devices. I've lumped some of my favorite mechanical and electro-mechanical gadgets into this chapter. In the next few pages you'll discover an esoteric mix of typewriters, aircraft, writing instruments, steam engines, time-pieces and bicycles.

The great thing about well-made mechanical things is that they're often reliable, tend to age well, and most are simple enough that a mechanically inclined person can repair them without having to call in expensive help. Unfortunately, many old devices have made their way to the scrap heap after years of faithful service. You rarely see a mechanical adding machine or cash register these days, for example, although they were once everywhere.

A close-up of a typical Russian Poljot chronograph. The mechanical movement is based upon classic Swiss designs.

Timepieces

Watches and clocks are beautiful machines. A good mechanical watch can last a lifetime if well cared for. Many of the world's best timepieces come from Switzerland, but remember that even a lowly $50 Casio G-Shock quartz digital keeps almost perfect time and should last a decade or more.

My advice? Keep it cheap. It's easy to find stylish and reliable vintage timepieces for less than $200. It's even possible to find brand new mechanical watches with jewelled mechanisms at decent prices. And it should come as no surprise that several Russian companies make decent mechanicals based on classic Swiss designs, although quality can vary considerably between production runs (and even between examples from the same batch).

Digital watches are a dime a dozen these days. Drop by a low-end department store and you'll find dozens of choices for less than $20. But don't forget that 30 years ago digital displays were new and exciting. People marvelled at tiny little LED digits. There's been a recent resurgence of affordable LED watches, probably driven by a realization that they can now be produced for next to nothing. I suspect this trend will soon flow into low-end department stores as well, so don't bother spending $100. Wait a few months and you might be able to pick up a new retro-style LED watch for a third of that.

Mechanical Watches

Poljot: The First Moscow Watch Factory

I often take a wrong turn on the web and find myself browsing items I'll never be able to afford. More often than not, this involves Swiss timepieces. Since I don't have thousands to blow on a 1964 Tag Heuer Carrera automatic, I'm forced to consider more reasonable wristwatches. You know, the kind with rubber straps.

The Poljot 31679 movement is accurate to about +/- 10 seconds per day and incorporates 23 jewels.

Poljot was founded in the 1930s as the First Moscow Watch Factory. Poljot means *flight* in Russian, and their timepieces were standard issue for Soviet pilots. Yuriy Gagarin wore a Poljot *Shturmanskie* (Navigator) watch on the first flight into space.

Poljot still offers a plethora of affordable mechanical timepieces, all made in Russia. They feature 17 to 31 jewel mechanisms in hefty metal cases, with steel or leather straps. The simple Poljot Aviator retails for $117 – a real bargain. Be warned that Poljot markets an ever-changing lineup of slightly more expensive chronographs and automatics. These are based upon a handful of mechanisms with varied case designs. Remember that there's not really any point in paying extra for a fancy case – what's inside is what counts – literally. [Visit the factory site at www.poljot.ru/en-index.html]

Vostok timepieces

The Vostok factory started making timepieces for the Red Army in the early 1940s. The factory got its start when one of Moscow's watch-making plants was evacuated to Chistopol in central Russia during WWII. In the mid-1960s, the factory became the official supplier of timepieces to the Soviet Department of Defence and began manufacturing their famed *Komandirskie* (Commander's) series.

The Vostok Kirovskie is a simple traditional design with a 31-jewel mechanical movement.

Vostoks tend to be simple and affordable, starting at under $50. For that price you get a serviceable 31-jewel wind-up mechanism that runs about 31 hours between winds. My favorite Vostoks are the replica *Kirovskie* models, based on Vostok's first design. They cost about $70 and have a stark elegance that suits everyday use. See www.rugift.com for dozens of Vostoks.

Watchismo: Vintage horology on the web

I stumbled upon the Watchismo site a few months ago. It's a fantastic place full of unusual vintage watches from the 1950s, 1960s, and 1970s. Many of the exotic collector's items are stratospherically priced, but there is a section of interesting under-$200 timepieces (including the fantastic $155 Pronto Sport GS) for mere mortals. [www.watchismo.com]

Spring Drive watches include over 80% of the components found in traditional mechanical designs.

Seiko Spring Drive: A revolutionary mechanical watch

The Seiko Spring Drive mechanism was initially developed in 1977, although it wasn't commercialized until 1999. The final result is a beautiful electromechanical wristwatch with a 72-hour reserve. The watch doesn't include a traditional escapement (oscillating mechanism), so the hands move with an eerily smooth motion. It's also incredibly accurate, designed to be an order of magnitude more precise than traditional mechanical designs.

The Spring Drive features a clever power reserve indicator on the face, so you always know how much energy remains. In case you get the urge to show off to your friends, each Spring Drive includes a see-through case back.

A manual-wind version of this 'everlasting' watch was introduced in 1999, but it took another six years and three prototypes to perfect the self-winding automatic mechanism. All this technology carries a price, however. Spring Drive assembly is performed by a team of five expert watchmakers, limiting production to about

1000 units in the first year. Expect to part with around $3500 for one of these hand-made works of art.

Pocket Watches

Stonehenge pocket watch: Druids only

When one of my co-workers left to live the life of a nomad, we sent him on his way with an engraved pocket watch. It was the perfect gift since he never wears a watch but always asks the time.

The Stonehenge watch opens to reveal a scale model of Stonehenge and includes a traditional watch face on the rear.

If a traditional pocket watch seems a tad stodgy for your New Age sensibilities, try the Stonehenge Pocket Watch. Pop this little artifact open and you're greeted by an exact scale replica of Stonehenge. The case includes a handy compass to help modern druid trainees align themselves properly with the sun.

For those (like me) who spend most of their time indoors, the watch includes a handy-dandy traditional analog clock face on the reverse side of the case. With a bit of practice, you'll be able to estimate the time fairly accurately and predicting the exact moment of the summer solstice will be a snap.

Stonehenge Pocket Watch ($42.95 from Sharpe Products, Inc. – www.stonehengewatch.com)

Wenger: Stylish Swiss pocket watches

Mention pocket watches and most people envision something out of the Victorian era – ornate and fragile. Modern pocket watches are anything but.

Wenger's Standard Issue pocket watch is accurate to 1/10 second per day and includes a handy calfskin leather lanyard.

If you prefer not to wear a wristwatch or you want to try something different, take a peek at Wenger's lineup. Their Swiss-made quartz movements are accurate to 1/10 second per day and include an alarm and date display. My favorite feature is the funky lanyard with quick-release clip. Oh, they're also water-resistant to about 100 ft. (30 m) in case you're overcome by the sudden urge to go diving fully clothed. Street price is around $150.

See the Wenger 73000 pocket watch at www.wengerwatch.com

LED & LCD WATCHES

LED calculator watches

A good example of a modern Retro LED watch. $85 from thinkgeek.com.

LED watches seem to be all the rage recently, with a sudden flood available in the sub-$100 range. Let's take a quick look at another market segment that died a quick death in the mid 1970s. Pulsar was first out of the gate with an LED calculator watch in 1975, followed in 1976 by models from Compuchron, Uranus, and even HP.

The strangest of all was the 1977 Wrist Calculator from Sinclair – it didn't include a built-in watch. Apparently, you were supposed to lug it around on your wrist while searching for people in need of emergency arithmetic.

Like their watch-only brothers, these little counting machines chewed through batteries so quickly that the display could remain on for only a few seconds at a time. The Compuchron's boxy metal housing hides four largish button cell batteries that provide the electrons for its careful pondering.

Lets hope some enterprising Chinese firm isn't gearing up to churn out remakes of these – it was bad enough the first time. They're occasionally available on the second-hand market as "new old stock" – the technology developed so quickly that many units were left unsold.

Affordable Casio LCD watches

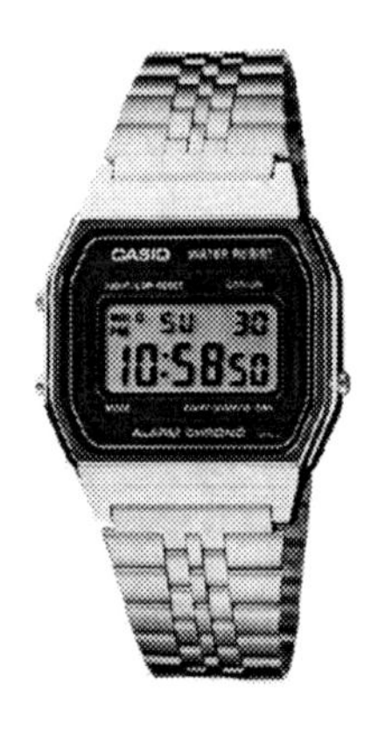

Casio still offers a remarkably affordable line of Casual Classic watches that includes more than a little 1980s style.

Once upon a time, watches were big clunky things that ticked. Most required daily attention or they'd grind to an awkward mechanical halt. Things changed forever with the arrival of mysterious and expensive digital watches in the early 1970s. These nifty gadgets had miniscule red LED displays that required you to poke a little button before offering up the time.

The digital watch became a runaway phenomenon in the early 1980s with the emergence of affordable LCD displays that always showed you the time, whether you wanted to see it or not. I was stunned to discover that Casio offers a Casual Classic line of watches harkening back to the angular days of the early 1980s. Most are pretty basic – simple retro silver or black, without fancy Sport doodads or complicated extras. You get the time, a calendar, maybe an alarm, and a little light for reading the display in dark caves or cupboards. Prices start at an almost silly $7.95.

Outstanding Clocks

CHRONOTRONIX IN-18 nixie clock

The $499 IN-18 looks like a chromed tissue box with nixie tubes poking out from the top. For the uninitiated, nixies are neon-filled glass tubes. They usually contain ten cathodes in the shape of the numbers 0 through 9, and a wire mesh anode. When electricity is passed between one of the cathodes and the anode, the corresponding number shines with an odd orangey-red glow.

A close-up look at the Nixie tubes on the Chronotronix IN-18 clock. Sadly, the tubes don't meet new European manufacturing standards and can't be sold in Europe.

Sorry. Enough technical mumbo-jumbo for today. The site's product descriptions are worth browsing because they're ever-so-slightly strange:

"The surface is very shiny and reflects the orange glow of the Nixie tubes -you won't be able to take your eyes off it. We will send a pair of cotton gloves along with your CHRONOTRONIX IN-18 NIXIE CLOCK in order to avoid leaving fingerprints on the case. Please wear them whenever you touch your Nixie clock."

Umm, OK.

The sales blurb proudly declares the clock accurate to around 0.0003 seconds per minute, which sounds incredibly good – until you realize it equates to about 12.96 seconds per month. Ahh, the wonder of marketing-speak. [www.nixieclock.net]

The Wil van den Bos flip clock shows off a plethora of exposed gears. It's available for $84.95 from www.shiptheweb.com

Wil van den Bos flip clocks

Mechanical things are fun because you get to muck around with cogs and springs and things. Usually this ends with a screamed obscenity and a few drops of blood. Through years of careful experimentation, I've discovered that clocks are relatively safe things to play with. They don't move unpredictably, and they tend not to spontaneously combust.

The Gear Flip Alarm Clock by Wil van den Bos of the Netherlands is a brilliant example of clever design and wicked engineering. Best of all, the numbers flip with a satisfying SNIK sound, just to remind you it needs mucking with. [www.littleclockshop.com]

The Kikkerland Capsule brings back memories of the Atomic Age.

Not quite your style? Try the aluminum and plastic Kikkerland Capsule. Just don't try to swallow it. It's backlit by blue LEDs, which are really annoying in a dark room. Really. [www.kikkerland.com]

If your tastes are a little more... umm... unusual, then perhaps you should consider Yoshitoma Nara's line of illustrated flip clocks. Known for animé-inspired sculpture and an intriguing fusion of art and technology, his work is "high fashion" Japanese art at its best. Not for children because of hard-to-explain grown up doodles. [awww.littleclockshop.com]

Inexpensive Timex flip clocks

Wouldn't you know it? Timex offers wonderfully affordable flip clocks. The Timex Corporation was founded in 1854 as Waterbury Clock in Connecticut. They began marketing affordable Waterbury pocket watches in the 1880s (complete with an amazingly long 9 foot hand-wound mainspring). By the early 1900s they were marketing the world's first $1 watch, the Yankee. Over 40 million were sold.

The Timex Flip Clock has a certain vintage air about it. It's also incredibly affordable ($34.95 list).

The company started manufacturing wristwatches in response to military requirements in WWI and introduced the first Mickey Mouse watches and clocks in 1933. They became the U.S. Time Company in the 1940s, and released the first Timex watch in 1950, becoming known for the slogan "It takes a licking but it keeps on ticking." (Hmm. In this case, it should be "Takes a licking but it keeps on flipping." Hyuck.)

The global watch industry was shaken by heavy competition from Asian manufacturers in the 1970s, along with the introduction of cheap digital quartz timepieces. Timex survived and continues to make hundreds of different quartz digital timepieces.

The $34.95 Timex Retro Flip Clock runs on one D-cell battery and features a quartz electronic movement. It's perfect for the office or living room – anywhere an easy-to-read conversation starter is needed. [www.timex.com]

Classic Mechanical Things

A typical manual typewriter. Note the the quirky open keyboard design.

Typewriters

Much like the creation of the incandescent light bulb, no one person can lay claim to the typewriter. There were many attempts at creating mechanical writing machines in the mid 19th Century. At first, designers built machines with 'index keyboards' – rotary dials that were used to select letters. This technique was simple but slow.

By the end of the 19th century, designers had hammered out the basic design of what we now call the 'manual typewriter' – each letter had its own key, and there was usually a large carriage return lever to advance to the next line (along with a bell to warn typists that they were reaching the end of the current one).

The biggest design challenge was ensuring that the type bars didn't collide with each other. This was eventually solved by introducing the QWERTY keyboard layout that is still in use on millions of modern computer keyboards. A popular myth is that the QWERTY key layout was designed to slow down typists, but a more likely explanation is that it was designed to reduce the frequency of type bars colliding and jamming.

The biggest challenge when using a typewriter is error-correction – making a mistake requires time-consuming manual alteration. By the late 1970s, many electric typewriters offered electronic type-ahead buffers and built-in error correction tapes to speed the correction process. Sadly, this wasn't enough to fend off the invasion of efficient computer-based word processors such as *WordStar* and *Word Perfect* in the early 1980s. These days, electric typewriters are rare in business environments – but they show up occasionally in shipping departments that require multiple carbon copies of documents.

Olivetti and Olympia were the last two major companies to produce all-manual typewriters, but they discontinued manufacture over the winter of 2004-2005. Several Chinese companies still produce cheap manuals, though of dubious quality.

You can usually pick up an affordable late-model manual for a reasonable price on eBay or at local flea markets. Be prepared to order replacement ribbons by mail order because they're impossible to find in the aisle of big-box retailers. Is it worth the trouble? You bet. Few things make an impression like a genuine typewritten letter – the color, spacing, and texture of type is unmistakable.

1928 Corona No. 4

Nothing beats the old-world charm of a restored vintage typewriter, like this $395 Corona from mytypewriter.com.

Back in the day, our grandparents had to bang letters onto paper one-by-one. It took ages and was wickedly error-prone. These days, young whippersnappers are more likely to text or e-mail. I'd always planned to pick up a manual typewriter so I could write The Great Suburban Novel or whip off the occasional pompous "Letter to the Editor" by candlelight during a power outage. Regrettably, both Olivetti and Olympia discontinued their manual typewriter lines late in 2004.

All is not lost. MyTypewriter.com offers a surprisingly broad array of vintage typewriters and ribbons. This one is a restored 1928 Corona No. 4 portable, also available in maroon, green, red and basic black. It's yours for $395 plus about thirty clams for a spare ribbon. Don't forget to pick up a dicshunary, since spel-correcsion is also manual.

Brother 'Webster' typewriter

The Brother Webster manual typewriter was built for the Webster dictionary company in the 1970s. It's built like a little tank – steel case and top-quality Japanese construction. The design offers an interchangeable special key to enable you to type various foreign squiggles or umlauts (replacement keys not included).

This is a new old-stock Brother Webster typewriter from www.sovietski.com. And, yes, replacement ribbons are still available.

Treat this as an opportunity to drive your significant other completely mad as you bang out copies of The Tinfoil Hat Gazette at the kitchen table. Just remember: The CIA knew Kennedy was an alien.

As of late 2005, Siegler & Co. had a few new-old-stock units for $199. Includes zippered leatherette carrying case, instructions and original factory test page. Unless you stumble upon an old stationary supply store liquidation sale, this may be your last chance to purchase a new manual typewriter. [www.sovietski.com]

Rotring - German precision writing instruments

Rotring was founded by Wilhelm Riepe in 1928. The Hamburg-based company initially made stylographs, but eventually became famous for their impeccable technical drawing pens and pencils. In case you're wondering, Rotring translates literally to 'red ring' – the trademark flash of color that sets these writing implements apart from others.

The Rotring Newton series is available in chrome-plated brass with matte black or matte silver finish.

The Newton lineup is available as a fountain pen, roller ball, ballpoint, or (recently discontinued) 0.5 pencil. Sadly, it is the pencil I covet most. For some odd reason, it tamed my meandering scrawl into something legible, artistic and organized. No mean feat. Priced from $30 to around $100. Your Moleskine notebook will thank you (see below). [www.rotring.de]

Moleskine notebooks

Before there were shiny battery-consuming handheld computers and PDAs, there were Moleskine notebooks. Van Gogh, Hemmingway, and various other dead people used one. And you can, too. They're available in sizes from pocket (3.5" x 5.5") through really large (7.5" x 10"). Perfect for hit lists, diaries, day planners, and obscene doodling. Prices start at under $10. Batteries not included or needed. [www.moleskine.com]

The Volta combines classic styling with a modern 250 Watt electric hub motor on the rear wheel.

Bicycles & Tricycles

Electric bicycles – The Mikado Volta

I am a sucker for electric vehicles. I have an especially soft spot in my skull for retro-styled electric transport. Like the Mikado Volta, for example.

The Volta is a classically styled electrically assisted bike. At first glance, it looks like something you borrowed from your grandfather because someone swiped your main wheels. A second glance reveals the 250 Watt electric hub motor on the rear wheel and the slim battery pack adorning the frame. It also offers a traditional 7-speed shifting mechanism and Shimano derailleur mechanism. The power assist will help you travel up to 45 km per charge (a good thing, since the frame is steel and might be a tad on the heavy side).

Oh, and it's the only electric bike I know of that hails from Canada. List price is CAD $1799 (roughly sixteen beaver pelts and a box of Tim Horton's donuts). [www.mikadobicycles.ca]

Tricked out tricycles

There's a slightly crazy-looking old lady who rides around my neighborhood on an elderly tricycle with an enormous wire mesh basket hanging from the back. I've never seen anything in the basket, and I've always been too scared of getting run over to ask what it's for. Why am I telling this tale? To point out that tricycles are not – usually – hip and happening transportation.

The Aerorider might make me change my mind. At first glance it appears that a tricycle, a raindrop, and a fighter plane got muddled up in a matter transporter – like Jeff Goldblum's experiences in *The Fly*, except with a happy ending. This little machine is electrically assisted: you pedal and the Aerorider's 600 W electric motor helps out. It has a respectable maximum speed of 45 km/h and a useful range of between 25 to 50 km, depending on local terrain.

The Aerorider seems like a great way to commute, as long as you don't have to contend with traffic.

Aerorider can be registered as a moped in many countries. In fact, the factory can easily limit the motor's output so it can pass as a motorized bicycle in the USA. It's biggest flaw? Unlike the similar-looking Twike, there's room for only one under the hinged canopy. Unless you're really good friends.

Steam & Stirling Engines

Boehm Stirling engine kits

Combining fire and pressurized steam is a recipe for disaster. In an attempt to make things a tad safer, Robert Stirling created the first steamless Stirling engine in 1816. By repeatedly heating and cooling gas inside a sealed chamber, he was able to avoid the nasty explosions and scaldings that were the bane of steam engine technology. While quite popular in the 19th Century, Stirlings were no match for the wave of new-fangled electric motors that appeared a few decades later.

www.ministeam.com offers a range of Boehm Stirling engine kits in North America.

These days, several manufacturers make Stirling toys – like the $340 Boehm HB12-AS2. It's elegantly crafted from stainless steel and aluminum, with dual machined brass cylinders. Boehm also makes several more affordable kit versions, starting around $200. These things run at 2,000 to 2,500 RPM – perfect for hooking up to the hamster wheel to give Hammy the ride of his life. [www.stirling-technik.de]

Mamod steam vehicles

Steam engines are magical. They're also increasingly rare. That's part of what makes Mamod steam toys so much fun. Their vehicles are completely piston driven; no batteries or wall transformers here. To ensure that things stay fun they burn easy-to-use solid fuel tablets and have safety valves to control boiler pressure.

Mamod's $450 William locomotive is currently the only train engine in their collection. I hope they produce more.

Oh – they also have working steam whistles that just beg to be pulled.

This engine is the £250 ($450) *William* locomotive. It's the only train in the Mamod collection; their other steam vehicles are cars, traction engines, buses, fire engines, and a steam roller. Mamod has been manufacturing toys for over fifty years and it shows: these vehicles are almost 100% metal and should last a lifetime. My Mamod steam roller is over twenty years old and still looks almost new. [www.mamod.co.uk]

The 1/32 scale Aster NKP 779 is sold in the USA by www.asterhobbyusa.com. These are the ultimate recreations.

Aster Hobby 1/32 scale steam engines

Aster Hobby in Japan makes incredible steam trains. The most stunning is their 1/32 scale NKP Berkshire, released in mid-October 2005.

Aster announced: "The NKP 779 will be produced in a limited quantity of 250 units for world wide distribution. It features alcohol firing, equalized main suspension, equalized tender truck suspension, working cylinder drain cocks, blow down valve, tender and axle pump, sufficient cab / tender space for RC servo installation etc. The locomotive and tender weigh in at 27 lbs dry and measures 40 inches over couplers."

779 is a meticulous scale reproduction of one of ten Berkshire 2-8-4 locomotives delivered to the Nickle Plate Road (Chicago - St. Louis) in May, 1949. There's no mention of price, although I would expect it to be in "small used car" territory. Don't forget to put aside a few thousand extra for rails, scale buildings, vehicles and other must-haves. [www.asterhobby.com]

Reproduction Dog Lock Pistols

This 'ere is a $289 reproduction of an early dog lock pistol, popular during the English Civil War. On second thought, they probably weren't that popular with the folks standing at the wrong end.

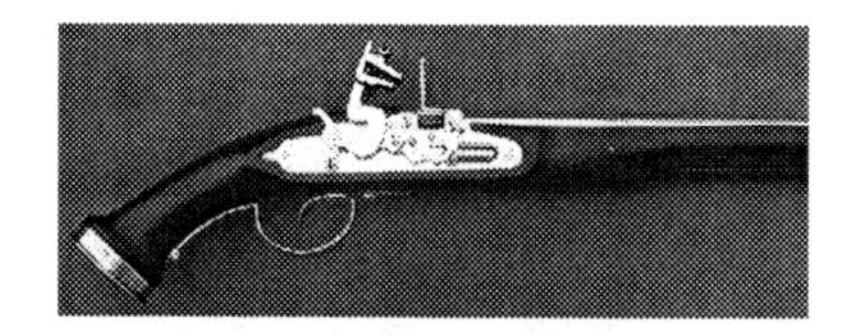

A Canadian-made reproduction of an English Civil War cavalry pistol. See www.militaryheritage.com for this and dozens like it.

I'll let Robert Henderson of The Discriminating General describe his handiwork: "With it's 16-inch, octagon-to-round barrel, this pistol must have been challenge to wield in the melee of battle. As with all of our flintlocks, this replica is made faithful to those of the period with tempered seamless modern steel with a threaded breech plug. The lock is made with strong durable springs and has a case-hardened frizzen (hammer) that throws good sparks. We use a cyanide case-hardening factory process that makes sparking both more reliable and longer lasting. Presently no other musket provider uses this technique."

In real life, Henderson serves as a consultant for the National Archives of Canada and numerous Parks Canada military sites. His replicas are historically accurate and can be altered to a firing state by a certified gunsmith. As with most items of this nature, don't point them at people, don't sneak them onto aircraft, and try not to spill black powder and shot all over the living room floor. [www.militaryheritage.com]

UPM Energy Meter:
Not mechanical, but neat

The UPM EM100 is an unassuming little energy meter (I was going to call it a 'black box,' but it's white) that plugs into a standard household outlet. Once installed, it quietly tracks the amount of energy used (in kWh), accumulated operation time, and other useful stats. Information is displayed on a rather slick LCD display.

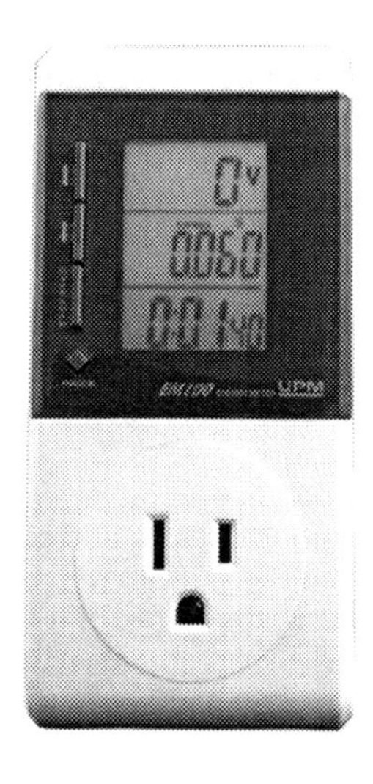

The UPM Energy Meter is a great way to find out just how much electricity your gadgets are munching on while lurking in "standby" mode.

The best thing? It costs a mere $25. A friend picked his up at a Canadian Tire superstore, but the UPM site hints it's available all over the place. Here's your chance to find out just how much power your ancient RCA TV gobbles. Finally, you'll have hard numbers to show how much you'll 'save' by replacing that clunky old 19" wood grain TV with a shiny LCD panel. Just don't blame me when the credit card bill arrives. [tinyurl.com/d77qg]

Flying Things

An Aero Vodochody L-39 Albatros two-seat jet trainer. Air Force experience is recommended.

Retro Aircraft

I can't resist writing about expensive toys, especially aircraft. Here are a few drool-worthy ex-military and reproduction planes to get your blood pumping. While some aircraft – like the L-39 jet – are the domain of the super-rich, others can be built for well under $50,000. That puts them within reach of dedicated aviation fanatics.

You'll quickly discover that factory-built aircraft are extremely expensive. To get the most for your money, take a look at the dozens of top-notch kit planes available today. Some are traditional tube-and-fabric tail draggers, while others feature rock-solid aluminum or ultra-modern carbon fibre construction.

If the kit plane bug bites you, I suggest joining the Experimental Aircraft Association (www.eaa.org). They offer high quality publications and technical resources for experimental builders. They also sponsor excellent fly-ins throughout the year. Fly-ins offer the opportunity to check out manufacturers up-close. You'll quickly discover who the dominant players are and advice from actual builders is priceless. I also recommend Kitplanes (www.kitplanes.com), an excellent monthly magazine.

L-39 and other ex-Soviet jets

Kids love toy planes. A few kids are lucky enough to buy the real thing when they grow up. That usually means a clunky used Cessna 172 or an old Piper Arrow. In recent years, wealthy enthusiasts have taken to importing and restoring old Soviet Block aircraft.

I am especially taken with the Aero Vodochody L-39 "Albatros," built in the Czech Republic as a two seat jet trainer. Over 2,800 were built following its 1972 introduction. Two hundred of them are now in private hands. It's powered by a single Ivchenko AI-25-TL turbofan engine and is capable of hitting a maximum speed of 485 mph (780 km/h). Ceiling altitude is 37,730 ft, so you'll have lots of sky to play in.

Jet Warbird Training Center [www.jetwarbird.com] offers 35 minute introductory flights in the L-39 for $1200. Flight training runs about $1950 per hour, including aircraft, instructor, and jet fuel. Expect to pay around $300,000 for a ready-to-fly late 1980s version.

Shopping for ex-military aircraft: Global Plane Search

The Internet can be a great place to get lost. Case in point: I stumbled across Global Plane Search yesterday. They list thousands of aircraft for sale, but the best part of the site is their ex-military section. [www.globalplanesearch.com]

Always wanted a restored WWII P-51 Mustang? One can be yours for a mere $1.5M. While you're shopping, don't forget to pick up a Mitsubishi Zero for dogfighting. It's only $695,000 but needs a little TLC. After something with a bit more kick? Some dude in Romania is selling a MiG 29 with a mere 717 hours on it. Better brush up on your Russian! And... If you need to do some heavy lifting, don't miss out on a pair of Lockheed C-130A Hercules.

A North American P-51 Mustang like this can be yours for a mere million and a half (flight training not included).

This is a photo of a real Supermarine Spitfire, not a reproduction. There are very few flying Spits left.

Supermarine Spitfire Mk26

If you happen to have AU $118,250 burning a hole in your IPO-enhanced wallet, here's the perfect way to while away your leisure time. Supermarine Aircraft has been producing Spitfire kits for about a decade. Unlike the original incredibly difficult to build wood and fabric versions, this recreation is fabricated from durable aluminum. It has a respectable 193 knot (222 mph) top speed, and a range of approximately three hours – enough to mount a quick early morning sortie to a neighboring city.

Most of the really hard work has already been done for you, but you'll have to put in about 700 hours of fiddly effort to turn your kit into a lean, mean playing machine. The final product will be an 80% scale easy-to-fly reminder of the original. Expect to spend a couple of hundred hours learning the ropes in more docile aircraft before hopping into your new toy. [www.supermarineaircraft.com]

Mifyter biplane

A brilliant way to relive the excitement of open air flying without the risk of getting shot.

I like to think I'd make a great fighter pilot, although the truth is I'd probably pee myself at the first sight of enemy aircraft. But that doesn't stop me from wanting my very own fighter plane.

While I'm at it, I might as well want the most ridiculous fighting machine I can find. Like this Mifyter kit plane, an original design that's loosely based on a WWI Fokker biplane. It's powered by a 64 HP Rotax engine, features a leisurely top speed of 95 mph, and weighs a mere 450 lbs empty. A "standard" kit costs $14,995 but doesn't include the engine, prop, instruments, wooden instrument applique, paint, upholstered seat cushion, static bomb or guns. I wonder where one buys guns and bombs for WWI biplanes these days, anyway? [www.biplanesofyesteryear.com]

RAF 2000 gyroplane

Canadian gyroplane manufacturer Rotary Air Force has just rolled out a new web site for their classic flying machines. They've been in business since 1987, and their RAF 2000 is touted as the world's most advanced gyroplane. It's powered by a 2.2 L or 2.5 L Subaru automotive engine and cruises around 70-90 mph (112 - 144 km/h). It's capable of landing in under 10 ft (3 m), as well.

Gyroplanes (or gyrocopters or autogyros) were invented in 1923 by Spanish aviator Juan de la Cierva. Propulsion comes from the small propeller sitting behind the pilots. They can take off and land in significantly less space than conventional aircraft and – despite the unconventional looks – have a reputation for being extremely safe. The RAF 2000 is available as a kit, starting at US $24,900. [www.rotaryairforce.com]

Fisher Flying Products Tiger Moth replica

Fisher Flying Products is – as far as I know – the only aircraft manufacturer in North Dakota. They market no less than fifteen aircraft designs. My favorite is the Tiger Moth, based on the classic WWII wood and fabric trainer. It's available with either a wood or steel tube fuselage.

The Tiger Moth was once the standard primary trainer for Commonwealth air force pilots. This one is a full-scale original.

Kit prices start at $12,950 for an airframe kit ($19,000 for steel tube). They estimate that an average builder can build a complete aircraft in about 700 hours. Once you're done, you'll have an easy-to-fly biplane that cruises at about 90 mph (145 km/h) and has a ceiling altitude of 10,000 feet (3000 m).

You can install a variety of engines including Rotax, Jabiru, and even – if you dare – a Geo Metro 3-banger. Just make sure you have an emergency landing field picked out. [www.fisherflying.com]

Automobiles

Top 25 Retro Cars

I wrote up a list of my favorite retro cars for *retrothing.com* a while back. This is an updated version of the original, with a few more must-have vehicles added for good measure. I restricted my choices to fairly common and affordable vehicles – don't expect to come across an Aston Martin DB5, 1962 Corvette convertible or Jaguar E-Type here.

One thing many of these vehicles share is simplicity, although several were technically flawed or suffered from massive variations in quality. Ranking these retrocars is almost impossible, so they're listed by date of release.

The Deux Cheveux was so named because it was powered by a tiny 2 cylinder engine.

Citroen 2CV6 (1948)

If you like insects, you'll probably love the 2CV6. Despite its prehistoric styling, it was famed as the Citroen that seemed destined to live forever. The original 2CV appeared in 1948 and remained on the market in various forms until 1991. Its main claim to fame was the hideously designed roll-back roof. Apart from that, you received a 602 cc engine that output a whopping 28 bhp. It puttered along with so much retro charisma that people didn't seem to mind its turtlish ways. Over 5,100,000 of these weird and wonderful creatures were produced.

The Rugged simplicity of a Land Rover. This is what all SUVs should be like.

Land Rover (1948)

The Land Rover was one of the first true SUVs. It was introduced in 1948, decades before the term was coined. By 1976 over one million of these workhorse machines had been produced. My family owned a Series II model for a short while in England's Lake District and I distinctly remember its utilitarian construction and lack of a viable heater. I wish today's manufacturers would revisit the utilitarian designs of the 1960s – off-road vehicles don't need heated leather seats or wooden dashboard accents. Instead, they should offer affordable bare-metal longevity.

VW Type II (1949)

I stretched the definition of 'car' a bit for this one, but the Type II is here because it's based on the classic Beetle (otherwise known as the Type I). The VW Bus is firmly entrenched in popular culture as the Ultimate Hippie Road Tripper. Part of that stems from its incredibly adaptable interior, and many did duty as affordable compact campers, chugging along the highway with a sound reminiscent of a happy tractor.

The VW Bus was built on the same platform as the Beetle.

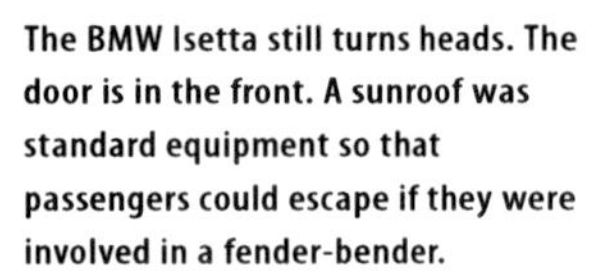

The BMW Isetta still turns heads. The door is in the front. A sunroof was standard equipment so that passengers could escape if they were involved in a fender-bender.

Up Close: The BMW Isetta (1953)

Imagine my surprise when I discovered that the diminutive BMW Isetta – introduced over 50 years ago – managed an incredible 50 to 60 miles per gallon. Following the devastation of WWII, there was a need for affordable and efficient transportation in Europe. Italian designers unleashed the incredibly successful Vespa motor scooter, along with an odd micro car called the ISO Isetta. After creating a sensation at the 1953 Turin auto show, German manufacturer BMW licensed and mass-produced the tiny machine in several different two and four seat configurations. BMW went on to produce over 160,000 of these strange little machines between 1955 and 1962. Sadly, it became a victim of booming worldwide economies – with money in their pockets, buyers migrated to more expensive traditional vehicles.

The original BMW Isetta 250 was powered by a modified 250 cc BMW motorcycle engine capable of reaching a mere 85 km/h (52 mph). The little 2-seater was followed in 1956 by a 300 cc model, and a 600 cc 4-seater became part of the family in the late 1950s. A mere 34,000 4-seaters were produced, in part because of stiff competition from the VW Beetle. Today, Isettas remain popular collector's items. And – as fuel prices continue to climb – a new generation of micro cars might soon take styling cues from these classics.

Incidentally, a company in the UK manufactures both BMW Isetta and Messerschmitt micro car replicas. Tritech Autocraft offers kits starting at £2650. You'll have to add donor parts such as the braking system from a MINI, steering from a Bedford Rascal and a Honda single cylinder 4-stroke engine. Expect to spend around £7000 plus a few hundred hours of labor to build your own. It looks like they're only available in the UK, but if your heart is set on one and you live in the nether-regions of the planet (like me), you should give them a shout to double-check. [See www.tri-techautocraft.co.uk for kit details.]

The original Mini had a stark simplicity that's sadly absent from most modern cars.

Classic Mini Cooper (1961)

Oh, the Mini. Built as Britain's answer to the ubiquitous VW Beetle, it was a capable and affordable everyday runabout that (with a few tweaks) could be turned into a respectable rally car. Even though they are tiny it is possible to fit four adults and 96 cans of Coca Cola inside (don't ask).

Volvo P1800 (1961)

Many people say "boxy" or "conservative" when asked to describe typical Volvo styling. Nothing could be further from reality when referring to the Italian-designed P1800. It was introduced in 1961 and for the first few years was manufactured in the UK. The engine was a 1.8L 4-cylinder that generated 100 bhp. It was followed in 1968 by a 2.0L with 118 bhp. By the end of production, over 39,000 had been built.

The P1800. A Volvo that was Italian designed and initially made in the UK.

The newest generation of Mustangs has taken styling cues from the original designs of the 1960s and early 1970s.

Ford Mustang (1964 - 1st generation)

Introduced in 1964, the Mustang caused a sensation. It's easy to see why, even by today's standards. It was small (for a mid-1960s American car), sleek, and muscular.

The unmistakable shape of an expensive Porsche, but with a much smaller price tag.

Porsche 912 (1965)

The inclusion of a Porsche on this list might seem like cheating, but the 912 was once known as the 'poor man's Porsche.' It combined the modern shape of the new 911 with the tried and true power plant from the classic 356. Its 1.6L engine put out a mere 90 bhp. Introduced in 1965, the 912 was phased out by the end of 1969.

An Italian work of art, yet its looks weren't enthusiastically accepted in the late 1960s.

Alfa Romeo Spider Duetto Series I (1966)

The Alfa Romeo Spider 1600 was officially named the Duetto in 1966. In North America, it became known as the Alfa Romeo Graduate thanks to its appearance in the 1967 Dustin Hoffman film *The Graduate*. The original round-tail Duetto featured a 1.6 L DOHC aluminum block engine and 4-wheel disc brakes. It was marketed until 1969. Surprisingly, the automotive press was unkind about its design in the late 1960s, although it looks beautiful to modern eyes.

BMW 2002 (1968)

If BMW marketed the 2002 in North America these days, I might seriously consider buying one. It owes its existence to North American exhaust emission regulations which dictated that BMW had to offer it with a clean-burning 2.0L engine, rather than an older twin-carburetor 1.6L design. The larger engine put out 100 bhp and made the affordable 2002 serious fun to drive.

BMW has done a remarkable job of keeping the front end styling of their cars consistent throughout the decades.

Datsun 240Z (1969)

Introduced in 1969, the Datsun Z became an instant success. It was a warning shot across the bow of European manufacturers: here was a Japanese-made sports car capable of 0-100 km/h in 8 seconds, yet selling for a mere $3,500. This stylish little car went on to sell over 100,000 units before production ceased in 1973.

A classic brochure image showing a couple admiring their new datsun 240Z.

AMC Gremlin (1970)

Like it or not, the Gremlin earns a spot on this list as the first American-made subcompact, introduced in 1970. What made it special was AMC's 6 cylinder engine that put out 128 bhp (impressive for the early Seventies). A three-speed column-mounted manual shifter was standard. Base price? $1879. I'll take two in lemon yellow, please!

Opel GT (1971)

The German-built Opel GT looks like a miniature Chevrolet Corvette. Over 100,000 were produced between 1968 and 1973. Trivia: It was the first production car to feature pop-up rotating headlights. The original 1965 prototype featured rectangular headlights – not nearly as endearing. List price was $3395, and you could upgrade to a 1.9 L 4-cylinder engine for $99 more. Those were the days.

A great shot of the Opel GT, showing off its trademark pop-up headlights.

A close-up of the luggage compartment. The air-cooled engine is in the rear.

VW Super Beetle (1971)

Driving a Beetle is guaranteed to put a smile on your face. Perhaps it's the shape or the strangely angled steering wheel that echoes the driving position in a city bus. They feature a rear-mounted air cooled engine, and everything about them was designed to be as simple as possible. The first few Beetles were made near Wolfsburg in 1945, and by 1971 over 1.3 million of the happy-looking little cars were churned out each year. German production ceased in 1978 (supplanted by the Golf), but the original Beetle was manufactured in Mexico until 2003.

Honda Civic CVCC (1972)

I'm not wild about the fender-mounted mirrors, but the Honda Civic remains a top seller to this day.

Small, simple and affordable to operate. Honda's fortunes blossomed with the 1972 introduction of the Civic. The key to their success was the clean-burning and economical new CVCC engine, which earned Honda a reputation for producing fuel efficient and reliable automobiles.

Fiat X1/9 (1972)

The Fiat X1/9 is the first of two mid-engine sports cars on my list. This car must have looked unbelievably modern when released in 1972. It included a 75 bhp 1290 cc engine and a removable roof panel. Because of US emissions regulations the motor was significantly detuned in all American cars. As a result, it became quite a popular car to "retune" for increased performance. Fiat discontinued the X1/9 in 1983 but it survived in Europe under the Bertone marque until 1988.

Triumph TR7 (1974)

When unveiled in 1974, the TR7's angular 'wedge' design was revolutionary. Unfortunately, early build quality was less than stellar and it was offered with an underpowered 2.0L slant-4 engine. Most important to TR purists: there was no soft-top version. Production ceased in 1981, but I think the TR's body has aged rather well – it still looks interesting rather than quaint.

1978 ad copy for the Triumph TR7, trumpeting a new level of comfort and handling. Unfortunately, it wasn't incredibly reliable.

Jeep CJ-7 (1976)

Produced between 1976 and 1986, the CJ-7 is considered by many to be the finest of the line. Over 370,000 were produced and the CJ-7 featured an automatic 4WD system known as Quadra-Trac. An automatic transmission was optional, as was a molded hardtop. Even though they've lived hard lives, you still see the occasional mud-spattered CJ on the road.

MGB Mark II (1976)

This is actually an MGB Mark I. It shares most of the styling cues of the later edition with a tad more chrome. Note the lack of a passenger-side door mirror.

In many ways, the MGB is a caricature of several generations of British soft tops, except better. It was well known for its tough and simple unibody design. This is the only MG known by many North Americans, which is a pity – the modern MG-F is tons of fun, too.

The Niva is a much underrated compact 4X4. Its no-frills approach adds to its charm.

Lada Niva (1977)

If I had to choose a vehicle to traverse the rough-and-tumble roads of rural Russia it might well be a utilitarian Lada Niva. Although many make fun of its boxy styling, I find the Russian minimalist approach to 4x4 design quite appealing. Production began in 1977 with a carbureted 1.6L 4-cylinder engine, manual 4 or 5 speed transmission, and full-time 4WD.

Suzuki SJ 410 (1982)

This tiny little off-road vehicle was incredibly popular as both a hard and softtop. It offered a 1.0 L engine which seemed well matched to its diminutive frame. The first SJ's were released for the 1986 model year in the USA as the Samurai. [yes, this is the Suzuki that was reported to have serious roll-over problems].

The Honda CRX was sold as a 2-seater in North America, but there was ample room for a large potted plant or an extra friend beneath the rear hatch.

Honda CRX (1984 - 1st generation)

This is a tremendously underrated car. I owned a 1987 model which one of my friends described perfectly as a full-sized slot car. In North America it was a two-seater, although Honda crammed in a tiny back seat elsewhere. In a pinch, one could easily stuff an unlucky spare friend into the flat cargo area beneath the hatch. It included a 1.5L engine that put out a mere 94 bhp, but its tiny size (and weight) made it incredibly nimble and zippy.

Toyota MR2 Mark I (1984)

The first version of this list appeared online. A few weeks later, my friend Martin pointed out that I'd missed the Toyota MR2. He's right – the first generation MR2 (known in casual conversation as the Mister Two) was introduced in 1984. It was Toyota's entry into the world of affordable mid-engine two seat sports cars, powered by a 112 bhp 4-cylinder. Its looks are a tad angular by today's tastes, but what an incredibly neat little ride! The first generation was produced until 1989, with a supercharged option appearing in 1986. Rumor has it that the MR2 design was based on the never-released Lotus X100.

Toyota Celica GT-S (1986 - 4th generation)

The 1986 Toyota Celica revitalized the flagging Celica line. It featured newly curvy styling and front wheel drive. The GT-S managed to squeeze 138 bhp from its 2.0L 4-cylinder, making for an unforgettably fun ride. Sadly, the Celica name was retired by Toyota at the end of 2005.

This Miata dates from the early 2000s. It's as beautiful as the original, with a couple of extra curves.

Mazda Miata (1989)

A sporty convertible that's affordable, fun to drive, simple, and easy to find. Debuting in 1989, the Mazda Miata built a loyal following. It has very neutral handling and makes an ideal first "real" sports car. They often turn up on the used market at reasonable prices.

A British Sports Car That Takes Things To Extremes

Ariel Atom

I couldn't resist sneaking in one last automobile. Allow me to introduce a car designed for blokes who rides motorcycles because cars are slower than turtles. It's called the Ariel Atom – no relation to the European laundry soap of the same name. Ariel is Britain's smallest auto maker, employing only seven speed-crazed souls. The Ariel name dates back to the 1870s, when the company made bicycles. They started making cars around the turn of the 20th Century. The Ariel name popped up from time to time over the decades. As far as I know, there is absolutely no connection between the modern company and its namesakes.

They market their cars with the slogan "No Doors. No Screen. No Roof." For most makers this would be the kiss of death: "Hullo, Mrs. Jenkins. Your new Toyota Flowerpot arrived at the dealership today. No, no... we don't offer boring old doors or a windscreen anymore."

The Atom has an amazing trick up its sleeve: zero to 100 mph (161 kph) in a blinding 6.8 seconds. Or – if you can shift fast enough – zero to 60 mph in a tad under three. The Atom costs about 35,000 euros and thoughtfully includes a passenger seat for a suitably insane friend. [www.arielmotor.co.uk]

The Little Guy camping trailer can be pulled behind nearly anything.

Teardrop Campers

Teardrop campers were all the rage in the 1930s and 1940s. By the mid-1950s they were replaced by gigantic aluminum things that cruised the highways like the fantastic space cruisers they were modeled after.

A new generation of miniature teardrop campers is taking the world by storm. The Little Guy Deluxe offers comfortable sleeping for two and extremely cozy sleeping for three, if that's your thing. They're equipped with pop-open rear storage, locking side doors, three battery-powered lights, optional roof vents, and even an interior cabinet for stashing your stuff. A double-wide version is available, as are motorcycle, cargo and camouflage models. I question the sanity of taking a camouflaged camper on your next duck hunt, though. [www.teardroptrailersexpress.com]

Nearly all Ural motorcycles include a sidecar. They have a tendency to work themselves loose, with an accompanying cacophony of squeaks.

Ural Troyka Motorbikes: A blast from the Soviet past

Even back in the late 1930s, BMW made great motorcycles. And they were decidedly better than those the Soviets had to suffer with. In a moment of strategic stupidity, the Germans gave blueprints and casting molds for BMW's outdated R71 motorcycle to the Russians. Throughout WWII, thousands of these bikes were manufactured for the Soviet Red Army.

By the 1950s, the Irbit Motorcycle Works was producing Ural motorbikes for civilian use. They survived the breakup of the Soviet Union and now operate as a privately held company. You can buy them new in North America or Europe quite easily, starting at around $10,000.

The vast majority of their bikes feature sidecars, like the Troyka shown here. Powered by a 745 cc twin engine, it offers sumptuous (by motorcycle standards, anyway) sidecar seating for your passenger.

The weight of the sidecar puts quite a strain on the Ural's antiquated dual-carburetor 40 bhp motor. Maximum speed is around 60 mph (96 km/h), so this isn't a good choice as a highway bike. The mechanical design is a throwback to the 1940s, with the dual carbs, grease fittings, and occasional loose bolts to prove it. Plan on becoming a backyard mechanic when you adopt one of these Russian wonders. [www.ural.com]

A look at some vintage gear, along with a few modern amplifiers, turntables and sonic gadgets.

The Wonderful World of Hi-Fi

The early days of recorded audio were anything but high fidelity. In the beginning, sound was captured mechanically on spring-driven wax cylinders or disks. The process was purely mechanical – artists spoke or performed into a large metal horn attached directly to a metal stylus.

I remember being captivated by the mechanics of sound as a child – records could be sped up and slowed down with the not-so-innocent touch of a fingertip. Tape recording didn't hold nearly the same wonder because the magic of magnetic encoding was well hidden from casual experimentation. There was no longer anything tactile about the sound medium.

Here's a look at some vintage gear and a few of the wonderful modern turntables, tube-enabled CD players and amplifiers available today.

This RCA Victrola plays almost modern 78 RPM records. Records ultimately proved more popular than Edison's wax cylinder format.

Phonographs: Spinning a Tune

Thomas Alva Edison patented the first cylinder Phonograph in 1877, but his equipment eventually proved less popular than disc-style Phonographs. This was most likely because flat discs were easier to manufacture (they could be stamped) and less expensive to ship. Edison bowed out of the market in 1929.

The market for Phonographs stumbled a bit from the mid-1920s through WWII. In part this was due to improved radio quality, but the Great Depression also ensured that money for entertainment remained tight. The end of the war saw a resurgence in turntable popularity which exploded with the arrival of rock and roll and transistorized amplification in the late 1950s.

Vinyl retained a firm hold on the marketplace with the introduction of stereo (and even quadraphonic sound) in the 1960s, although it faced increasing competition from pre-recorded cassette tapes in the 1980s. Alas, the appearance of the Compact Disc in 1983 signalled the beginning of the end.

LP records had virtually disappeared from store shelves by the mid-1990s, replaced by the bright digital sound of Compact Discs. Don't fret, though. There's been a resurgence of interest in vinyl over the last few years, driven by a healthy dose of nostalgia, the growing profile of club-style DJ performance, and a respectable array of modern turntables.

There's something mesmerizing about the sight of a turntable in action.

Vinyl recording formats

Modern records are recorded at one of two speeds: 45 RPM (revolutions per minute), or 33 1/3 RPM. A third speed, 78 RPM, was used in early recordings. Most modern turntables can't handle 78s and those that can will require you to install a different needle. The fidelity of a recording is a factor of the turntable speed and groove spacing. Consequently, the highest fidelity recordings will usually be 45 RPM 10" or 12" discs. Seven inch discs are commonly referred to as Singles. They usually contain one or two songs per side, recorded at 45 RPM. Think of them as the 1970s equivalent of going to iTunes and plunking down 99 cents for the latest single from your favorite band.

Ten inch discs were termed EPs and offered three or four songs to a side. They're often recorded at 45 RPM, although some were tracked at 33 1/3. The EP was usually the domain of the

Indie band looking for their first big break. Since studio time was ludicrously expensive before the advent of home recording, a band often couldn't scrape up the money to record a full album's worth of material.

Twelve inch disks were known as LPs (Long Play) or albums. A typical album included nine or ten songs and great thought was often given to the track order to ensure that the break between sides A and B followed logically with the music.

The LP record was the heart and soul of the recording industry until the arrival of Compact Discs in 1983.

The physical nature of vinyl caused no end of headaches for recording engineers. They had to limit low-frequency bass sounds to prevent the stylus from being bounced out of the groove. You'll never hear a rhythmic bass tone panned hard left or right on a record for the same reason.

These days it's possible to pick up reissues of many famous records from the past, although they're usually extremely expensive. But used record stores still abound, especially in larger urban centers. And you can often find a gold mine of vintage music at garage sales – people often sell off their vinyl collections for mere pocket change.

Turntable preamplifiers

Records are far from perfect. The physical nature of vinyl limits frequency response and dynamic range. In an effort to improve sound quality, the Recording Industry Association of America (RIAA) agreed on an equalization standard in 1954 that reduces low frequencies and increases highs during manufacture. On playback, the process is reversed. Since vinyl captures bass much more effectively than treble, this dramatically improves quality.

This is the reason that most stereo amplifiers from the 1950s through 1980s had Phono inputs – RIAA equalization was applied to the signal appearing on these inputs, while other inputs (usually Tape and Auxiliary) were unmodified. Many modern amplifiers exclude Phono inputs, making it impossible to connect a turntable.

Some modern turntables get around this problem by including a user-selectable preamplifier circuit. To interface older players you'll need an external preamplifier that plugs between the turntable and your snazzy new amp. Prices range anywhere from about $30 through hundreds of dollars for artfully designed tube models. I've listed several options below, including two that connect a turntable directly to a computer (perfect for ripping your vinyl to mp3).

You can pay hundreds of dollars for an audiophile tube Phono preamplifier, but this one does admirably for a fraction of the price.

ART DJ PRE II

Pro-audio manufacturer ART sells a top-quality Phono preamp called the DJ PRE II. This affordable aluminum wonder box lets you hook an old-school turntable to any shiny new stereo system that lacks Phono inputs.

The unit offers switchable input impedance, adjustable signal gain and optional low-pass filtering to mask turntable rumble. ART is well known for their pro recording gear and the DJ PRE II retails for around $50 at pro music retailers. [www.artroch.com]

TERRATEC Phono Preamp Studio USB

I threw out most of my vintage LPs during a move four years ago – a fit of momentary insanity that I've regretted ever since. The flip side of this tragedy is that many others are doing exactly the same and affordable record collections regularly surface at garage sales and flea markets.

This Terratec Phono preamp includes bundled audio restoration software to remove clicks and rumble.

Once you've (re)built your vinyl collection, the big question becomes "How do I get this stuff into my computer?" Terratec has a great solution. Their 100 euro ($130) Phono PreAmp Studio USB is a little box that contains a Phono preamp, an extra Line-in (for cassette players or what-have-you) and a USB output. When connected between your turntable and computer, it automagically creates digital backups of your classic LPs, 45s, and EPs. The package thoughtfully includes Sound Rescue, a sound restoration package that removes pops, crackle, rumble, and hiss. [www.terratec.com]

The ART USB MicroPre is a low-cost vinyl to digital interface. And yes, it looks incredibly like its brother on the last page.

ART USB MicroPre Phono/Line Preamp

ART introduced the $99 USB MicroPre Phono/line preamp in early 2005. It shares the same curvy case as their all-analog DJ PRE II. Like the Terratec interface mentioned above, this model is intended to interface your turntable (or any other audio source) directly to your computer. It even has an S/PDIF digital input so you can gorge on digital sources, too.

No sound cards or audio interfaces are required – it outputs a digital signal over USB. You can use an external power adapter (preferred) or power the unit directly from the USB connector. The MicroPre includes a front panel gain knob and clipping light to fine-tune the input signal. Thoughtfully, ART included a headphone jack so you can monitor the digital output – a perfect way to make sure your recordings don't suffer from ugly digital clipping if you accidentally exceed the unit's headroom.

I like the idea of these units as a way to transfer valuable record collections to a computer-based audio library. Just remember that one of the wonderful things about vinyl is its smooth analog sound – for best results, hook your turntable up to a good amplifier/speaker combination and listen "the natural way." [www.artroch.com]

Affordable Turntables

Buying vintage turntables

You can often find vintage turntables for sale. Most from the 1960s and 1970s are belt-driven models produced by companies that have long since gone out of business. Several companies on the Internet offer replacement diamond cartridges of sapphire needles for thousands of different models – make sure that you can get your hands on the right model before purchasing.

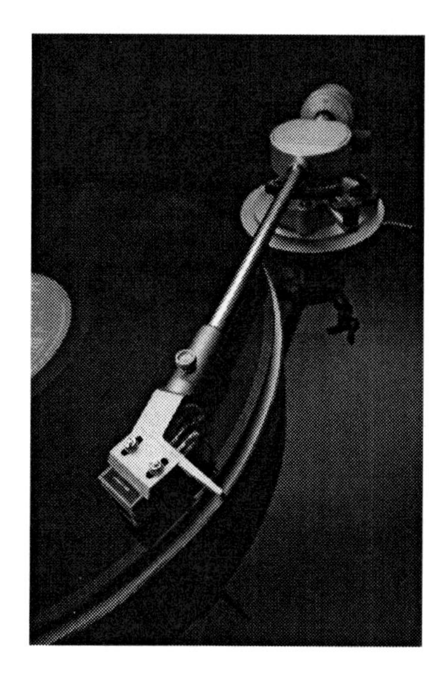

A bigger problem with vintage turntables is the belt-drive mechanism. Most turntable platters were driven by a large rubber belt. This did an excellent job of isolating the platter from the potentially noisy electric motor. Unfortunately, these belts don't age well; they stretch and become brittle over time. The only solution is to replace the belt, but suitable replacements might be hard to come by. Check out Jerry Raskin's Needle Doctor [www.needledoctor.com] for replacement belts, cartridges and needles.

New models

The vinyl resurgence brought an explosion of turntables to market. As with anything in the hi-fi world, prices range from under $100 to several thousand bucks for 'audiophile' styling and sound. It's possible to get excellent quality at a decent price, though. Here's a quick look at some modern units in the sub-$150 range.

DJ-friendly Turntables

In the DJ world, the Technics 1200 line (and its brothers) are the de-facto standard. They run $400+, which is a fair chunk of change. Here are a couple of inexpensive DJ turntables that would also work wonders with your home system.

Numark TT1650 (approximately $160)

This direct-drive entry from Numark is an excellent starter model. It has a strong and consistent motor, which is important if you're planning to DJ. The TT1650 can be mounted horizontally or battle-style and features an aluminum platter with plastic body, just like the Stanton on the next page. Plays 33 1/3 & 45 RPM. Competent and curvy. [www.numark.com]

This ain't your parent's turntable. A strong direct drive motor and variable speed makes it suitable for DJ duty as well as spinning vinyl at home.

The T.60 is the least expensive direct-drive variable speed turntable in Stanton's line. A T.60X model is also available if you wish to buy without the stylus cartridge.

Stanton T.60 (approximately $150)

The T.60 is the least expensive direct-drive turntable in the Stanton line. It offers basic features for DJing and a reasonably high-torque motor for OK scratching capability. You'll find a +/- 10% pitch control, removable target light and a clever cloth dust cover. The body is weighted plastic with an aluminum platter, but that's to be expected in this price range. 33 1/3 & 45 RPM compatible. [www.stantondj.com]

Home Stereo Units

The DJ models mentioned above could serve admirably in a home rig, but if you're into something more traditional, several well-known manufacturers make decently priced home components.

Sony PS-LX250H (approximately $100)

The Sony PS-LX250H includes a built-in Phono preamp, just in case your modern stereo system doesn't have one.

Sony's low-cost entry is an automatic belt-drive system with respectable sound. It features a built-in preamp for compatibility with newer stereos that don't have a Phono-in jack. I bought one of these several years ago and my only gripes are a slightly out-of-true platter and the cheap plastic feel of the controls. Decent quality at a bargain price. Plays 33 1/3 & 45 RPM. [www.sonystyle.com]

Audio Technica AT-PL50 (approximately $100)

This is the lowest cost unit in the Audio Technica range. It's belt drive, which means lower torque, slippage, and potentially more rumble. Includes a built-in Phono preamplifier. At this price, don't expect zillion-dollar quality; some users comment it skips quite frequently and doesn't have the best sound. Plays 33 1/3 & 45 RPM. [www.audio-technica.com]

The belt driven Audio-Technica includes a switchable Phono preamp and an aluminum platter, which is standard for this price range.

Teac P-A688 (approximately $130)

This is another strong entry-level offering from Teac, a brand with a long history in the hi-fi market. The P-A688 is a semi-automatic turntable with built-in switchable Phono preamplifier. Plays 33 1/3 & 45 RPM. [www.teac.com]

Portable Turntables

Yes, you read that right. These little beasts are designed to travel – great for trying out used vinyl before laying down your cash or for dropping by a friend's place.

If I was in the market, the PT-01 would be a strong contender. There's something about being able to power a hi-fi turntable with batteries that is irresistible.

Numark PT-01 (approximately $100)

This capable little turntable plays 33 1/3, 45 and 78 RPM discs. It measures a very compact 12"x12"x4" (30x30x10 cm) and includes a built-in speaker and protective cover. It offers up a hi/lo tone control, varispeed, and can run on 6 D batteries. My only gripe is a slightly weak headphone amp, but that could just be a sign of my impending deafness. The PT-01 is a well thought out portable that could easily serve double duty as your main home deck. [www.numark.com]

The Vestax Handy Trax is beginning to show its age, but it offers great portable playback.

Vestax Handy Trax (approximately $125)

The Handy Trax was first in the modern generation of portables. It features a clean and powerful headphone amplifier, built-in speaker, and runs on 6 C batteries while you're out and about. Like the Numark PT-01, it plays 33 1/3, 45 and 78 RPM records and has hi/lo tone controls and varispeed. It's a definite contender, although not nearly as stylish as the Numark. In fact, it reminds me of the borkish players I was subjected to in early grade school. [www.vestax.com]

Conclusion

If I were buying again, I'd probably take a hard look at the direct-drive DJ models from Stanton and Numark. They're excellent quality for about the same price as a lowly iPod Shuffle. It's proof that good things do come to those who wait.

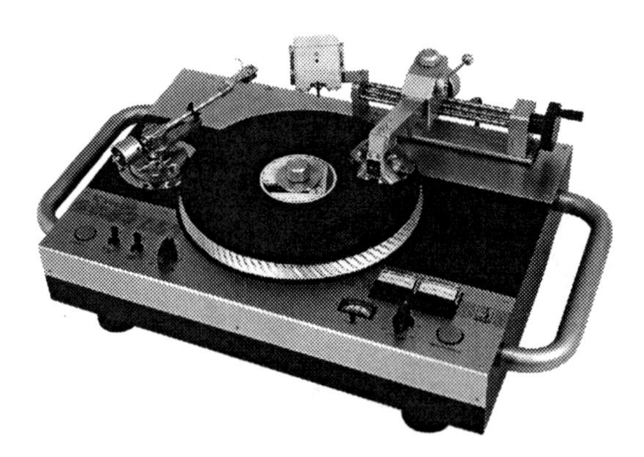

Now here's a great business idea. The Vestax VRX-2000 lets you cut short-run records for a relatively reasonable rate. Just remember that mastering vinyl is a tricky task.

Cutting Your Own Vinyl

Bored with burning CDs and ripping mp3s? Got the urge to make real records?

You're looking for a Dub Plate – a machine that inscribes music onto special vinyl blanks. They produce one-off records durable enough to handle repeated playing or scratching. The only hitch is the price. There are several turntable add-ons available in the $5000 to $7000 range, but the Vestax VRX-2000 is the only all-in-one solution on the market – for a cool $10,000.

Cutting vinyl is an art - you're limited to 12 to 15 minutes per side and the source material has to be compressed to match the limited dynamic range of vinyl. Any really low frequency sounds (bass, kick drums) must be panned to the center of your stereo mix or there's a good chance they'll cause the needle to skip. [www.vestax.com]

Build Your Own Gramophone

The $60 Gakken Gramophone Kit from VeryCoolThings.com is a unique way to reuse that stack of discarded CDs and CD-Rs that everyone seems to have lying around.

The idea of making gramophone recordings on old Compact Discs is too good to pass up.

Assuming you have the manual dexterity to successfully complete the one-hour kit, you'll be rewarded with a gramophone recorder/player that uses old CDs as recording platters. Simply place a fresh CD on the platter, speak into the paper cup, and your voice is cheerfully etched into the surface of an unsuspecting and unwanted CD.

The company also makes an Edison-style player that scratches sound onto a spinning plastic cup, much like Edison's famous wax cylinder recorders. [One of many neat products on sale at www.verycoolthings.com]

Neo-Retro Portables

Forty years ago it was impossible to grab some tunes and go for a jog (unless you had a pet marching band). Without iPods and Walkmen, all you could hope for was the right tune on the car radio. Sure, there were portable record players – but they weren't exactly pocket-sized.

Don't laugh, a suitcase style record player like this Crosley CR89 reproduction was perfect for visiting friends or playing music outside.

The Crosley CR89 Traveller is an 18.5 lb (8.4 kg) reminder that "portable" had a different meaning in the 1960s. It can handle LPs, 45s, and even 78s. Unlike the original players of the era, this modern model has closely spaced stereo speakers behind the front grill. The grooviest feature of all is the Stack-O-Matic record changer that lets you stack and play six records in a row.

The $179 Traveller won't offer a room-rocking hi-fi experience, but it's a great excuse to dust off some old 45s and have a laugh. [www.crosleyradio.com]

One significant reason that vacuum tubes still appear in audiophile equipment (apart from their unique sound) is that they look beautiful, especially when switched on. Unfortunately, they're also fragile and require frequent replacement. Audio tubes are still manufactured in Russia and China.

Tube Amplifiers

Once upon a time, vacuum tube circuitry was the only way to efficiently amplify sound with respectable fidelity. Tubes are fickle things – they generate a lot of heat, a little bit of light, and they're subject to slight manufacturing imperfections that render some of them useless for audio applications.

Tube audio fell out of fashion for a while in the 1980s as home listeners became enthralled in the grips of the pristine digital sound from their newly acquired CD players. Surprisingly, those players gave new life to analog technology. Purists quickly decried the digital players as harsh and brittle sounding. This might have been the case, although there was also a steep learning curve for recording engineers who had to learn how to tweak the best possible sound out of their new digital wonder boxes. Tube amplifiers smoothed the newly bright and dynamic sound a little, making it easier to enjoy.

The mid 2000s saw a resurgence of interest in vacuum tubes – I've even seen fake tubes adorning the top of cheap retro-styled clock radios. Audio manufacturers in China have discovered the tube mystique and a series of progressively more refined Chinese tube amps have begun to make their way around the world. Rather than provide a laundry list of modern tube amplifier manufacturers that will quickly become outdated, I've selected only a handful of interesting amps for you: a fantastic bargain from Thailand, a tiny low-power amp from the USA, and a high-end iPod accessory from Germany.

nOrh SE-9 Integrated tube amplifier

Tube amplifiers are shrouded in high-end mystique, probably because hi-fi manufacturers like to keep it that way. Maybe this will change, thanks to an influx of affordable and (apparently) well-built tube amps from the Far East. The $450 SE-9 integrated amplifier caught my eye immediately. It's from the nOrh Loudspeaker Company, improbably located in Bangkok, Thailand. Even at this bargain price, you get dual inputs, four Electro Harmonix tubes, platinum coated switches, and a whole host of other audiophile features. Suffice it to say that it puts out an honest 9 watts per channel of smooth Class A sound. With some fairly high-efficiency speakers this looks like the ideal box to rediscover *Kind of Blue* by Miles, or perhaps induce some nasty drug flashbacks courtesy of Pink Floyd. [www.norh.com]

The SE-9 is a rare bargain in the audiophile world. It's also nOrh 's best seller.

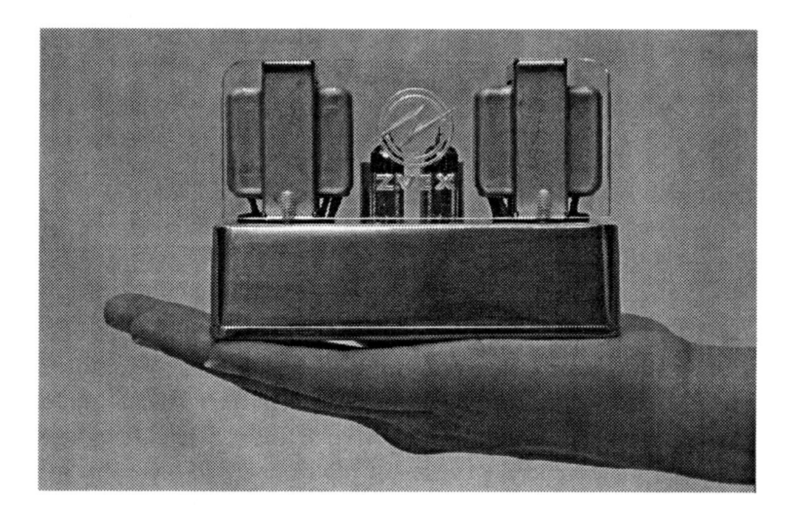

The Z.Vex iMPAMP can be tucked almost anywhere. It's the smallest tube amplifier I've encountered.

iMPAMP micro tube amplifier

The iMPAMP is a truly tiny stereo tube amplifier from designer Zachary Vex. Intended for use with iPodish things, it puts out an itty-bitty 1W per channel. To squeeze everything into such a tiny space, the iMP uses a pair of sub-miniature Philips JAN 6021W vacuum tubes manufactured in the mid 1980s. Vex comments "These tubes represent the height of civilization's investment in tube technology. There was nothing better ever made."

Some might question the sanity of hooking a tube amplifier to an mp3 player, but you can feed it more refined audio sources as well. Vex also uses the iMP with his Clear Audio turntable, a preamp, and a pair of Monitor Audio Gold speakers with surprisingly good results. The iMP sells for $525 and measures an almost sub-atomic 4.4"x 3.3" x 3.3" (that's 111 mm x 76 mm x 76 mm in the metric world). [www.impamp.com]

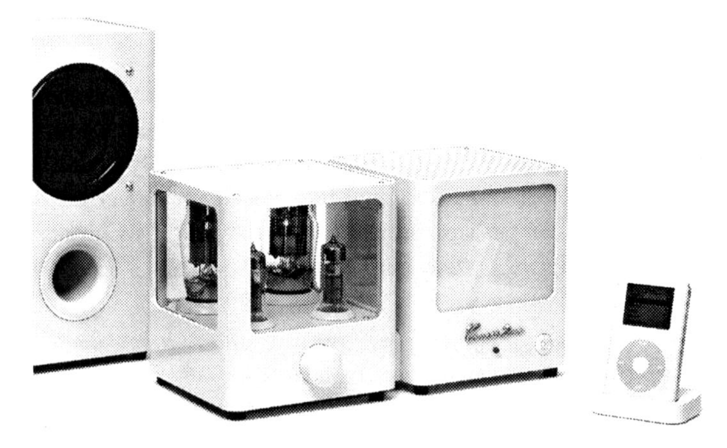

If your iPod has been good to you this year, why not splurge on an incredibly high-end tube amplification system?

Concertino iPod tube amplifier and speakers

This rather snazzy-looking setup is the Concertino iPod tube amp, complete with a couple of speakers and a few feet of speaker wire. The price is equally snazzy: a shade over $4,100 (including shipping). The German-made Concertino weighs in at 22 lbs, plus about 13.5 lbs for the speakers. Sound is processed through a four tube system before being pumped out of the speakers in all its analog tube-warmed glory. Concertino includes a second audio input so you can attach a CD player or turntable, although at this price we'd expect a plethora of inputs and add-ons (plus in-home installation by a German technician in a white lab coat). [www.goldster-audio.com]

JoLida vacuum tube CD, DVD, and tuner components

JoLida offers a vacuum tube DVD player, CD player, and AM/FM tuner. I wonder if they're planning a tube-based mp3 player?

I spend considerable time figuring out how to sneak electronics into the house. This is one of the reasons personal computers are such popular DIY gadgets – it's easy to add an extra gigabyte of memory or a new motherboard without anyone noticing. I suspect this also led to the proliferation of tiny satellite/subwoofer speakers in the mid 1990s. Your partner's Financial Overload Meter goes into high alert at the sight of huge Klipsch tower speakers coming through the front door, yet no one seems to notice a set of cute little cubes sitting on the shelf.

This is an incredibly long-winded way to admit that I couldn't figure out how to slip vacuum tube stereo components into the house. I lived in fear of my wife noticing an eerie glow from the little light bulbs beside the CD player. Thankfully, JoLida understands my plight. They market a line of tube-enabled CD / DVD / AM-FM components that look suitably inconspicuous. Only you and I will know that a pair of ludicrously expensive 12AX7A tubes live behind that unassuming grey aluminium front plate. It's better that way, trust me. Prices start at about $499, see www.jolida.com for detailed specifications.

Solid State Amplifiers

Vintage solid state amplifiers at bargain prices

I have mixed feelings about including vintage solid state (transistorized) stereo amplifiers in this book. Technology has advanced so much that mass-produced modern amplifiers routinely outpace their elderly low-end audiophile cousins from the 1970s and 1980s.

Here are a couple of relatively low-cost solid state amps that had an enormous impact on home audiences. They appear occasionally on the used market at reasonable prices. Assuming you can find one in good condition, it might prove to be the cornerstone of an affordable audiophile system. Just don't expect to find modern niceties such as remote controls, surround sound decoders, or digital inputs. These are strictly two-channel stereo, with decidedly analog inputs and outputs.

NAD 3020 stereo integrated amplifier

British manufacturer NAD (originally New Acoustic Dimension) was founded in 1972. Over the decades they've offered a progression of stunning audiophile equipment. Unfortunately, their new components carry stunning prices, too.

The NAD 3020, designed by Bjorn Erik Edvardsen, was created in 1978-1979 as a low-cost introduction to audiophile sound. It is an integrated design that combines a pre-amplifier and power amplifier in the same box, like most modern components. The 3020 is conservatively rated at 25 Watts per channel, but in reality it pumps out considerably more.

The 3020 was an incredibly popular little amplifier that turns up quite frequently on eBay and in used equipment shops in the $100 range. If you find one, the contacts will probably need cleaning or replacing – nothing was gold plated at this price point.

Don't forget that the great thing about buying classic hi-fi equipment is that you can enjoy it for a few years and then resell it without losing too much.

Mission Cyrus stereo integrated amplifier

Mission's Cyrus One integrated amplifier took simplicity to new heights. No unnecessary switches or flashing lights here!

I subconsciously placed the Mission Cyrus underneath the NAD 3020, but that is only because I owned an NAD while one of my friends bought into the Mission mystique. The Cyrus offered cutting-edge 1980s design that hasn't aged well – they look angular and awkward in comparison to today's sleek components. This awkwardness can work in your favour – others might pass them over without realizing their true beauty lies within.

Based in Cambridgeshire, England, Mission (now Cyrus) still produces top-class hi-fi equipment. The Cyrus was introduced in 1983 and the ground-breaking Cyrus One (30 W per channel) and Cyrus Two (50 W) models arrived in 1985. Mission also produced a matching AM/FM tuner and a series of progressively more refined (but unremarkable) CD players. The Cyrus units have a very dynamic sound that is clear and bright, requiring careful matching of speakers to make sure you don't end up with an overly harsh system. They work wonders with vinyl.

The Cyrus Model Three was introduced in the early 1990s. While it was more attractive than the Model Two it replaced, most judged it to be sonically inferior. Model Ones and Twos occasionally appear on the second-hand market for several hundred dollars – a bargain if they're in good shape.

JoLida hybrid integrated amplifiers

JoLida is famous for their modern tube amplifiers. I was originally planning to mention a model from their tube lineup, but I had a change of heart. Perhaps the best value in their product line is the $350 JD-1301A hybrid integrated amplifier. This simple unit incorporates a vacuum tube preamplifier circuit hooked to a 30 W + 30 W solid-state stereo power amplifier. The result is a great trade-off – the warmth of tubes and the low cost of transistors.

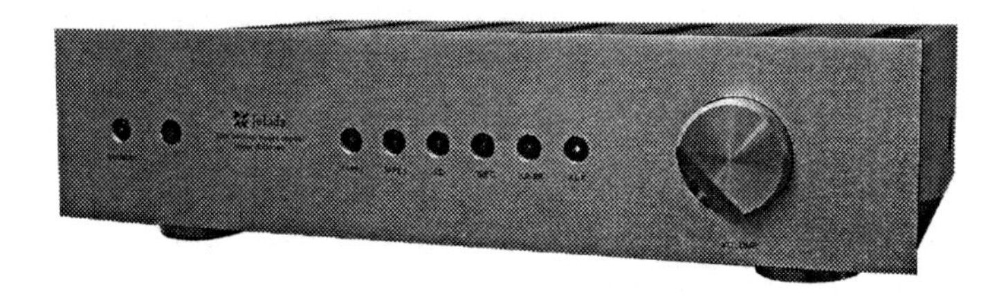

One knob and seven push-button switches. Audio doesn't need to be more complicated than this.

If your pocket book stretches a bit further, be sure to check out JoLida's JD-1501RC. This upscale hybrid looks great and offers 100 W of power per channel, along with a remote control. The front panel offers a power switch, 6-way selector buttons and an ALPS stereo volume control. If you're a tweaker at heart, there's nothing to stop you from replacing the 12AX7 tubes with some higher-end Electro Harmonix models, upgrading the internal wiring, or replacing the volume control with a fancy low-noise stepped attenuator.

Be warned that tube-based electronics require care and feeding that modern home listeners might not be used to – the preamp tubes are like light bulbs and occasionally burn out, requiring replacement every thousand hours or so. [www.jolida.com]

Low cost hi-fi: Some swear by the Sonic Impact T-Amp

The T-Amp is an extremely low-cost digital amplifier that has been generating quite a bit of excitement around the web. I've done a bit of digging, and it appears this is one of those rare cases where you get considerably more than you pay for.

The low-down

1. The T-Amp uses a Tripath TA2024B digital audio power amplifier. This respected chipset is incorporated into LCD TVs from Samsung, Sharp and several others. They use it because it sounds good, doesn't require expensive low-pass filtering, and is extremely efficient (~90%), which means it produces less heat and doesn't require a bulky heat sink.

The Sonic Impact T-Amp isn't much to look at. It only puts out about 5 Watts per channel of clean sound, so you'll need high-efficiency speakers to make it shine.

2. Tripath chips (TK2050) are used in the Sonos Digital Music System as well as hi-fi integrated amps from Bel Canto. Car stereo manufacturers are also beginning to take notice – several manufacturers are using Tripath chips, including Panasonic and Blaupunkt.

3. Tripath introduced the TIO Digital Amplifier card for PCs in 2000. It was a clever idea: mount a TA2024 audio amplifier on a PCI card that connects between a sound card and some good passive speakers. Sadly, it didn't catch on.

4. The Sonic Impact T-Amp appears to be designed around a low-cost version of Tripath's reference board for the TA2024 chipset. This explains the T-Amp's almost non-existent feature set (a single set of inputs, one plain-Jane volume knob/power switch). But remember - simple designs are great for DIY tweaks.

5. In the audio world, there's no such thing as a "Class T" amplifier. This is a trademarked Tripath buzzword. The design appears to be a highly modified Class D circuit that resolves some of the traditional problems associated with digital amplifier designs.

6. The T-Amp design works best in small rooms driving extremely efficient (>90 dB) speakers. THD+N (distortion & noise) is quite respectable until you drive the Tripath chip above 5 W output per channel. If you crank it up, THD+N rises to an icky 10% at full power (15 W into 4 Ohms).

7. For best results, use a stabilized AC power adapter that puts out no more than 13.2 V DC at 1.2 amperes. The Tripath chip *will* be damaged if you overdrive the voltage. While we're in warning mode – continuous operation at high volume *will* shorten the life of this amp – the circuit board doesn't have a heat sink and will get quite warm if you pump a lot of power through it.

Conclusion

The T-Amp is basically the same design as the $125 Tripath TA2024B evaluation board, but selling at a bargain price. Sonic Impact cut corners on the case and connectors, but the internals are top-notch.

You'll have to put in a bit of DIY effort to make the T-Amp really sing. I suggest attaching a good stabilized power supply, installing an ALPS volume knob, and upgrading to gold-plated RCA inputs and speaker posts. Make these changes and you'll be impressed as long as you keep the volume to moderate levels and use high-efficiency speakers. Rumor has it that Sonic Impact will introduce more powerful models based on other Tripath chips in 2006. I can't wait! [www.si-5.com]

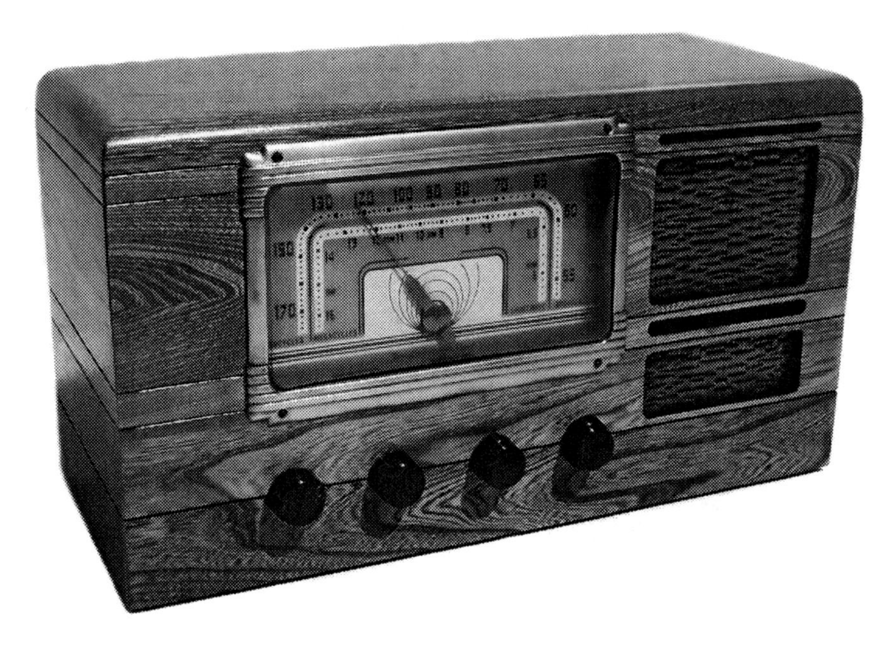

This 1929 Spartan is a wonderful example of vintage radio. The case is beautifully constructed from wood, making the Bakelite knobs look slightly out of place for modern taste.

Tube & Transistor Radios

Until the 1940s, radios were based on vacuum tube technology. This made them bulky and power-hungry. They were often built-into large stand-alone living room consoles or bulky desktop cases. The idea of a pocket radio seemed out of reach. The invention of the transistor in 1948 changed everything, and within years the world was flooded with newly miniaturized electronic devices.

Until the 1950s, home radio sets received only AM and possibly Shortwave broadcasts. In many ways, Shortwave was the mid-20th century equivalent of Internet newspapers – it became possible to listen in on broadcasts from half-way around the world.

FM radio sounded much better than its AM counterpart. Although the technology was invented in 1933, it wasn't until 1945 that the modern American FM broadcast band was defined (88 to 108 MHz) and the United States FCC didn't approve FM stereo broadcasts until 1961. By the end of the 1960s, high fidelity FM radio stations were commonplace, dramatically altering how people experienced music.

The Regency TR-1 was the first mass-produced transistor radio. It was made in the USA, but many of its successors came from Japan. Its plastic case was manufactured in a rainbow of colors. Special thanks to Dr. Steve Reyer for allowing me to reproduce this fantastic photo.

Regency TR-1: Igniting the transistor revolution

The invention of the transistor ensured that the last half of the 20th Century would be filled with ever-shrinking and more complex gadgetry. In fact, nearly every electronic gadget and gizmo that exists today incorporates anywhere from a few to a few million transistors.

Bell Labs announced the transistor to the public on June 30, 1948. Initially, the devices proved challenging to build, and it took four more years before industrial giant Raytheon began mass production. Their first commercial transistorized product was a hearing aid.

The first commercial transistor radio – the $49.95 Regency TR-1

– was introduced in late 1954 by the Regency division of an Indianapolis-based manufacturing company. They were the first to bite when Texas Instruments went looking for a company willing to incorporate their transistors in pocket radio designs. Interestingly enough, industry giants such as RCA turned them down because of the transistor's 'inferior' sound.

Converted into today's dollars, the TR-1 cost about the same as a modern iPod digital music player. And – like the iPod – the TR-1 dramatically changed how people listened to music. Prior to the TR-1, the radio was treated like a piece of furniture that sat in the living room, under the control of watchful and selective parents. Suddenly, the radio became a personal fashion accessory. It's no coincidence that the birth of rock and roll followed so closely after the invention of the transistor.

More than 100,000 TR-1 radios were manufactured over the course of little more than a year. The unit used expensive components and relied upon relatively expensive American labour for assembly. In the end, Regency failed to achieve long-term commercial success.

Find out more about this little bit of history by visiting Dr. Steve Reyer's TR-1 site at people.msoe.edu/~reyer/regency/

Radio Age: Restored tube radios

These days it seems every audio manufacturer is releasing something with tubes. You can even find tube amps for your car and iPod. Before the commercialization of the transistor in the early 1950s, tubes were a sonic necessity. They were bulky, hot, and required frequent replacement. They were also magical. The soft golden glow from the back of the family radio cheerfully illuminated living rooms around the world, and many old-timers argue the sound was smoother.

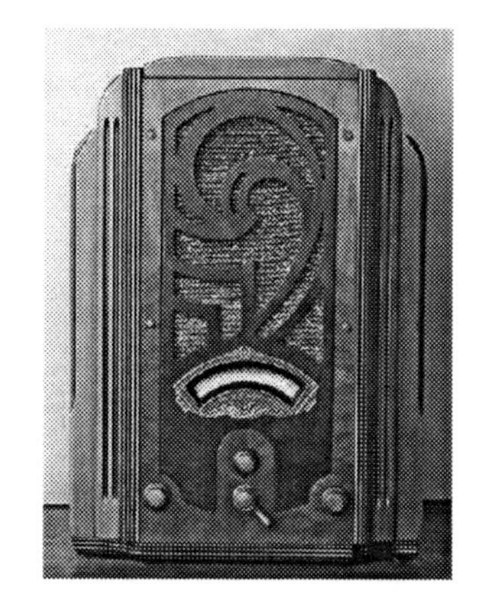

This 1933 Stewart Warner 'York' radio echoes the design of skyscrapers. It receives AM and two Shortwave bands and contains seven tubes to warm your parlor.

Radio Age refurbishes and sells classic tube radios from the 1930s, 1940s and 1950s. Many feature ornate wooden cases or quaint Bakelite exteriors. Most receive AM and Shortwave only because they predate the introduction of FM radio. Prices range from a few hundred to several thousand dollars, depending on the rarity and quality of the set. Take the time to visit the collection – they're beauties. [www.radioage.com]

The 1955 Sony TR-55 was Japan's first transistor radio. Sony had phenomenal success two years later with the pocket-sized TR-63, selling over 100,000 units worldwide.

The birth of Sony Corporation

The true victors of the mid-1950s Transistor Revolution were the Japanese. They perfected another revolutionary concept – miniaturization. While the Regency TR-1 attempted to cram relatively large components into a small case, the Japanese designed components and controls to be as compact as possible. This subtle shift enabled Japanese designers to build smaller and less expensive equipment that was bound to capture the public imagination.

And so it was that a small company called Tokyo Tsushin Kogyo K.K. (Tokyo Telecommunications Engineering Corporation) introduced Japan's first miniature transistor radio, the TR-55, in mid-1955. It was sold on the Japanese domestic market, but didn't exhibit quite the fit, finish, and quality that their later radios were known for. All that changed with the international release of their TR-63 "Transistor Six" shirt-pocket radio in 1957. Instead of shoehorning in traditional components, the TR-63 was designed around all-new miniature devices. It was the smallest radio ever manufactured and went on to sell over 100,000 units in four different colors, setting the standard against which future radio sets were judged. But this was only the tip of the iceberg.

TTK changed their name to Sony Corporation in 1958 (Incidentally, Sony is meaningless in Japanese – they took the bold step of creating a name that would exclusively define their brand). In what was to become typical Sony style, their next pocket radio was even smaller and sleeker. The TR-610 sold over 430,000 units – an astounding figure at that time. And, most importantly, Sony established itself as a dominant force in the consumer electronics world. American companies found themselves unable to compete against a flood of affordable and highly miniaturized devices from Japan.

Modern Neo-Retro Radios

Early transistor radios make great collector's pieces. Because of their age, many have fallen silent and those that still work are not always in top shape. But don't despair – there are still companies out there that offer the quality and simplicity of a good old-fashioned transistor radio, except with high-quality modern components. Here are a couple.

Famed audio designer Henry Kloss co-founded Acoustic Research in 1952. He created the timeless Tivoli Audio Model One tabletop radio in 2000, at the age of 70.

Tivoli Audio Model One

Satellite radio frightens me, and not just because of Howard Stern. It's their sneaky subscription model that has me quaking in my boots. Y'see, I figure that after dropping a few thousand rubles on a nifty new radio, I shouldn't have to fork out my hard-earned kopecks every month for the privilege of keeping the music coming. Of course, this argument is just a ruse to hide the cold, hard truth: I'm a cheapskate.

So, instead, I drool over 'classic' tabletop radios. Some of the best come from Tivoli Audio, a company originally set up to offer products created by famed audio wizard Henry Kloss. His Model One radio is a legend – one speaker, one huge tuning knob, one box, and one very reasonable hundred dollar price tag. By using discrete components instead of off-the-shelf integrated circuits, this radio is able to precisely tune stations that lesser radios might miss. Reviewers appear quite impressed with its sound quality, too. [www.tivoliaudio.com]

If your audiophile tendencies lean toward modern conveniences like stereo, CD players, and garishly colored plastic, Tivoli can oblige you with slightly more sophisticated units as well.

Crosley Radio was founded in 1920 and went on to become one of the world's largest radio manufacturers. The Crosley name was licensed in 1993 to produce a modern line of neo-retro electronics.

Crosley CXRM satellite radio

Crosley's CRXM Explorer 1 satellite radio is the audio equivalent of VW's New Beetle. At first glance it reminds you of something from the fifties. When you take a closer look, all you see is wickedly cutting-edge design. It offers AM/FM/XM radio, a smattering of presets, dual alarms, EQ, and a headphone jack. The crowning glory is the wooden cabinet made from actual trees. [www.crosleyradio.com]

Sinclair Z1 micro radio

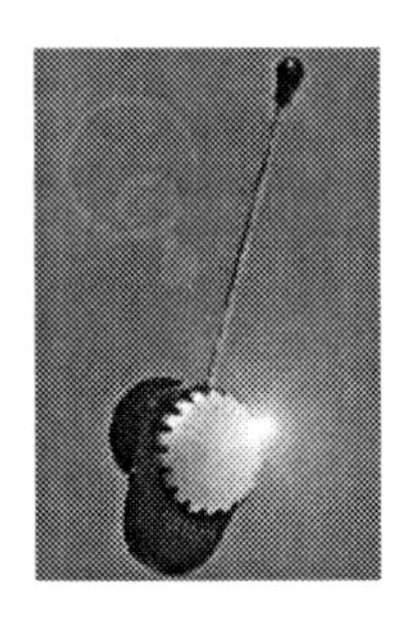

The Sinclair Z1 micro radio is the ultimate in radio miniaturization. If you're in an area with strong signals, you can even remove the antenna completely.

Before the famous Sinclair computers and calculators, Sir Clive Sinclair made radios. He still does.

The half-ounce (14 g) Sinclair Z1 Micro AM Radio is the smallest radio I've ever seen. To make things even more compact, the antenna can be removed when used in areas with good reception. It runs for 40 hours on one SR44 button cell, and a key-chain carrying case is included to keep this little widget from getting lost.

Sir Clive released a similar FM ear radio in 1997, although its clip-on design was elephantine in comparison to this. And now, the best part. They're still available directly from Sinclair Research for a mere £9.95 (approximately $18). [www.sinclair-research.co.uk]

Vintage Candle 1218 portable transistor radio

The story goes that some 1970s vintage Candle 1218 transistor radios were abandoned in the back of a Texas warehouse. After a quick glance, it's obvious why. They feature newfangled AM/FM/SW reception, complete with a genuine Eye Stabber 1000 telescoping antenna. These things are apparently available in equally hideous shades of red or green. The AC adapter and 4 AA batteries are not included (not that you'd want 30 year-old batteries shipped to your house anyway). Personally, I think it'd look great sitting on your trendy new IKEA coffee table. Given the $99 price tag, check out a few garage sales first – I suspect you could find one of these somewhere for a buck and a handshake. [www.sovietski.com]

Not everything from the past was beautiful, of course. The Candle 1218 radio is an endearing example.

Delonghi toaster radio

I include this item as an example of wretched marketing excess. Why else would one build a Flash Gordonesque radio into a perfectly serviceable toaster? Sometimes it makes sense to combine appliances. Take the toaster oven, for instance. It toasts and it ovens. Easy to explain, easy to use. The $50-ish Delonghi toaster/radio isn't so easy to explain.

It's a rather nice looking 2-slice toaster with a built-in Kenwood FM radio. I suppose it would be handy in a cramped apartment kitchen, but who in their right mind puts fiddly radio knobs right next to a couple of poker-hot electric heating elements? On the other hand, it's the only radio with a slide-out crumb tray. [www.delonghi.com]

Toast and music have never looked so good together. The Delonghi TT756 is available in blue, red, yellow and silver. They won't say which color makes the best toast.

Build Your Own Radio Station

PCI Max 2005 FM radio transmitter

Forget Internet podcasting. It's time to consider starting a real pirate radio station.

PCS Electronics would love to outfit your PC with the PCI Max 2005 card. This 149-euro ($183) 300 mW stereo FM transmitter fits inside a PC for easy access to your mp3 collection. If you want a bit more power, you can add a 15 Watt booster for another 179 euros ($220). The resulting 11 km (7 mile) range should bring the Radio Police to your door within hours.

The PCI Max FM radio transmitter even works in stand-alone mode (no PC required).

This would be perfect for broadcasting the *Bee Gees Greatest Hits* across your estate for the serf's enjoyment. Just don't blame me for the uprising. Panicky Legal Dislaimer: FM radio transmitters are illegal in many countries. Check with local authorities if in doubt. [See www.pcs-electronics.com – a new 2006 model is slated for release about the same time this book goes to press. It offers a new 15 kHz lowpass filter for dramatically better sound, along with a few redesigned features.]

Building A Radio Out Of Household Odds & Ends

Scitoys.com

Let's jump back to the dawn of radio. First introduced in the early 20th Century, crystal radios are incredibly simple devices powered directly by radio waves. That means they need no batteries, require few parts and can be built quickly by bored do-it-yourselfers. I built one as a kid, but not like this.

Simon Field's scitoys.com offers instructions for building radios using common household items – as if McGyver decided to drop by for the afternoon. You'll discover how to make a simple coil antenna using a plastic water bottle, craft a tinfoil and wax paper capacitor, and assemble a lethal-looking diode out of a rusty old razor blade. If that's not enough, he guides you through the assembly of a simple AM radio transmitter using little more than an electronic oscillator and an audio transformer. Field claims it can be built-in a mere ten minutes.

The Kosmos Radiomann kit is perfect for teaching older kids about radio technology. Of course, nothing is stopping you from buying one for yourself.

We live in a world where we're encouraged to see technology as magic. These simple designs help to anchor us to the science behind the mystery. They're also way cheaper than an iPod.

Radiomann Crystal radio kits

Kosmos Radiomann kits were first introduced 70 years ago. A lot has changed in the world of technology since 1935, but you can still build an updated version of the German original. It comes complete with glowing vacuum tube and wooden case. Because you construct it yourself, the set can be quickly modified (instructions for over 30 experiments are included). The unit is battery powered so you don't have to worry about accidentally zapping yourself with high voltage, and can be configured to receive AM and Shortwave broadcasts. [www.hammacher.com]

Build Your Own Loudspeakers

Building your own stuff is an awesome way to get high quality at a decent price. Hi-fi aficionados have known this for decades. In the 1960s, wannabe NASA scientist-types built their own Heathkit amps and radio receivers. These days, soldering together your own THX Certified Digital Home Theater System just isn't feasible. It *is* possible to make a great set of speakers, though.

The Audio Review speaker kit includes everything you need to build your own audiophile-quality bookshelf speakers.

Madisound offers everything a reasonably sane do-it-yourselfer could ever need, including dozens of different speakers, crossovers, capacitors and inductors. For those (like me) who don't know the first thing about speaker design, they offer ready-to-build kits. I was quite taken with the $340 Audio Review speakers, available in clear, black or red oak finish. Each cabinet houses a 1" tweeter and 6.5" mid-woofer. Their sensitivity is a decent 89 dB and they can handle a solid 100 Watts RMS. The great thing about building from a kit is that you have the freedom to spend a little extra on gold-plated mounting posts, snazzy metal oxide resistors, and a Kenny G album to suck up to your significant other. Shudder.

[Check out the kit at www.madisound.com/ar_com.html]

Tape Machines

The first magnetic recorders used wire instead of magnetic tape. A thin wire was passed over a recording or playback head at an incredibly fast 24 inches per second (61 cm/s). The end result was passable for speech, but not good enough for high-fidelity reproduction.

The Germans started the quest to perfect magnetic audio tape in the 1930s. Key German technology was brought back to the United States after WWII. Companies like Ampex worked hard to perfect it. The first time-shifted broadcast was a Bing Crosby radio show in 1948 (Crosby invested in Ampex, since he saw the advantage of recording his shows on his own schedule). Ampex went on to introduce the first broadcast videotape recorder in 1956.

Reel-to-reel recorders remained popular audiophile devices until the end of the 1970s, when advances in audio cassette formulation and noise reduction led to its adoption as the de-facto home recording standard. Reel-to-reel analog recorders continued to be used in professional recording studios, where high tape speeds and tape widths of up to 2" allowed pristine multitrack recording. Even today, many artists record on two-inch 24-track tape, insisting that it offers a more appealing sound than digital.

There were numerous cartridge-based tape formats released over the years, but many are now impossible to find. One of the most popular was the 8-track cartridge system that was introduced in 1965 as an accessory for Ford cars. Ampex, Bill Lear (of Learjet fame), and RCA Records backed the format. 8-Tracks sold well throughout the 1970s in North America, although they weren't nearly as popular in Europe. Their design split the tape into 4 separate stereo tracks which played in a loop. It was impossible to rewind the tape, and the track order of albums was frequently rearranged to avoid awkward silent pauses at the end of a track.

Reel-to-Reel

Reel-to-reel recorders were known simply as tape machines until the introduction of compact audio cassettes in the early 1960s. The heyday of reel-to-reel was the late 1970s, when companies like Sony, Akai, Nakamichi, Revox, and Technics offered high-quality stereo recorders for home use. Home recorders captured audio on ¼ inch tape at either 3 ¾ inches per second or 7 ½ inches per second.

The first transistorized reel-to-reel tape machine was Sony's TC-777. Later models such as the Sony TC-630 were designed to be part of modular home stereo systems, usually accompanied by a high-quality amplifier, stereo speakers and a turntable.

Reel-to-reel recorders were made in large numbers and can be great yard sale bargains. Be sure to check the condition of the playback heads – they wear down over time. If you like analog audio, I guarantee you'll enjoy the sound of a top-notch reel-to-reel deck. Expect to pay $100 to $300 on eBay for high-end equipment in good condition.

By the way, tape manufacturer Ampex was eventually spun off and renamed Quantegy. For a while they existed as the only analog

The Sony TC-777 transistorized professional reel-to-reel tape recorder was state of the art in 1961.

tape manufacturer in North America. They declared bankruptcy in 2004, signalling the possible end of the line for audiophile reel-to-reel tape. Fortunately, there continued to be significant demand for their product from professional recording studios and they resumed production in early 2005.

There are no mainstream manufacturers of home reel-to-reel recorders left (except for one system that uses a modified cassette mechanism) so you'll have to resort to eBay and vintage equipment specialists if you're intent on tracking one down. If you believe in Karma, you might just find one for sale in the classified section of the local newspaper.

Revox A77: My favorite reel-to-reel recorder

The Revox A77 was introduced in 1967 with a list price of around $900. It accepts up to 10 ½ inch reels and runs almost silently. The first thing that will strike you when you hear one of these is the quality of sound – far beyond what one has come to expect from the more common cassette format. The machine remained on the market until 1980, when it was replaced by an updated version with similar sound quality.

Revox lives up to the legendary Swiss reputation for quality – many of these old machines are still functional and enjoyed by tape connoisseurs. Even though it's well designed, the A77 will require

An artistic shot of the Revox A77 from an old sales brochure. Tape reels could be plastic or metal, with many enthusiasts opting for expensive metal reels because they look wonderful.

tweaking and repair from time to time. Surprisingly, spare parts remain relatively easy to come by, although not always affordable.

There's something almost religious about re-recording CD versions of classic jazz and rock records back to analog tape. The result is organic – mild tape compression of the high end and a slight thickening of the bass.

Nagra SNST-R miniature reel-to-reel tape recorder

It's hard to get an idea of just how small the Nagra SNST-R is without actually holding one.

The Nagra SNST-R miniature reel-to-reel tape recorder is a Swiss work-of-art weighs that weighs a mere 21 oz and measures a svelte 5.75" x 4" x 1" – not much larger than an iPod. It runs for a respectable 5 hours on a pair of rechargeable AA batteries, and the Nagra site recommends the SNST-R as "the ideal candidate for all portable, location or discreet recording applications."

They conveniently forget to mention that you need to be a gazillionaire to afford one; it retails for a stratospheric 9599 euros. [www.nagraaudio.com]

An icon: The Compact Audio Cassette

Creating mix tapes of songs was a favorite pastime for many in the 1980s. It took incredible skill to mix and match moods, tempos and bands in a way that really captured the essence of your musical personality. Suddenly, your music could accompany you anywhere – at home, in the car, and in portable players like the Sony Walkman.

The youth of the 1980s were the second generation weaned on portable audio. Their parents lived through the birth of the portable radio in the 1960s. But this was different. Unlike their parents, these kids had full control over the music they listened to, thanks to the ubiquitous Sony Walkman that exploded onto the market in 1979. For the first time, people could seal themselves into their own little musical universe. The boombox took things even further – we became able to share our musical world with others, whether they wanted to hear it or not.

The cassette tape is becoming increasingly rare these days. They're commonly available in lengths up to 120 minutes, although the thin tape used in longer types is more prone to breaking.

Philips Compact Audio Cassette: An early open standard

Philips developed the Compact Audio Cassette in 1963. At the time, it was just one of several competing cartridge-based formats designed to simplify home tape recording. RCA had developed a magazine-style system in 1958, and Grundig began pushing to develop a German standard in the early 1960s.

Philips approached Sony Corporation in Japan after realizing that Japanese acceptance of the new format would vastly improve the chance of success. After some heavy negotiation, Philips agreed to license the system to Sony without royalties. In fact, by 1965 Philips had opened the format up to other manufacturers free of charge.

The cassette initially offered fairly poor fidelity and was marketed for voice recording and dictation. Technology improved quickly and advances in noise reduction technology, stereo recording, and new tape formulations soon assured high-quality sound from the compact format. Incidentally, Philips went on to codevelop the Compact Disc.

Dolby Noise Reduction

The popularity of cassettes was driven in part by a noise reduction system developed by Ray Dolby, who had been part of the team that created the first rotary-head videotape recorder for Ampex.

Most reel-to-reel and cassette players produced throughout the 1970s and 1980s offered one form or another of Dolby noise reduction and pre-recorded tapes often included Dolby B encoding. These systems were simplified versions of Dolby's professional Type A 4-band system. They offered single-band noise reduction – reducing noise above 1KHz by 10 dB (Dolby B) or 20 dB (Dolby C).

Dolby B and C are the most common noise reduction systems in the consumer tape world. They both work in a similar manner by companding an audio signal – reducing the dynamic range of a signal during recording, and expanding it on playback. While Dolby B and C gained considerable popularity, a third system called Dolby S arrived too late – cassette tape was on the way out, superseded by pristine and extremely portable compact discs. Dolby went on to create digital encoding systems that are common in modern movie theatres and home entertainment systems.

Budding entrepreneurs should take note: Dolby chose to license the system, rather than waste resources on manufacturing. It was a smart move that made Ray Dolby a billionaire.

Sony Walkman: Revolutionizing the Audio Experience

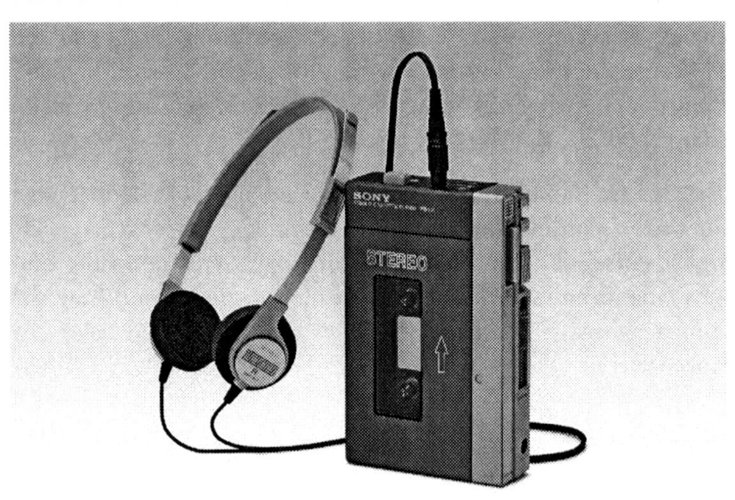

The Sony TPS-L2 Walkman was initially priced at 33,000 Yen because it was released during Sony's 33rd year.

Sony Corporation introduced the TC-100 portable cassette recorder in 1966. My father owned one and it was a magnificent piece of engineering. It accompanied us in the car on many long drives, perched on the back seat between my sister and I. Of course, it had several limitations. The first was that it was monaural. The second and most serious issue was that most of its body was taken up by electronics and a hefty speaker. This limited its practical application to home listening and the occasional car trip. Jogging with one of these under your arm was out of the question.

In the late 1970s, Sony introduced the Pressman – a very small portable cassette recorder. It was a monaural unit designed for media gathering, with a correspondingly high price tag. Sony's then-Honorary Chairman Masaru Ibuka wanted a compact music player that he could take on trips and asked the company's Deputy President Kozo Ohsone to modify the Pressman to create a portable stereo music player. The device was a stunning success and impressed everyone who heard it.

By early 1979, Sony Chairman Akio Morita clearly saw the possibilities of this tiny device and assembled a design team to create a smaller and less expensive player that could be carried everywhere, hoping to emulate the success that the transistor radio had enjoyed in the 1960s. There was only one problem: the new unit dwarfed the massive earmuff-style headphones of the 1970s.

Ibuka found the perfect solution to the headphone problem on one of his frequent visits to Sony's research labs. An R&D team had almost finished development of an ultralight headset that weighed a mere 50 g. The timing was perfect, and these were released with the TPS-L2 Walkman on July 1, 1979.

The Walkman was introduced to the USA in mid 1980 as the Sony Soundabout. By 1984, sales of pre-recorded cassettes outpaced vinyl and the Walkman was an established global phenomenon. By its 20th anniversary, Sony had sold 186 million units. Even though other technologies have taken its place, Sony still produces a handful of affordable Walkmans starting at a mere $17.95.

Sony made an enormous variety of Walkman models – many barely larger than the cassette they house. They are great collector's items and many of the smaller second-hand models make excellent everyday listening devices, too.

Television brought the excitement of world-class entertainment into the home.

Exploring the Television Age

The ethereal world of television has shaped the lives of several generations. A mere sixty years ago newspapers, radio reports and newsreels molded our understanding of the world. That all changed in the 1950s when television invaded households throughout North America and Europe. TV made the world feel smaller and less isolated. It also became an incredibly powerful tool to influence public opinion and sell products.

And – for the first time – viewers could experience the sights and sounds of world-class entertainment from home. It was the beginning of what Faith Popcorn eventually termed *Cocooning* – the trend of retreating to the safety and comfort of one's own home. If you pause for a moment, you'll realize that most of the items in this book owe their existence to this trend toward home entertainment.

The first B&W television from Philips, introduced in 1951.

Early Electronic Television

Early TV broadcasts were in black & white. Television gained popularity in the United States after World War II at a phenomenal rate, with over 50% of American households owning a TV by the end of 1954. Videotape wasn't perfected until 1956, so shows were either performed live or shown from film using a conversion device called a Telecine.

Television offered miniscule screens in the late 1940s – 9 inches (22 cm) was considered huge. The display tube was extremely curved in front and far from rectangular. In fact, some Zenith models from the late 1940s featured round picture tubes. By the late 1950s, technology had advanced to the point that RCA was able to make enormous 21" color screens, although the price was comparable to a modern 60-inch plasma set.

Development of the Sony TV8-301 pushed the Sony R&D team to the limit. Its revolutionary all-transistor design stunned gadget lovers when it first appeared.

Sony Corporation introduced the first 5-inch all-transistor television in 1960, foreshadowing Japan's future dominance of the television industry. The TV8-301 was black & white and has just about the coolest Jetson's styling I've ever seen. By the time Sony's R&D team had finished their design, they had created 9 brand new transistor devices, including a high-frequency tuning transistor that was completed only a month before the set was released. It goes without saying that the set was extremely expensive and its bleeding-edge components were prone to frequent failure. Seventeen years later Sony would once again revolutionize the color television industry with the introduction of the Trinitron picture tube.

These days, you can pick up a portable B&W TV for under $20, like Coby's 5" portable with AM/FM radio (available from Toys 'R' Us). I added one to my Christmas list as the perfect set for playing Atari Flashback 2 games.

Ampex VRX-1000: The first commercial video tape recorder

The world's first practical videotape recorder was released in 1956. It was as large as a dining room table and cost a cool $50,000. The Ampex VRX-1000 featured an incredibly modern-sounding model number, too.

The Ampex VRX-1000 videotape recorder is on the right, beside a rack of broadcast video equipment.

Ampex discovered that the secret to recording video on tape was to use a rotating head. This enabled them to fit 90 minutes onto a single reel, making the VTR practical for TV broadcast use. The tape ran past the head at 15 inches per second, so those reels must have been huge! They hit on the right approach: Modern VHS and minDV recorders use similar rotating head mechanisms.

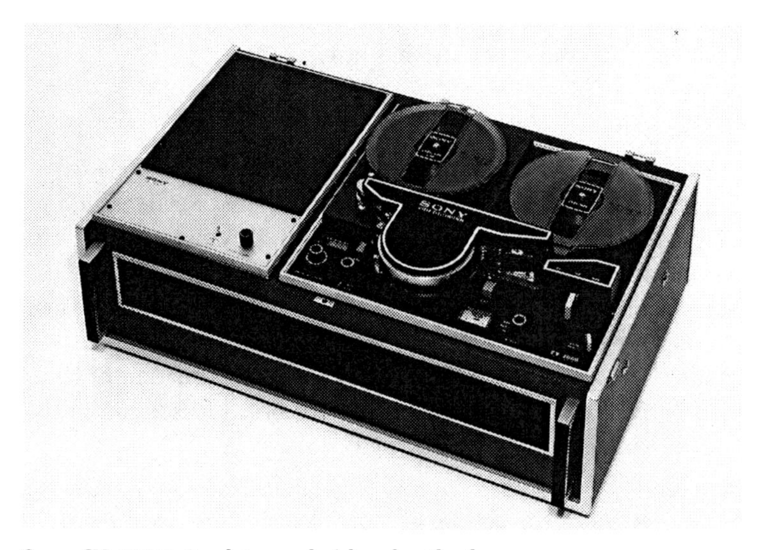

Most Sony CV-2000 VTRs found their way into commercial or educational settings.

Sony CV-2000: Reel-to-reel video for the home

I rarely go nuts over a gadget, believe it or not. But rest assured that I would be like a kid in a candy store if I had a chance to play with the Sony CV-2000 reel-to-reel home video tape recorder (launched in August, 1965). This $695 unit enabled the average

Joe or Jane to record their favorite television shows on half-inch reel-to-reel tape for future enjoyment. In actuality, most CV-2000s were sold for industrial or educational purposes.

The CV-2000 recorded in black and white, matching the technology of the day. The tape ran at 7.5 inches/second, allowing a maximum of 1 hour on a 2,370 foot reel. Rewinding took seven minutes, and I dread to think what would happen if the tape transport jammed – you'd have a roomful of tape spaghetti. Additional reels of tape cost $40, a princely sum at the time.

Sony also offered the compact VCK-2000 TV camera kit, including camera, tripod and microphone. I suspect that somewhere out there a few lucky people have home videos recorded in the mid 1960s. Of course, the quality was laughable by today's standards. Sony used rotary heads and double sideband FM recording to capture the video and audio signals, but the result was a mere 200 lines of horizontal resolution.

An essential feature of the modern VCR is conspicuously absent: the clock timer. The designers were so focused on creating the video equivalent of the hi-fi reel-to-reel recorder that they missed the importance of unattended recording. Funnily enough, the clock was still missing when Sony rolled out the first Betamax VCR in 1975. But that's another story.

Television goes color

Color television systems had been demonstrated for decades, but early color systems were incompatible with existing B&W sets. A compatible system was developed in the early 1950s, and the Tournament of Roses Parade on January 1, 1954 became the first nationally broadcast color show in the United States. In Europe, conflicting broadcast standards delayed the introduction of color by over a decade – the first regular color broadcasts began in the United Kingdom on July 1st, 1967.

Sony announced the closure of most of their tube-based television plants in 2005. This wasn't much of a surprise, given the sudden popularity of LCD and Plasma flat panel displays.
The Trinitron KV-1310 was introduced in 1968 and met with rave reviews because of a new color tube technology that was far superior to the standard shadow mask tube. It featured a stunning 13-inch screen, received VHF and UHF transmissions, and

The Sony Trinitron picture tube offered an incredibly bright and clear color image. This is their first Trinitron, the KV-1310, dating from 1968.

became the first consumer electronic device to win an Emmy award in the early 1970s.

Betamax vs. VHS:

BATTLE OF THE VIDEOTAPE FORMATS

Sony Betamax

I take the ability to time-shift my favorite shows for granted these days, although I use a hard drive based PVR rather than tape. Back in the mid-1970s, the idea was revolutionary. Sony was the first company to mass market a cartridge-based videocassette recorder, based upon their professional U-Matic system. They introduced the SL-6300 VCR in 1975. Aiwa, NEC, Pioneer, Sanyo and Toshiba eventually licensed the technology.

Japan Victor Company's VHS (Video Home System)

In 1976, JVC introduced VHS as a competitor to Sony's Betamax format. The technology was similar to Sony's – both used half-inch tape and rotating recording heads. JVC's licensing policy was reportedly less strict than Sony's, resulting in more companies adopting the format even though it offered a slightly lower quality picture.

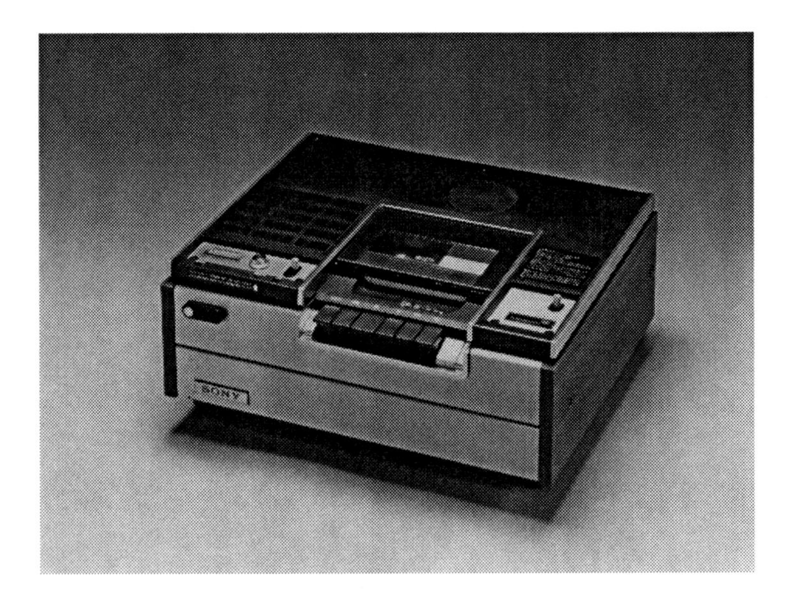

Sony's first top-loading Betamax VCR, introduced in 1975. It offered better quality than competing VHS decks, but Sony eventually lost the format war.

The video format war

The battle between Betamax & VHS was intense. The Sony system was widely regarded as technically superior and Sony held the initial lead in sales. There were several problems with Sony's technology, though. The video rental industry was in its infancy in the late 1970s, so most VCRs were purchased by people who wanted to record off-air shows. VHS had a distinct edge here, since early Betamax tapes could record only one hour of high-quality video, versus two hours on each VHS tape. Betamax tapes also took noticeably longer to rewind because the tape head could not be disengaged. VHS recorders were much faster because they automatically disengage the head before rewinding.

The unfortunate result of the tape differences was that consumers and retailers perceived VHS to be a better format, even though this was certainly not the case technically. The final nail in Sony's coffin was that JVC made it easier for manufacturers to adopt their technology, resulting in far more companies adopting the format. This doesn't seem like a significant stumbling block until you realize that consumers are more likely to buy a format that offers a choice of 100 models over a 'lesser' type with only a few dozen. Sales of Betamax recorders and tapes began to nosedive around 1984, and Sony threw in the towel and introduced their first VHS VCR in 1989.

Sony didn't completely lose the fight, however – a high-quality version of the Beta format went on to dominate the professional market.

MCA Laserdisc

The MCA DiscoVision format – as Laserdisc was originally known – was developed in the late 1960s. Philips first demonstrated a prototype player in 1969. The format was released as the first commercially available consumer optical storage medium in 1978. Movies were stored on huge 12-inch (30 cm) double-sided discs. Video was stored at a resolution of 400 lines (440 in Europe) – almost twice that of VHS tape. And – unlike future optical media – Laserdiscs stored analog video rather than digitally encoding it. This means that Laserdiscs don't suffer from the blocky artefacts that often mar DVD.

Philips VLP 720 Laserdisc player from 1983. The discs measured an enormous 30 cm (12 inches) in diameter.

The format was reasonably successful in Japan but met with indifference in the United States, where players sold at a premium. Adding to the format's troubles, it wasn't possible to record on discs and they stored a maximum of 60 minutes per side, necessitating several flips and swaps during a film.

Pioneer still manufactures several Laserdisc players for the Japanese market, and their DVL-919 dual LD/DVD player is still listed on their US website with a list price of $1275 (I was able to find it at B&H Photo in New York in late 2005). Online stores such as www.discountlaserdisc.com offer thousands of movies, although very few new titles appear in the format apart from Japanese Anime.

RCA SelectaVision

RCA introduced the SelectaVision format in 1981. It has the distinction of being one of the last consumer electronic standards developed entirely in the USA. Movies were encoded on large VideoDiscs that were read mechanically using a replaceable stylus.

Front-loading RCA SelectaVision player playing a demo disc on an RCA TV. My apologies for the hideous wood grain.

VideoDiscs were encased in plastic sleeves because they were extremely susceptible to dust and contamination. Technically the format was similar to VHS tape – about 240 lines of resolution. Each side held a maximum of 60 minutes of video, requiring a flip halfway through a feature film.

The format was discontinued in 1984, after selling about 500,000 units. VideoDiscs were probably doomed by their short playing time and inability to record – most households chose tape-based VHS recorders instead. There's still a thriving online community of collectors who buy, sell, and trade old players and movies, although none have been produced since the mid-1980s.

Predicta manufactures a line of beautiful 1950s-styled televisions with modern color tubes and components. They're not cheap, but they sure are pretty.

Predicta televisions

Through an unfortunate geographical accident, my family didn't own a television until I was about seven years old. When the boob tube finally arrived, I cheerfully bathed in the warm black & whiteness of the intense gamma radiation emitted by the glowing screen. My mother warned me many times not to sit so close, lest I receive a fatal dose.

I miss those days. Which is probably why I'm so excited that Predicta has released a line of truly beautiful retro-style televisions. The tubes bulge out of the cases, cheerfully flaunting their lack of lead shielded plutonium injectors (that's a joke, by the way). This is the *Holiday*, although I'm especially fond of their *Meteor*, which looks like it was involved in a NASA rocket experiment sometime in 1957. Apparently, these beasts are made with new-fangled solid-state components and a color picture tube. Lethal radiation not included. [To check out Predicta's stunning lineup, visit www.predicta.com]

Retro Enterprises – Reincarnated Japanese televisions

Retro Enterprises in Tokyo offers an interesting lineup of vintage televisions. They replace the innards of stylish boxes from the 1950s and 1960s with brand new color TV components. The result is a remote-controlled vintage TV with state of the art picture quality. The lineup includes funky models from Toshiba, Hitachi, Matsushita (Panasonic), Sanyo and others.

A beautiful NEC RT-33 television, upgraded with modern components from Retro Enterprises in Tokyo.

The star of Retro's lineup is the 168,000 Yen ($1450) Model RT-39 with a way-too-modern 15-inch Fujitsu LCD screen. It has VGA, S-Video and standard inputs and receives both NTSC and PAL transmissions, ensuring worldwide compatibility. As with all of Retro Enterprises' updated TVs, you'll have to use the remote to change the channel and volume – the ancient front panel controls aren't connected to the modern internals. Retro Enterprises also stocks an enormous number of Fuji Single-8 cameras and film. Owner Tak Kohyama speaks English, so e-mail him with questions if you're interested. [Visit film.club.ne.jp/english/englishindex.html for the full scoop.]

End Of The Television Age – Antennas

While looking around my neighborhood this morning, I realized there were no TV antennas poking out from the rooftops. They were replaced by cable TV or little round satellite receivers in the blink of an eye.

I suppose this is another sign that the Television Age is well and truly dead. Thirty years ago we were limited to a small handful of off-the-air programs. If a good movie or show was on, half of the neighborhood was watching. Now viewers are faced with the daunting task of choosing from hundreds of boutique channels. And – worst of all – we have to pay a significant monthly fee for the privilege of watching commercial-splattered shows.

All is not lost. You can still pick up an excellent analog TV antenna such as a futuristic $99 model from Radio Shack. It can be installed in your attic so your neighbors don't make fun of your old-fashioned ways. And – best of all – there's no $30 per month access fee.

The incredibly compact Terk HDTV indoor antenna will soon be popping up in a living room near you.

The introduction of digital broadcast TV means that people in metropolitan areas will be able to receive great looking (and sounding) digital TV with indoor HDTV antennas like Terk's sleek little $50 unit. It's cool to think that digital TV will encourage the redeployment of a sea of antennas.

Making Better Video: Digital Film Restoration

Lowry Digital Images

This was going to be a section about the restoration of *Casablanca, Star Wars,* and the *Indiana Jones* films. But when I started investigating the background of John Lowry, the magician who restores these old films frame-by-frame, I discovered something far more interesting.

In the beginning, Lowry ran a little company in Toronto called Image Transform. One of his earliest successes was cleaning up the dodgy black and white images broadcast from the moon by NASA astronauts. At that point there was no digital television, so all manner of analog ghosting, fuzzing, and waviness crept in. By transferring images to film through a fancy set of electronic filters he was able to bring out details that were previously invisible.

These days, he runs Lowry Digital Images (recently acquired by DTS), the leading digital film restoration company. The company uses racks of Apple PowerMacs to process terabytes of scanned images. In addition to color correction, dust and scratch removal, the company has developed proprietary software to eliminate frame jitter and weave. The results are unbelievable – rock steady images without any of the flaws we've lived with for so long. I own a restored copy of *Casablanca*, and can heartily recommend any of their other restorations, including *North by Northwest* (their first restoration), *THX 1138*, the *Indiana Jones* DVD boxed set, and the re-re-re-released *Star Wars* trilogy. [Lowry is now a division of DTS – drop by www.dts.com/digital_images/ for their full restoration catalog.]

Camcorders & the Fisher-Price Pixelvision

You might have noticed the distinct absence of handheld video cameras in this chapter. That's because I'm unsure of their place in history. The first camcorders were certainly revolutionary, but the low quality and awkwardness of many early portable video recorders makes them virtually useless today. We merely interpret their output as "cheap video."

Oddly enough, I suspect that video recording technology will advance over the next ten or twenty years to the point that video cameras will capture imagery that far exceeds even the best film equipment. At that point, quirky lo-fi video from the early 1980s will begin to have value as a Retro format. People will use it just to emphasize its imperfections.

There is one camcorder I'm willing to include here. It's the Pixelvision PXL 2000 from toymaker Fisher-Price. The PXL 2000 appeared in 1988 as a low cost kid's video camera. It records decidedly lo-fi video on standard audio cassette tapes running at very high speed (approximately 4X normal). The PXL 2000 captures a mere 100 lines of resolution (versus about 500 from a modern miniDV camcorder) and grabs only 15 frames of video per second. To top everything off, the camera features a cheap fixed-focus plastic lens. A tiny matching 4" B&W monitor was available as an accessory.

The result? A unique and totally charming device with a cult following. It sucks low-definition images from a dreamy and hazy parallel world in which fast-moving objects and people leave ghostly contrails. These things are now the domain of artsy-fartsy collectors and video dreamers – expect to pay hundreds for one in good working condition. [See www.jm3.net/pxl/ for a Pixelvision FAQ and links.]

Travel back to a time when hundreds of unique computers battled for the hearts and minds of technology enthusiasts.

Invasion of the Microcomputers

The history of microcomputers often gets told something like this: First, there were confusing boxes covered in switches and blinking lights. Then came slightly less confusing boxes with keyboards from Atari, Apple, Radio Shack and Commodore. They were crushed a few years later by the combined might of Microsoft and IBM, although Apple is still clinging to life. End of Story.

The real tale is a tad more interesting. Browse through computer magazines from the late 1970s and early 1980s and you'll discover literally dozens – maybe even hundreds – of microcomputer companies. All but a few systems were based on incompatible designs. Software written for a Commodore 64 couldn't run on an Atari 800, for instance. Technology advanced so fast that even machines from a single manufacturer were rarely compatible with each other.

The Apple Macintosh introduced millions of people to the graphical user interface and the mouse.

The 1970s: In the Beginning

Scelbi + Mark-8

The Scelbi and Mark-8 computers were offered in kit form in 1974. Both machines were based on Intel's early 8008 microprocessor. They were intended for hobbyists, but the high cost and relative simplicity of early components made it difficult to build capable systems. Still, these machines had a lasting impact on computer-minded engineers. Young programmers and designers formed computer clubs like the *Homebrew Computer Club*, where members Steve Wozniak and Steve Jobs demonstrated the Apple I in 1976.

MITS Altair 8080

The Altair was the first mass-produced Intel 8080-based home computer, introduced in 1975. The newly introduced Intel 8080 microprocessor was intended as an industrial controller for elevators and traffic lights but proved ideal as the brains for a home machine. In actuality, most Altairs incorporated the improved 8080A processor. The price was a reasonable $595, although the system offered nothing more than a front panel of blinking lights and toggle switches at that price, along with a meagre 256 bytes of memory. An optional video card offered 64 character by 12 row text output in UPPER CASE ONLY. You could also connect the machine to a serial terminal, assuming you had one kicking around your research lab.

The company went on to produce the more professional looking Altair 8080B in 1976, as well as a Motorola 6800-based machine called the Altair 680 in late 1975. The clock speed of the 680 was a mere 500 kHz – just about the slowest machine I've ever stumbled across.

Incidentally, the first microcomputer BASIC was written for the Altair 8080 by Paul Allen and Bill Gates. Allen served as the company's Associate Director of Software for a short while, dividing his time between MITS and a little company he co-founded with Gates called Micro Soft.

In the end, MITS gained a reputation for releasing faulty hardware, ultimately leading to the company's collapse.

IMSAI 8080

The IMSAI 8080 was the second mainstream Intel 8080-based microcomputer, hot on the heels of the MITS Altair. Nearly 20,000 were built before succumbing to a wave of easier-to-use products from the likes of Apple, Radio Shack, and Commodore. There was no built-in keyboard, just a front panel full of switches and lights. You had to connect a terminal if you were planning any meaningful programming.

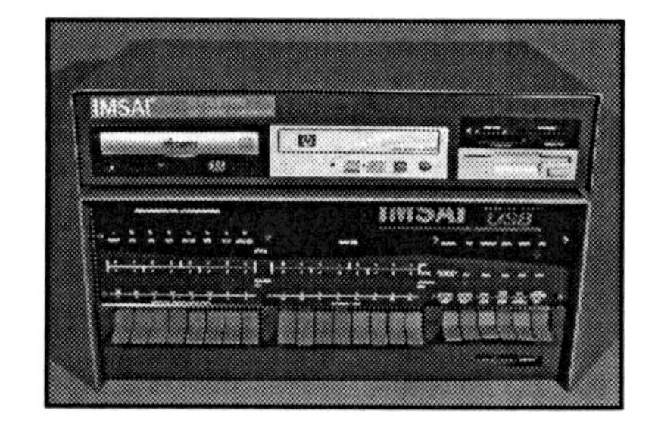

An IMSAI Series Two USB machine (bottom) with the mini drive subsystem perched on top. It doesn't get much geekier than this.

IMSAI recently announced an updated version of their original system. The new IMSAI Series Two is a hybrid – it can function as a vintage S-100 computer running the archaic CP/M operating system, but there's room for a modern Windows & Linux compatible motherboard as well. The motherboard has been upgraded significantly – it now includes a Zilog eZ80 Acclaim 50 MHz microprocessor with built-in Ethernet network capabilities.

In essence, you're buying the ultimate retro case mod with a bonus CP/M computer thrown in for kicks. If you're a true Ubergeek, a USB port can be used to interface the vintage system with an external PC.

The machines are made by the Fischer-Freitas Company, formed by a couple of IMSAI employees who bought the rights to the system in the late 1970s. This may be the best way to taste vintage computing – not only does the re-released system offer USB and modern components, but you get support and software from the old company. Try that with your MITS Altair 8800 or Intertec Superbrain Jr.

The IMSAI Series Two starts at $995 and includes a classic (long) cabinet, power supply, USB-enabled front panel with blinky lights and flippy switches, S-100 system motherboard, and enough software to get you started. You'll have to provide your own ATX motherboard, hard drive, and accessories if you want to add a modern PC alongside the vintage system.

If you have the urge to expand your new IMSAI, the Series Two Mini Drive Subsystem is a retro-styled case to house floppy, CD-ROM/RW and DVD-ROM/RW drives. I know the idea of adding DVD compatibility to a 1970s-vintage CP/M system sounds a bit whacky, but don't forget there's room for a seriously modern PC-compatible ATX motherboard behind all those switches and lights. [www.imsai.net]

Apple I (June 1976)

Fake wood is very much in fashion these days. Several of Dell's laptops can be outfitted with wood panels, and enterprising do-it-yourselfers have started to churn out teak laptops, oak iPods and mahogany PDAs. None of these hold a candle to the original Apple 1 computer, Wozniak and Jobs' first crack at creating a true mainstream personal computer, typically built into homemade wooden boxes (it didn't come with a case)

Do you remember the original Apple rainbow logo? I still have an old Apple sticker glued to my toolbox. Here's a slightly more whimsical interpretation:

Their revolutionary approach involved placing everything onto a single circuit board, rather than in a huge box full of backplanes, connectors, and tangles of wire. Only a few were made, but everything they learned from their first machine went into making the Apple II an earth-shattering success. They chose not to use Intel 8080 processors because, at $175 a piece, they couldn't afford them. They went with the lowly 6502, available for a mere $25. Wozniak was also hung up on the daft idea of including a keyboard instead of a good, solid panel of switches and blinky lights. Computers have never been the same since. Loaded with 4K of memory, it was announced on April 1, 1976 priced at $666.66 (I'm not making this stuff up!) Many of them didn't work properly – par for the course back then.

These days, the Apple I is a priceless collector's item. Have no fear, h4x0rs! Tom Owad and John Greco have written *Apple I Replica Creation: Back to the Garage*. This 416 page how-to guide leads you through the process of building and programming your very own Apple I replica. I can't see many people actually going through with it, but picking up a copy to understand the innards of a simple microcomputer can't hurt. Now if only you could hook a PlayStation controller up to this thing.

If you want something ready-built, a company called Briel Computers [www.applefritter.com/briel] offers the Replica 1 – a $159 DIY version of the Apple I. It's much smaller than the original, relying on modern components to replace outdated and discontinued integrated circuits.

Apple II (1977)

The Apple 1 would have become a footnote in computing history if it had not been followed by the incredibly successful Apple II. This $1298 machine set the benchmark for serious home and office use in the late 1970s. It could accommodate a very respectable 48K of memory and initially relied on an external cassette recorder for program storage.

A 1979 Apple advertisement encourages people to buy the Apple II because it won't "limit" them to an array of pre-programmed cartridges or restrict them to monochrome graphics.

An external 143K floppy drive followed in 1978, making the Apple II one of the first home machine systems to include "standard" floppy disk storage (you could add a total of two). By mid 1978 Apple was offering the Apple II Plus, which came with 48K standard.

Steve Wozniak's design did many things right: it incorporated a user-friendly keyboard in an era when most machines offered a baffling front panel of lights and switches, it included bit-addressable color graphics, supported low-cost floppy drives, and included a good BASIC language interpreter.

By 1979, over 50,000 Apple II machines had been sold. But that was nothing compared to the success Apple was about to have because of an innovative piece of software named *VisiCalc*. It was the world's first spreadsheet program, a prehistoric forerunner of programs like *Microsoft Excel*. *VisiCalc* was first released for the Apple II, giving a huge boost to business sales. By 1982, a stunning 750,000 Apple II systems had been produced.

Even though it was superseded by the Apple Macintosh in the mid 1980s, variants of the Apple II proved extremely popular in the education market. The last Apple IIs rolled off the line in 1993, a full fifteen years after the system's introduction.

Commodore PET (June 1977)

The MOS 6502-based Commodore PET was introduced in 1977 with a meagre 4K of memory. This model earns a special place in my heart as the machine I learned to write spaghetti BASIC on.

An early Commodore PET 2001 with built-in tape drive and horrendous rectangular keyboard. At least they used a QWERTY layout.

It offered stunning integration: the motherboard, keyboard, monitor and tape drive all shared a single 'stylish' case. The PET also had its share of quirks – while later PETs had keyboards designed for Earthlings, early versions used something akin to a cash register keypad. But – since I didn't know any better – I thought it was fabulous.

The first series of PETs offered white phosphor monitors, but at some point these were exchanged for trendy green-on-black *Matrix* displays. All Commodore models featured a secondary set of graphic icon characters that could be displayed instead of letters and numbers. This allowed simple graphic display without requiring a bit-mapped graphics controller.

I've had a recent hankering to find a dead PET and replace its innards with something a tad more modern. It'd be worth it, just to see people do a double-take.

Radio Shack TRS-80 Model I (August 1977)

In 1977, Radio Shack was at the forefront of the home computer revolution. Their Model I computer was shipped as a ready-to-use system. The motherboard was built into a bulky keyboard unit and shipped with a plug-in B&W monitor and a portable cassette recorder for program storage. The basic unit could support up to 16K of memory, although an expansion dock was available that increased memory to 48K and supported 5 1/4 inch floppy drive storage. I liked the crisp 64 character x 16 line display – far better than squinting at fuzzy television displays of the era.

The machine was a surprise success for Tandy/Radio Shack – more than 200,000 were produced before it was withdrawn from the market in early 1981, having failed to meet new electromagnetic emission standards in the USA. Its direct replacement was the all-in-one Model III, but times had changed and the replacement's crude B&W images and lack of sound were no longer competitive. The $3500 Model II was introduced in late 1979, but it was aimed squarely at the business market (with two 8-inch floppy drives, offering an unprecedented 500K of storage each).

Atari 800 & 400 (November 1979)

By 1979, Atari was well known for its arcade and home videogame consoles. The Atari 800 computer was an attempt to extend their success into the home computer market. It was also the first mass-market microcomputer to incorporate a custom chipset. The ANTIC chip handled video configuration, GTIA took care of displaying the video data, and the whimsically named POKEY scanned the keyboard, generated sound, and handled serial communication. Atari created their own pared-down version of BASIC, issued as a plug-in 8K ROM cartridge.

Atari countered Apple's advertising strategy by increasing the standard memory in their Atari 800 to 48K and selling it for half the price of a comparable Apple system.

The 800's biggest drawback was its strange serial-based peripheral system. This made add-ons extremely expensive, unnecessarily increasing the cost of must-have peripherals such as a cassette or 90K floppy drive. Its best features were the two plug-in cartridge slots under the top panel – simply plug in a program and go.

The Atari 400 was the 800's little brother. It shared the same general design, and was envisioned as a low-cost game machine. It had an absolutely despicable membrane keyboard, a mere 8K of memory, and less expandability than the 800. To their credit, Atari offered a decent selection of their popular games on cartridges that snapped into the machine's single cartridge slot.

The 8-bit Atari lineup went through countless changes and model numbers in the early 1980s before being supplanted by the technically superior 16-bit Atari ST series in 1985.

The 1980s: Joining the Mainstream

Radio Shack TRS-80 Color Computer (July 1980)

The CoCo was Radio Shack's belated foray into the world of color computing. It offered a palette of only four colors.

Radio Shack followed up the success of its TRS-80 Model I, which featured an underwhelming B&W display, with the Color Computer (CoCo) in July 1980. It was designed to connect to the antenna input of a TV using an RF modulator to reduce cost.

The keyboard was a bizarre full-sized chicklet-style unit that was challenging to touch type on, and the basic configuration offered a mere 4K of memory and could display only mediocre 4-color graphics. It did have a few things going for it: a game cartridge port, a low price ($399), a multi-tasking operating system (OS-9), and the support of the Radio Shack sales network.

Sales were respectable and the CoCo 2 and CoCo 3 eventually followed. The white-cased CoCo 2 arrived in 1983 and included a much-improved keyboard, smaller case, more memory, and the ability to display lower case characters. The CoCo 3 was introduced in the face of stiff competition in 1986. It included an upgraded processor that could run twice as fast as the previous model and a custom graphics processor that supported up to 64 colors.

Commodore VIC-20 (January 1981)

The Commodore VIC-20 wasn't much to look at, but it was affordable and capable. Commodore eventually discounted it to as little as $99.

Commodore followed up their incredibly successful PET line with the VIC-20. This $299 machine featured a custom chipset (seeing a pattern yet?) and included only 4K RAM – barely enough to hold a respectable program. Like the TRS-80 Color Computer and the Atari 800/400, it included a cartridge slot for programs and supported cassette program storage, although the cassette drive wasn't introduced until 1982.

The VIC-20 was immensely successful, eventually selling more than 1 million units. It also had significant limitations: the display showed a mere 22 characters of text on each screen line and could display only 176 X 184 pixels.

Commodore's experience with the VIC-20 helped to pave the way for the immense success of its successor, the Commodore 64.

TI 99/4A – Sixteen bits of popularity (June 1981)

Texas Instruments supplied transistors for the world's first pocket radio in 1954. Twenty-seven years later, they were manufacturing one of the most popular home computers in the United States – the TI 99/4A, an immensely successful follow-up to their 1979 99/4 model.

Texas Instruments enlisted the services of popular comedian Bill Cosby to promote their TI 99/4A computer. They weren't nearly as cool as Commodore, who hired William Shatner of Star Trek fame as their pitchman.

The machine was extremely well specified: it featured a TMS9900 16-bit processor, a minimum of 16K memory, 16 color graphics, and a convenient expansion port. About 2.8 million 99/4A machines were produced through 1984.

The system debuted with a list price of $525, although the cut-throat market of the early 1980s required steep discounts and rebates to keep the machines rolling out of the door. Eventually, the system was redesigned (much like the inexpensive late-1980s Commodore 64C) to reduce production costs. The newer machines sported a beige color scheme.

Texas Instruments could have had far more success with the 99/4A line if they had shared details about its operation and interface design. This would have enabled third-party developers to design add-on accessories. As it was, TI chose to keep this information to themselves – probably in an attempt to increase add-on sales.

IBM PC Model 5150 (September 1981)

I almost didn't include the IBM PC, because I don't consider it to be a home computer. It was expensive and most were sold with a high-resolution monochrome card designed for word processing and spreadsheeting. The system was to have a phenomenal long-term impact on the computing industry, however.

The machine was based on a 4.77 MHz Intel 8088 processor with 64K RAM, 64K ROM, and one or two built-in 5 ¼ inch 160KB floppies. Buyers could select between a high resolution monochrome graphics card or a lower-rez 4-color color graphics adapter (known as CGA).

The original IBM PC was built like a tank, setting it apart from "lesser" home computers that tended to use plastic cases. The keyboard case was solid metal and featured incredibly noisy "tactile" keys.

Several things made the 5150 successful: IBM's marketing clout, Microsoft's compact PC-DOS operating system, a vast array of time-saving business software, and a card-based expandable architecture. Microsoft's implementation of MS-BASIC had a fairly significant impact in the early days, too, but this became less important over time.

While the PC was a big success in the business market, most home users gravitated toward much more affordable offerings from established home computer companies such as Atari, Commodore, and even Apple (although Apple made significant inroads in business, thanks to *VisiCalc*).

The PC didn't start to conquer the home market until the late 1980s, when a proliferation of capable clones sparked a price and feature war that continues today.

BBC Micro (Late 1981)

Determined not to be left out of the coming "computer revolution," the British Broadcasting Corporation decided to produce a series of television and radio shows focused on microcomputers. They published a list of specifications and set about looking for a company to design and produce a reference platform. A tiny company called Acorn won the design competition and the BBC Micro was introduced in early 1982 at a price of £235. It was based on the 6502 microprocessor and came with 16K of RAM (later expanded to 32K). It could display color graphics at up to 640 x 256 pixels, and the built-in BASIC interpreter was excellent.

With the support and credibility of the BBC behind the little company, they went on to sell more than one million systems. The BBC Micro became the standard educational computer in the UK and was supported by a broad range of software titles.

Acorn produced a lower cost version called the Acorn Electron in 1983. They underestimated demand and it was in short supply throughout the 1983 Christmas season. Time marched on, and Acorn introduced several good computers in the late 1980s – the BBC Master (1986), and the brilliant 32-bit ARM RISC-processor equipped Acorn Archimedes (1987). Neither achieved the runaway success of Acorn's early machines.

The ZX81 was seen as a toy because it had no moving parts. The keyboard is a printed membrane. The ZX Spectrum offered an "improved" raised rubber keyboard.

Sinclair ZX Spectrum (April 1982 in UK)

The $200 Sinclair ZX80 and subsequent $99 ZX81 introduced over half a million people to affordable home computing. They had low cost membrane touchpad keyboards, hardly any memory (as little as 1K) and displayed only black and white characters.

Sinclair's follow-up ZX Spectrum could produce a rainbow of color (OK, not quite – 8 colors at two different brightness levels) and featured an almost-normal rubber chicklet keyboard. It sold for £99 with 16K of memory, but could accept up to 48K. While Sinclair sold millions of these machines in Europe, they didn't have similar success in the USA where Timex had only moderate luck marketing their own version.

Commodore 64 (September 1982)

The Commodore 64 is an icon among 1980s home computers. I have no firm idea how many were sold, but my guess is over 20 million. The success of the C64 is a direct result of selling a brilliant design at a reasonable price (initially $595, eventually much

Commodore was able to sell their C-64 for only $595 because it incorporated an incredibly cost-effective custom chipset. It was estimated that Commodore's per-unit cost for later versions of the machine was less than $50.

less). It came equipped with a 1 MHz 6510 microprocessor (a Commodore-manufactured 6502 derivative), 64K memory, a good BASIC interpreter, a ground-breaking 3-channel programmable analog synthesizer and a capable custom graphics chip.

You had a choice of cassette tape program storage (slow) or an enormous external 5 ¼" floppy drive (also slow). The disk drive was an interesting piece of work – it contained its own microprocessor and communicated with the main computer via a serial cable. The design was definitely more attractive than a wide ribbon cable, but loading and saving files was a tedious process. To alleviate boredom, many games took advantage of the machine's brilliant sound capabilities and played high-energy tunes while loading.

Microsoft MSX – The Japanese standard (Late 1983)

The MSX reference standard was extremely popular in Japan during the mid-1980s. All MSX machines were based on a common reference design and ran MSX-DOS – an early command-line based operating system from Microsoft. A standardized Microsoft BASIC programming language was embedded in ROM and all MSX machines featured at least 32K of memory and a 3.58 MHz Zilog Z80 microprocessor. It was a clever idea in a market fragmented by incompatible competing systems that allowed manufacturers to introduce new machines with the benefit of pre-existing software libraries.

I was digging around in my basement a while ago and came across a box of forgotten music gear from the 1980s. The most exciting discovery was my old Yamaha CX5M MSX-compatible music computer. Released in 1984, this little beast offered a built-in FM synthesizer and MIDI IN/OUT ports. It also includes Microsoft Extended BASIC for programming. Methinks I'll have to dust it off, power it up, and hack up a few strange little MIDI mangling synthesizer programs.

Apple Macintosh (January 1984)

Like the IBM PC, I have a hard time placing the Macintosh on this list, although it is also one of the most influential designs of all time. The Mac is now a common home computing platform. This certainly wasn't the case in the mid-1980s, though. When it was introduced, the Mac was too expensive for all but the most serious home hobbyists.

The original 128K Macintosh debuted at a price of $2495. It included a built-in 9-inch monochrome display, a speedy Motorola 68000 16-bit microprocessor, a single built-in 3 ½ inch floppy drive, mouse, and a ground-breaking graphical user interface.

The original Mac shape is one of the most recognized design icons of the early microcomputer era; elegant and understated, much like its operating system. It's possible to pick up used Mac Classics (an early 1990s update of the original design) in good shape for around $100. I've been thinking about picking one up to run some ancient music sequencing software, actually.

In many ways, the Macintosh was the mid-1980s equivalent of Apple's modern iPod music player. It ensured Apple's survival when nearly every other manufacturer fell by the wayside.

Atari 520 ST (June 1985)

The Atari ST was a well-designed 16-bit "next generation" home computer. It was also the first home machine to include built-in MIDI ports to connect electronic music synthesizers and sound generators. It didn't take long for the ST to become the preferred platform for musicians and computer-based sequencer packages such as Cubase became immensely popular (Cubase is still available today, running on Windows and Mac OS).

The Atari 520 ST was the first 16-bit platform from Atari. It included MIDI interface ports, making it a favorite with musicians.

The Atari ST series owes its existence to former Commodore boss Jack Tramiel. He left Commodore in 1984 and set about acquiring then-struggling Atari, with the intention of releasing a Motorola 68000-based 16-bit personal computer. He negotiated an agreement with the Amiga development team, but it collapsed when his first act upon buying Atari was to fire all of the company's old (and well respected) engineers.

Tramiel's new Atari Corporation went on to develop the Atari 520 ST in about a year. It ran TOS, an operating system that combined Digital Research's GEM window-based environment with a Microsoft DOS-like system called GEMDOS. Amusingly, GEMDOS was based on the old CP/M system used in systems like the IMSAI 8080. One advantage of GEMDOS was that it could read and write MS-DOS format disks.

The 520 ST was released in June 1985. It featured 512K RAM, a full-sized keyboard, and interfaced with one or two external floppy drives and a hard drive. Most of the components were off the shelf, including a Yamaha-designed sound chip. The exceptions were the graphics chip and several "glue" chips. The 1040 ST was introduced in 1986, with 1MB memory and a built-in floppy.

The ST series offered excellent performance at a reasonable price, making it a popular platform. Its biggest competitor turned out to be the Amiga, which was snapped up by Commodore.

The Amiga 2000 looks like a boring beige PC, but it was one of the most powerful multimedia machines of the 1980s.

Commodore Amiga (July 1985)

The Commodore Amiga (originally the Amiga Lorraine) was a stunning piece of work. It was originally envisioned as the ultimate game machine, but the design worked well as a general purpose computer, too. The Amiga project was originally begun in 1979, although it wasn't demonstrated to the public until 1984.

The Amiga 1000 ($1295) was the first model to see the light of day. It looked strikingly like a PC-compatible: a beige case with an external keyboard and monitor. It was based on the Motorola 68000, but what made the Amiga magic was its custom chipset. It had three coprocessors: Denise (video), Agnus (memory management), and Paula (4-channel 8-bit sampled sound playback) Consequently, it was one of the first affordable machines capable of displaying high-resolution full-color graphics while playing realistic multi-channel sampled sound.

The Amiga became popular because of its amazing capabilities, but it wasn't until the release of the all-in-one Amiga 500 that it became an affordable mainstream computer. Its Kickstart operating system was based on a system originally designed for minicomputers, with an ingenious boot sequence that loaded the Kickstart low-level system routines first, then a set of Amiga DOS graphic and interface libraries second. As a result, applications (usually games written in assembly language or C) could be loaded without requiring unnecessary operating system components in memory.

Ugly Ducklings: Oddball Microcomputers

Designing hardware for simple home microcomputers became a relatively trivial exercise in the early 1980s. It was nearly always quality software (or the lack of it) that predicted a machine's success in the marketplace. It's easy to laugh at the massive blunders made by even the largest manufacturers in those early days, but don't forget that we have the benefit of 20/20 hindsight. Back then, technology was changing at a breakneck pace and it wasn't at all clear where the market was headed.

Intense competition in the industry meant that prices dropped significantly each year while capabilities skyrocketed. Unfortunately, it also meant that consumers frequently got handed the short end of the stick. They paid hundreds of dollars for systems advertised as "expandable and future-proof" only to find them obsolete and discontinued within a year. By 1984, faced with a slowing economy, people stopped buying all but the most popular systems and the market imploded. It took several years before a new crop of brilliantly designed machines – the Commodore Amiga, Atari ST and Apple Macintosh, along with a growing number of IBM PC clones – pulled the market out of its slump.

Here are a few slightly odd or misguided machines for your amusement. Several were quite popular, although most of these were budget machines rushed into production in the lead-up to the 1984 market collapse.

Rockwell AIM 65 (1977)

I scrawled a comment into a notebook a few weeks ago about the $375 AIM 65: "Insane cash registerish thing." That pretty well sums it up. Rockwell was better known for its defence contracts than its microcomputers. The AIM 65 was a 6502-based machine with a built-in single line LED display and a cash register style thermal printer on the top panel. It came with either 1K or 4K of memory, dual cassette interfaces for storage, and three empty internal ROM slots for programming languages or user programs.

The AIM 65 was a decidedly strange looking machine that proved useful for industrial and scientific purposes.

The AIM 65 was quite successful because it filled a wide range of industrial needs by being cheap, simple, and extremely compact.

Sinclair ZX80/81 & Timex 1000 (February 1980)

I love the Sinclair ZX80/ZX81 computers. I bought a ZX80 by mail order when they were first advertised in BYTE magazine, unable to resist the bargain-basement price. These machines were cheap for a reason: The keyboard was printed on a large flat membrane, much like you'd see on a microwave oven. They had 1K of memory and displayed B&W text on a TV set. No graphics, no sound. The display memory was shared with program memory, so the display of an unexpanded machine included "garbage characters" that were actually part of your BASIC program. Still, it offered a Z-80 compatible processor and an OK version of BASIC. Around 100,000 were sold before the introduction of the ZX81.

Sinclair was brave enough to offer the ZX81 as a $99.95 mail-order kit. It was possible because the design was so simple that it required only 4 integrated circuits.

The follow-up ZX81 featured an even simpler design with only four integrated circuits (some had an extra RAM chip, for a total of five), an RF modulator, and some discrete components. Because of its simplicity, Sinclair offered it as a kit for $99.95, or fully assembled for $149.95. Hundreds of thousands were sold, and I remember seeing it discounted to as little as $49.95.

One interesting Sinclair quirk was the use of tokenized BASIC for programming. Instead of typing commands like PRINT or INPUT, you entered a special key sequence to select the statement that was printed on one of the keys.

Zebra Systems in New York [www.zebrasystems.com - (212) 675-8414] still markets the ZX81 kit at $99.95. I'm not sure how many they have in stock, but this is a great opportunity to build a seriously Retro piece of computing history.

Jupiter ACE (April 1983)

The incredible success of the Sinclair ZX81 led many manufacturers into the dangerous world of cheap and cheery low-end computers. The Jupiter ACE was the doomed child of one of these expeditions.

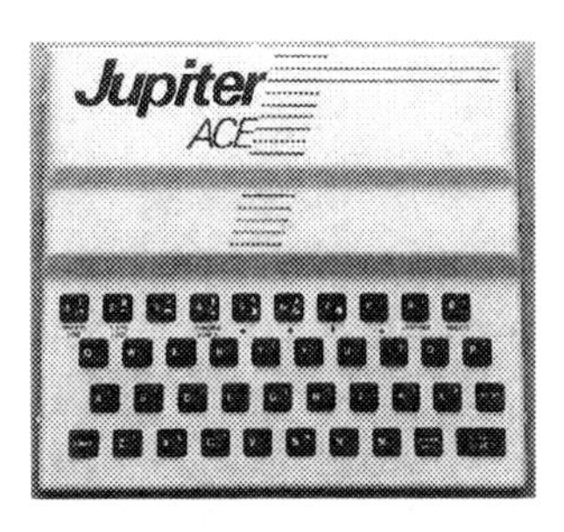

The Jupiter ACE was designed by some of the members of the Sinclair ZX team and it reminds me in more than one way of a strange cross between the ZX81 and ZX Spectrum.

The ace up Jupiter's sleeve (groan) was that instead of including a built-in BASIC language interpreter, it was based on a nifty but obscure language called FORTH. This must have been very cool for the engineers who developed the system, but the public accepted it with as much glee as they would accord to a three week old rotting fish.

Pity, because the £89.95 machine was a respectable piece of work. It could generate beeps and included 3K of memory (expandable to a rather odd 51K). A useless factoid: the machine's designers also worked on the Sinclair ZX Spectrum.

Texas Instruments 99/2 (1983)

This shot of the TI 99/2 was taken from a magazine ad featuring Bill Cosby (yes, those are his hands).

By 1983, Texas Instruments faced fierce competition at the low end of the microcomputer market. Commodore had reduced the price of their popular VIC-20 to the hundred-dollar mark and Sinclair & Timex were making a name for themselves with low budget home machines. Texas Instruments didn't want to be shut out of the low-end market, figuring that low-end sales would lead to future upgrades within the TI line. They designed the TI 99/2 to fill this gap and placed splashy magazine ads featuring pitchman Bill Cosby.

The 99/2 was designed to retail for $99.95. It had B&W graphics, no sound and only 4K of memory. The keyboard had 48 calculator-type keys. An underwhelming offering.

By its release in the spring of 1983, things were so competitive that TI had already discounted their mainstream 99/4A model (sometimes selling below $200), and it made no sense to flog a less capable machine for only a few dollars less.

Mattel Aquarius (June 1983)

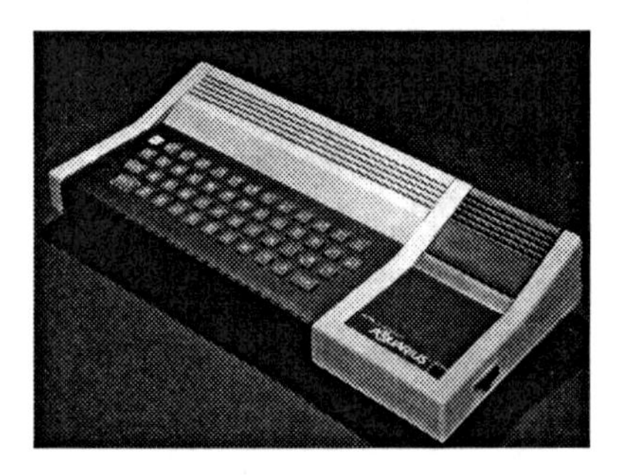

Cartridges for the Aquarius were strangely angled to plug inconspicuously into the back right side of the console.

Mattel is best known for creating the first 16-bit videogame console, the Intellivision. Like Coleco, they saw an opportunity to leverage their success into the home computer market. The $159.95 Aquarius was designed by Radofin Electronics, the Hong Kong company that manufactured the Intellivision. The machine featured the common Zilog Z-80A processor at 3.5 MHz, and accepted either 4K or 16K memory packs. The Aquarius graphics display was much the same as the Intellivision – it would have been impressive in 1981, but 40x24 column text and blocky 16-color graphics at 80 x 72 pixel resolution were hardly a head-turner in mid-1983.

The Aquarius was just one more in a sea of almost-good-enough machines released in 1983. It met with indifference and vanished after selling only a handful of units. Strangely, Mattel's 1983 Aquarius Home Computer Catalogue lists an Aquarius II with a full-travel keyboard (rather than the chicklet style model on the lower cost unit) and up to 64K memory, along with a 4-color printer. No word on price or whether they actually reached production.

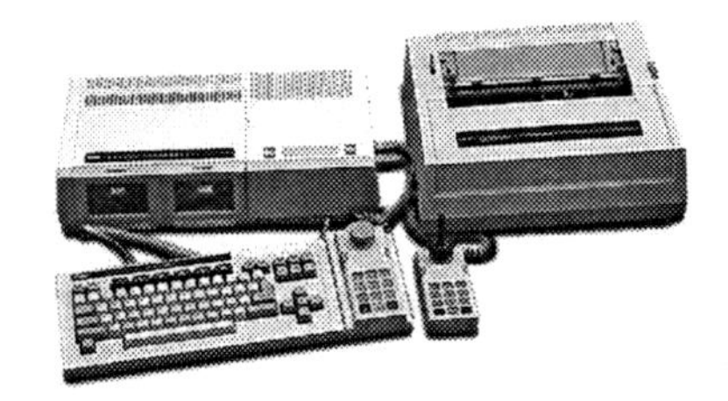

The Coleco Adam featured two front-mounted tape drives. They looked like standard cassettes but required special tape.

Coleco Adam (October 1983)

The Colecovision was a successful and quite capable videogame console introduced in 1982. The Adam was an attempt to capitalize on this success by adding a full-fledged computer system to the main unit. You could buy it in two configurations: A standalone system, or as an add-on for your Colecovision unit.

The system included a daisywheel printer and external keyboard, with a serviceable word processing package in ROM. It also included a high-speed tape drive for program storage. For some peculiar reason, the power supply was in the printer case – it wouldn't turn on without the printer attached.

The system was priced at $595. It included 80K memory, a respectable 3.58 MHz Zilog Z-80A microprocessor, and full compatibility with Colecovision game titles. Unfortunately, the system just wasn't ready for prime time – a significant number of Adams were returned to the factory because of defects, and Coleco lost millions.

In an effort to rescue the PCjr, IBM released "PCjr Booster" which included a mouse and enough RAM to let it run most popular Microsoft titles. It was too little, too late.

IBM PCjr (November 1983)

IBM attempted to crack the home market in late 1983 with the PC Junior. This not-so-cheap PC-DOS machine was an attempt to capitalize on the popularity of their business-oriented but expensive PC.

The PCjr was an expensive ($1200) flop. It featured a clever wireless keyboard design, but IBM used ghastly plastic chicklets instead of proper full-sized keys. To make things worse, they'd attempted to simplify the various interface ports on the back, making the PCjr incompatible with generic accessories and cables. To add insult to injury, it didn't run many popular PC software titles and required an add-on if you wanted to display 80 columns of text per line. The final nail in this machine's coffin was the name; who wants to invest $1200 in something that's merely a 'junior' computer?

The TRS-80 MC-10 was a bargain-priced machine that was discounted to $79.95 in 1984, as Radio Shack tried to clear out unsold inventory.

TRS-80 Color Computer MC-10 (End of 1983)

The MC-10 was pitched as an entry-level machine to compete with ultra-cheap designs like the Sinclair ZX81. It arrived in late 1983 at a price of $119.95. Unfortunately, its tiny keyboard was even harder to use than its big brother's , it offered an equally deficient display and only 4K of memory. It was definitely a better machine than the ZX81, but didn't have the power to be a Really Useful Computer. It vanished quietly in early 1984.

At least the Commodore Plus/4 had a proper keyboard. It sported an odd brown and beige color scheme and wasn't compatible with the popular Commodore 64.

Commodore Plus/4 (1984)

Commodore was one of the most prolific microcomputer design companies of the 1980s. They're famous for the VIC-20 and Commodore 64, but designed literally dozens of machines (such as the VIC-21 SuperVIC). Their creation that intrigues me most is the Plus/4 – it just doesn't make sense.

The Plus/4 was built around Commodore's TED single-chip computer concept. TED was envisioned as a way to profitably produce extremely cheap computers, although the Plus/4 was at the high end of the product line. The Plus/4 was intended as a follow-up to the C64 and VIC-20 but used a different microprocessor and system architecture (making it incompatible). It had a better built-in BASIC programming language and could display more colors, but did away with the sound generator and hardware-based graphic sprites that made the Commodore 64 so successful. Oh, and it included a suite of low-quality built-in applications.

Regrettably, there was only so much fun to be had with a home machine focused on word processing, spreadsheets, databases, and a drawing program. One can only imagine the boardroom politics that resulted in this disaster making it to production.

Early Portables

Osborne I (April 1981)

This $1795 machine weighed in at 24.5 lbs and just fit under a standard airline seat, qualifying it as a 'portable.' It ran the CP/M operating system and was one of the first machines to come bundled with an array of useful software (*Microsoft BASIC, SuperCalc spreadsheet,* and *WordStar*).

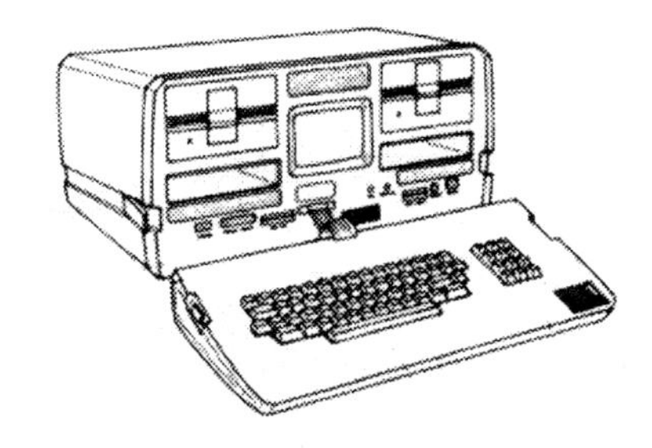

The Osborne One demonstrated that miniaturization still had a long way to go. Still, it served the needs of business people admirably.

Osborne earns a place in the Essential Retro Hall of Fame for putting themselves out of business by pre-announcing a new 'executive' model many months before it was ready to ship. The result? Everyone said, "Ohh... I'll hold off buying until the new one's out." Predictably, sales plummeted and they filed for bankruptcy in 1983.

Their lasting legacy was the term "Osborne Effect," to describe the damage inflicted on current sales by announcing future models months or years in advance.

Compaq Portable (1983)

Join me on a trip back to the Dark Ages – January 1983, to be precise – and the introduction of the Compaq Portable computer. The Portable has the distinction of being the first IBM PC clone to include a legally reverse-engineered version of the IBM BIOS (low level system routines). The work-alike system software cost $1 million and took a year to write, but avoided the wrath of IBM's legal department.

Check out the two full-height 5 1/4 inch floppy drives on the right side of the case. The first version didn't have a hard drive (this was back in the days when MS-DOS fit on a single floppy).

The Compaq was actually the second MS-DOS compatible to market. The Hyperion, an attractive Canadian-built MS-DOS machine, was released several months prior. The Hyperion was a well-designed machine with a 7-inch amber monitor. I suspect it would have been a smash hit, except for the fact that its BIOS wasn't 100% IBM compatible, causing many popular MS-DOS programs not to run.

The luggable Compaq gave users the ability to take a truly IBM compatible computer with them wherever they travelled and was an instant hit. Compaq sold 53,000 units by the end of 1983, bringing in over $110 million.

The machine's specifications are laughable by today's standards: 4.77 MHz processor, 128K RAM , and two 5 1/4" floppy drives.

The Plus model (October 1983) added a 'gigantic' 10 MB hard drive. The 9-inch CRT display came in a gorgeous shade of green and featured the revolutionary ability to switch between MGA (hi-rez monochrome) and CGA (ghastly low-rez "color" mode).

At 34 lbs, this machine stretches the meaning of 'portable,' but it did offer a wicked arm workout.

Radio Shack TRS-80 Model 100 (1983)

The key to the Kyocera-built Model 100's success was it's full-sized keyboard. It was perfect for touch-typing almost anywhere.

Radio Shack was a major player in the early 1980s home computer market. I once owned a TRS-80 Model 1 with 16K memory and a crude B&W video display. The company was famous for marketing house-branded machines from other companies. This was the case with the TRS-80 Model 100, designed and built by Kyocera.

The $799 Model 100 was introduced in 1983. It offered a 40 character by 8 line screen, 8K memory (enough for about 11 pages of text), ran for 15+ hours on four AA batteries, and featured a built-in 300 baud (approximately 30 characters per second) modem. It included a version of the Microsoft BASIC programming language, and rumor has it this was the last product to feature code crafted by Bill Gates. I've heard similar rumors about the Japanese MSX computer series, though.

The Model 100 was an incredible hit with journalists, who quickly realized the power of this early notebook. Stories could be typed up anywhere and transferred back to the publisher using the built-in modem – a revolutionary approach. Over six million of these portables (and their offspring) were manufactured and they still have legions of dedicated users.

Texas Instruments Compact Computer 40 (1983)

The CC-40 might have been a great financial and scientific computer, had TI provided a way to store programs.

I've always had a soft spot for tiny computers. The CC-40 was a gem – it demonstrated the advantage of blending TI's home computer and pocket calculator expertise. Unfortunately, it offered no external program storage. It was intended to work with a miniscule wafertape drive which turned out to be too unreliable for real-world applications.

The CC-40 was built around a single-line 31-character LCD display and included a version of TI BASIC that was largely compatible with the 99/4A. The base configuration offered 6K memory but could be expanded to 18K.

I suspect this system could have made a huge impact on the engineering and scientific markets. It was small enough to carry around and powerful enough to run specialized programs.

Commodore SX-64 (1984)

Strangely enough, the first color portable computer came from Commodore. The SX-64 was a luggable 23 lb version of their smash-hit Commodore 64 desktop. Sadly, the SX-64 didn't fair well in the marketplace, probably because Commodore was better known in gaming circles than in the boardroom. And who wants to play games on a tiny 5-inch diagonal screen?

I remember being incredibly impressed when I first encountered the SX-64. Its 5-inch screen was incredibly sharp, although hardly ideal in a home computing environment.

The SX-64 shared many specifications with the Commodore 64: A MOS 6510 processor running at a blazing 1MHz, 3-channel SID chip sound, 64K memory, and an internal 170K 5 1/4" floppy drive. It listed for $995 when introduced at the Winter Consumer Electronics Show in January, 1984. At that same show, Commodore announced they had sold over $1B worth of personal computers in 1983 – becoming the first company to break the billion dollar barrier in the home PC market.

Cambridge Z88 (1987)

Sir Clive Sinclair made millions from his incredibly cheap line of ZX80 and ZX81 computers in the early 1980s, followed by even more success with the rubber-keyed ZX Spectrum lineup. His interests went far beyond computers, however. He got his start building transistor radios and progressed to introduce an enormously popular line of affordable electronic calculators and digital watches. He even dabbled with vehicle design, coming up with the ill-fated C5 electric scooter and even a futuristic sea scooter that is sold by watercraft giant Bombardier.

The Cambridge Z88 is one of the few retro-portables I would consider for everyday use. Its molded rubber keyboard is quiet and modern erasable memory packs are available.

Now that's out of the way, allow me to introduce my favorite Sinclair creation. The Cambridge Z88 is a sleek notebook computer that was introduced in 1987. It runs on four AA batteries and features 32KB of memory (upgradable). The display is a 640 x 64 monochrome LCD capable of three (count 'em!) shades of grey. A decent productivity suite was included: word processor, spreadsheet, calculator, BASIC interpreter, and various PDA-like widgets. To round off the package, software is available to transfer files to and from a PC or Macintosh.

Rakewell Limited still offers the Z88 and numerous accessories online. Prices start at £80.00, so this might be a perfect solution for someone needing a cheap writing machine with an almost full-sized keyboard. Or, if you're like me, you can use it to write incomprehensible spaghetti code in BASIC. [www.rakewell.com]

Dana takes some of the best ideas from notepads of the past and combines them with affordable modern technology. The result is a truly practical portable.

The Dana: A modern retro portable (2004)

I love classic notepad computer designs. Machines like the Cambridge Z88 and TRS-80 Model 100 were lightweight yet included full-sized keyboards and compact screens. I've been considering a Cambridge Z88 for a while, but the idea of lugging around such an elderly machine terrifies me.

Alphasmart makes a machine that harkens back to the notepads of the 1980s. The $429 Dana Wireless runs Palm OS, ensuring compatibility with thousands of programs. It features a full-sized keyboard, built-in 802.11b wireless capability and a respectable 7.25 x 2.25 inch (18.4 x 5.7 cm) monochrome screen. Dana's *Documents To Go Professional* software ensures compatibility with *MS Word, Excel* and *PowerPoint*. Palm OS productivity software is included along with a simple web browser and e-mail capability.

This machine is compact without being cramped: 1.9" x 12.4" x 9.3" (4.8 cm x 31.4 cm x 23.5 cm). It runs on 3 AA batteries or a rechargeable pack and the entire system weighs a modest 2.0 lbs (908 g).

Dana has a decidedly old-school feature set: No hard drive, no color screen, minimal memory and a lightweight OS. And guess what? She looks like an excellent low-cost replacement for a full-fledged laptop. [www.alphasmart.com]

Pocket Computers

Rapid advances in miniaturization made pocket computers a reality in the early 1980s. The first of these candy bar shaped machines were basically calculators on steroids. They usually offered a single-line LCD display, miniature QWERTY chicklet keyboard, and a cut-down version of the BASIC programming language. Bizarre tape printers were available as add-ons, in case you wanted to print out something that looked like a grocery store receipt. If you needed to store programs, micro-cassette interfaces could link to tape recorders. You just had to remember not to record the latest Kajagoogoo LP over top. Believe it or not, people actually wrote minuscule videogames for these things, too.

Radio Shack sold re-branded versions of many Sharp pocket computers in the early 1980s. This is the TRS-80 PC-3.

Sharp PC-1210 BASIC Computer (1981)

The most famous pocket computers were made by Sharp – they released the ground-breaking PC-1210 BASIC computer in 1980 (with 1K of memory) and continued making vastly superior variations until 2001. The PC-E500 shown here dates from about 1990 and is one of the more interesting models in their lineup - 32K RAM, scientific built-ins, and a gigantic (for the day) 4 x 40 display. Other manufacturers jumped into the game, too – Casio, Psion, NEC, Panasonic, TI and Seiko released a few models with varying success.

The Sharp PC-E500 was a fairly advanced pocket computer introduced around 1990.

Worth picking up if you can find one at a garage sale or on eBay.

A Japanese advertisement for the RC-20 wrist computer. Somehow, I can't see this thing becoming a fashion accessory.

Wrist Computers: Seiko Epson RC-20

I recently stumbled upon Pocket Calculator Show's "For Sale" page. They're offering a plethora of vintage wrist computers and digital watches to the unwashed masses (that's us).

The strangest is the Seiko Epson RC-20 Wrist Computer. It packs a Zilog Z-80 microprocessor and a touch screen interface in a package small enough to strap to your wrist. The idea was that you wrote some incredibly cool programs on your home PC, downloaded them to your watch, and then ran around the neighborhood demonstrating your coding prowess until the police arrived to subdue you. Very cool, nonetheless.

Other offerings include a copy of the Seiko digital watch worn by James Bond in *The Spy Who Loved Me*, a red Seiko wrist computer, and the tremendously daft Casio GM-1 10-in-1 Game Watch. [www.pocketcalculatorshow.com]

Atari Portfolio (1989)

Write-ups for the 1989 Atari Portfolio always describe it as "about the size of a VHS tape." Not much help in our tapeless world. These days, we'd have to compare it to a stack of DVDs or a half-dozen (or more) iPods.

The Atari Portfolio was a marvel of late 1980s miniaturization. Designed by DIP in Guildford, UK, it was more-or-less IBM PC compatible. The biggest compatibility challenge was the monochrome 40 x 8 character non-backlit screen – few programs could run acceptably with so little screen real estate, and even fewer developers produced Portfolio versions of their work. The machine featured an NEC V30 processor (Intel 8088 clone), a meager 128K RAM, and a Microsoft DOS 2.2 compatible operating system that was idiotically named "DIP-DOS." There was no room for internal floppy or hard drives, so everything was stored on battery-backed memory cards. A special card reader was available to transfer information to your desktop PC.

The Atari Portfolio was a great idea, except it ran very few of the most popular MS-DOS programs.

Oddest quirk: When turned off, the screen flashed briefly every couple of minutes as the machine woke itself to check the calendar.

The Portfolio was years ahead of its time, but its non-standard design kept it from being adopted by the business community. It (and the Atari Corporation) disappeared quietly into the mists of time in the early 1990s.

Apple Newton MessagePad (1993)

The Apple Newton MessagePad was one of the first mainstream PDAs (Personal Digital Assistants) to feature touch-screen handwriting recognition and full programmability. Its closest competitor was the Tandy/Casio Zoomer, a forerunner of the Palm Pilot that was introduced several months prior to the Newton's launch. Sony also dabbled in the early 1990s PDA market – the Japan-only PTC-500 Palm Top handheld was released in 1991.

The Newton MessagePad would have been a runaway success if Apple had waited another five years for smaller, faster components and better handwriting recognition software.

Most people know the MessagePad simple as the Newton, although that was merely the name of its operating system. The Newton captured the imagination of journalists when it was first shown in 1993. For a while it seemed that touch-screen tablets were poised to take over the computing world. Even though it looks like something from Steve Job's imagination, Newton was released five years before he returned to Apple as interim-CEO in 1997. Interestingly, it was Jobs himself who terminated the Newton project in March 1997, as an attempt to cut costs at the cash-strapped company.

Newton OS was one of the first affordable mobile platforms to include built-in handwriting recognition. Unlike Palm's later Graffiti system, the Newton required a few brief training sessions to learn the nuances of your writing style. Sadly, I was never able to achieve fantastic reliability with its recognition architecture. The MessagePad used an ARM 610 RISC processor at 20 MHz, offering 482K of system memory and 158K of non-volatile user memory. Applications and the operating system were stored in 4MB of read-only memory. The 336 x 240 pixel display was reflective – no fancy backlighting or color here. Later versions (such as the 2000 series) offered larger backlit displays and up to 8MB RAM.

While some users became devout MessagePad disciples, the Newton ultimately proved to be a slow-burning failure. I think there were several reasons: priced at $700, the original unit was too expensive to become a geek stocking stuffer. They were too bulky and heavy to slip into a pocket (later MessagePad models weighed as much as 1.4 lbs and measured a pocket-unfriendly 8.3 x 4.7 inches).

Perhaps most damaging to the Newton's reputation, early versions of the handwriting system (written by a team of Russian programmers at Paragraph International Inc.) didn't work well and became the brunt of many techie jokes. Even though Apple added a nice new print recognition engine to Newton 2.0, the old rumors persisted.

Finally, in early 1997, Apple tried to target the educational market with the laptop-like Newton eMate 300. It was discontinued 11 months later as the Newton line disappeared forever.

The Casio Zoomer looks remarkably like an oversized Palm PDA from the 21st Century, even though it was introduced back in 1993.

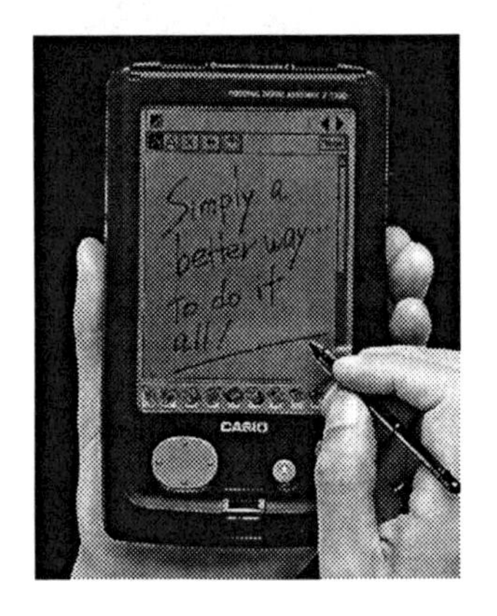

Casio / Radio Shack Zoomer (1993)

Long before the PalmPilot became a household name, Radio Shack introduced a PDA called the Zoomer. It featured a touch-screen display with handwriting recognition, along with a set of personal productivity programs. Best of all, it beat the Apple Newton MessagePad to market by several months.

Early sales were strong, but software problems and a $700 price tag resulted in slow sales (less than 10,000 units shipped). The machine was as slow as molasses. Palm founder (and Zoomer developer) Jeff Hawkins called it "the slowest computer ever made by man," the handwriting recognition wasn't fully baked, and it was too large to fit in a pocket.

The Revo Plus offers long battery life and the ability to check e-mail or browse the Internet.

Psion Revo Plus (1999)

Psion was founded in 1980 as a software company focused on home computers like the Sinclair ZX Spectrum. They began dabbling with handheld devices and eventually developed a handheld operating system called EPOC. A series of quirky little handhelds followed, although they're best known today for transforming EPOC into the Symbian OS that powers mobile phones from Nokia, Ericsson and Motorola.

I spent a lot of time wandering European airports in the late 1990s. Puttering around airport electronics shops was a wonderful and costly way to kill time, and Psion handhelds repeatedly caught my eye. Sadly, Psion withdrew from the handheld market in July 2001, but many of their sleek little machines live on.

This is the Revo Plus. It wasn't the largest or most powerful of their line, but it offered a tantalizing balance of respectable features, low price, and reasonable battery life. It was introduced in 2000 and originally sold for $399. Revo Plus came with 16 MB RAM, an early version of the Opera web browser, and ran a 36 MHz ARM processor. The display is crisp but not backlit in an attempt to stretch battery life (and keep the price down). A souped-up suite of PDA-ish software is included. Standout programs include an *Excel*-compatible spreadsheet and a serviceable word processor.

Psion handhelds are becoming quite inexpensive on the web, and chances are there's one on eBay that was purchased by a marketing boffin and tossed unused into a desk drawer.

The Treo 90 may go down in history as one of the most streamlined Palm OS machines. It makes up for a lack of wireless capability with its small size and integrated thumboard.

Handspring Treo 90 (2002)

PDAs no longer hold the mystique they once did. In the beginning, these clever widgets were touted as the ultimate way to categorize, synchronize, and simplify your life. Millions of us soon realized this was marketing hogwash. Batteries died quickly and only a dedicated UberNerd could write intelligible graffiti with the little stylus. The rest of us pathetically scribbled vital notes in gibberish.

Palm was originally a software company, but company founder Jeff Hawkins took what he learned from the Casio Zoomer experience and applied it to the PalmPilot in 1996: smaller, simpler, cheaper and quicker. It was a recipe for success, and the PalmPilot personal digital assistant became the fastest selling computing device in history.

One of my favorite Palm OS machines is the often-overlooked Handspring Treo 90. Although it was svelte and shared the color screen and QWERTY thumboard of its big brothers, it didn't include the hot features of 2002 – a smartphone and wireless browsing. As a result, it was quietly taken behind the barn and shot.

Strangely enough, it is close to the ideal PDA. The Treo 90 is compact, includes the WordSmith word processor, a reasonable 16MB of memory, offline browsing and e-mail, and a rechargeable battery. I've been watching eBay for a bargain, but decent units still fetch around $100. Get one if you can and your life will be more categorized, synchronized and simplified than ever. Honest.

Extending your PC or Macintosh's life

There comes a point when your old machine doesn't cut it anymore. Movies stutter, games sputter and you fear it may be time for an expensive replacement. Replacing the processor might be a good way to keep your old system running a year or two longer. I recently upgraded my machine and the result is fabulous: a speed increase of almost 50%. Here are a couple of options for late model PCs and Macintoshes.

Upgrading an Intel-Based PC: PowerLeap processor modules

I'm on the verge of needing a new computer. Unfortunately, the idea of losing a day or two while setting up a new machine fills me with dread. PowerLeap turned out to be my savior. They offer a range of modern processor replacements for less-than-new machines. Their top-of-the-line upgrade is a 3.2 GHz module for computers that can't quite handle the latest generation of hyper-threading Pentium 4 processors. It sells for $249 ($179 for a Celeron version). They also make less expensive models for older Slot 1, Socket 370, and Socket 423 systems.

Not sure what you need? PowerLeap's site includes an online hardware scanning utility that checks your machine and suggests suitable upgrades. They also have an online chat function so you can sanity-check your choice before purchase. [www.powerleap.com]

Apple Mac processor upgrades: PowerLogix

PowerLogix offers a series of drop-in processor replacements for PowerMac G3 and G4 machines. Their PowerForce kits cost from $139 to $749.99, depending on your machine and the processor speed you're after.

Their low-cost PowerMac 7300 – 9600 upgrades are the best bang for the buck. The $139 upgrade increases the processor speed by as much as 9X, to 900MHz. That should be sufficient to boost an aging machine to almost modern performance. Check them out; these are a great way to add a bit of rabbit to turtle-like systems. [www.powerlogix.com]

The 1970s saw the birth of the arcade phenomenon, and people rushed to bring the technology home.

The magic of Videogames

Videogames changed the way people played in the 1970s and 1980s. Even though they enjoyed considerable popularity, early games were incredibly crude because they lacked programmable digital logic circuits. By the late 1970s, simple microprocessors were cheap enough to serve as the heart of quite sophisticated home gaming units.

Home videogame systems were an incredibly clever application of early microcomputer technology. They required no keyboard, no tape or disk storage, no operating system or programming languages, very little memory, and no expensive video display (apart from your living room TV set). And, since there were no third-party developers (until Activision in the early 1980s), users had to buy all of their games from the manufacturer. Simply brilliant.

Classic 8-bit Videogaming

Allow me to introduce a handful of ground-breaking game consoles that defined the industry until the introduction of sophisticated 16-bit consoles in the late 1980s. Millions of these units were made and they often sell for only a few dollars at garage sales. The games are incredibly simple compared to today's sophisticated offerings, but that is a significant part of their charm.

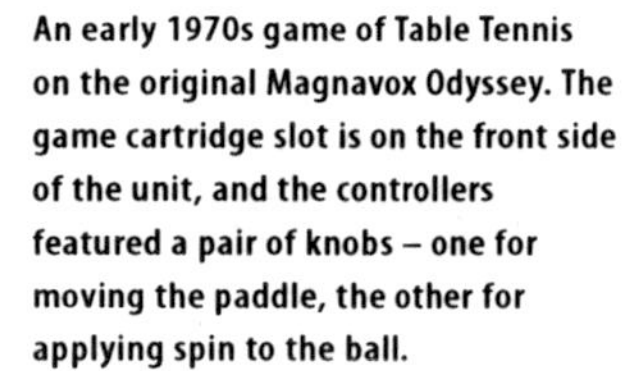

An early 1970s game of Table Tennis on the original Magnavox Odyssey. The game cartridge slot is on the front side of the unit, and the controllers featured a pair of knobs – one for moving the paddle, the other for applying spin to the ball.

Magnavox Odyssey : Computerless gaming (1972)

The Odyssey was the first home videogame console, released in 1972. The unit was best known for a 2-player game called *Table Tennis*, although a total of 12 game cartridges were available (six shipped with the console itself). The system didn't use a microprocessor, relying instead on an intricate network of discrete electronic components to generate a couple of paddles, a tennis net and a bouncing ball. The game cartridges had a series of jumpers that modified the game play by moving or removing the net and controlling how the ball and players interacted. To make the games more visually interesting, a set of transparent screen overlays were provided.

There was considerable public confusion about the system – many people mistakenly believed that it only worked with Magnavox televisions, an inaccuracy that Magnavox was in no hurry to correct. Over 350,000 Odyssey systems were sold before Magnavox replaced it with the simplified Odyssey 100 system in 1975.

Atari Pong comes home (1975)

Atari was founded by Nolan Bushnell, designer of *Computer Space*, the first arcade videogame. After trying out the Magnavox Odyssey in early 1972, he set about building his own version of electronic ping-pong and named it *Pong*, after the sound the ball makes when hitting the table. It was a runaway success. Magnavox quickly claimed that Atari had infringed on their ball-and-paddle gameplay and sued. The case was eventually dropped when Bushnell agreed to pay royalties on each *Pong* unit sold. Almost 40,000 *Pong* coin-operated games were manufactured.

The modern Atari Flashback 2 console includes PONG as a hidden 'Easter Egg' game. It requires a couple of classic Atari 2600 paddles to play.

Bushnell continued to build Atari's arcade business, but was determined to crack the home market as well. Atari designed a home version of *Pong* that included digital on-screen scoring, something the crude Magnavox Odyssey didn't offer. The scoring system was based on a single chip, something that no other manufacturer had managed up to that point. They struggled to find a distributor until Sears & Roebuck took a risk and purchased 150,000 units for the Christmas 1975 season. They sold out.

Atari released a number of *Pong* derivatives in 1976 and 1977, including a 4-player version. One such game – *Video Pinball* – replaced the simple *Pong* chip with a microcontroller. This enabled it to play pinball and a breakout game in which a ball and paddle were used to knock down a wall of bricks. Even after these early successes, the best was yet to come.

Velleman Classic TV Pong kit

Electronics kit maker Velleman markets a Classic TV game kit that lets you build a modernized version of *Pong*. The graphics are black & white and extremely rudimentary, but that's part of its charm. The kit features single and two player modes, so you can include your significant other in your latest electronic obsession. Simple though it is, I find myself wanting to build one into an old upright arcade case. [www.vellemanusa.com]

Velleman's Classic Pong kit may not be sensible, but it certainly looks like a great way to brush up one's soldering skills.

The Coleco Telstar Colortron added the excitement of color to the Coleco experience.

Coleco Telstar (1976) & Telstar Arcade (1978)

The Coleco Telstar sold for $49.99 and shipped over 1 million units in 1976. It was built around the AY-3-8500 digital game chip from General Instruments, which had been recommended to Coleco by Ralph Baer (creator of the Magnavox Odyssey). According to industry legend, Coleco called in Baer at the last second because the Telstar had failed FCC radio frequency emission tests. This was a potential nightmare because Coleco had a warehouse full of systems ready to ship. Nothing he tried made the problem go away – until he looped the antenna cable through a Ferrite bead as an "RF choke." The Telstar passed testing with days to spare and became a smash hit during the holiday season.

Baer parlayed his success with the Telstar into a design contract for a later Coleco product – The uniquely triangular Telstar Arcade. Each side of the unit featured a different set of controls – a steering wheel, a set of paddle controllers, and light-cell gun. Game cartridges (there were four) featured a custom digital game chip with three or four games – at least one for each side of the console.

Fairchild Channel F (1976)

The Fairchild Channel F goes down in history as the first cartridge-based microprocessor videogame system. It was based on the Fairchild F8 multi-chip microprocessor and included 64 bytes RAM. A total of 21 cartridges were released by 1978, but its blocky graphics didn't compare well to the Atari VCS and it vanished quietly from the market by the end of the 1970s.

The Atari VCS 2600 shipped with a pair of incredibly simple controllers featuring a rubberized joystick.

Atari Video Computer System 2600 (1977)

By 1976, Atari chief Nolan Bushnell realized that the future of videogaming lay in cartridge-based systems. As sales of Atari's various *Pong* systems declined, they started work on a console code-named Stella. Stella was built around a 1.19 MHz 6507 microprocessor (a stripped-down version of the CPU that would eventually power the Apple II, Commodore PET, and Atari 800 home computers). It featured a custom TIA (Television Interface Adapter) capable of displaying 304 x 192 pixels at up to 16 colors (with many limitations), 128 bytes of RAM memory, and each cart contained up to 4K of game ROM. Many later cartridges used a bank-switching technique to allow games to fill up to 64 K of memory, although only one cartridge from Dynacom was that large – most bank-switched games fell in around the 8K mark. The best thing about the console was the joystick design. It was remarkably simple, with a single red fire button and an 8-direction rubber-coated plastic stick. They proved remarkably resilient, standing up well to the abuse of energetic game play.

The console retailed for $299, a reasonable price for such advanced technology. I first saw the unit marketed as the Sears Video Arcade, sold through Atari's old friends at Sears & Roebuck. The system sold respectably for the first several years, but the industry as a whole was struggling. Videogames faced stiff competition from low cost handheld electronic games such as Merlin, Simon, and the various sports titles from Mattel.

I can still remember the excitement of bringing home a brand new Atari VCS, although the only cartridge I owned for a while was Combat.

The big breakthrough for the VCS came in 1980, when Atari licensed the arcade hit *Space Invaders*. The next big milestone for Atari came with the defection of some of their top programmers to form Activision, the first third-party developer of console games. Activision started releasing games in 1980 and the public soon realized that many of them were better than anything from Atari. Activision went on to sell millions of titles, including *Pitfall, Freeway, Kaboom!, River Raid,* and *Chopper Command.* These games offered innovative multicolored sprites and frequently included scrolling play fields.

The 1980 version of Space Invaders proved to be an incredibly hot title for Atari and helped to sell millions of consoles. Most Atari games included dozens of variations that subtly altered game play and often included two-player versions.

Atari lost a significant number of game sales to Activision, but the incredibly high quality of Activision's titles helped to drive the unit's popularity against tough competitors such as the Mattel Intellivision. In the end, the reputation of the VCS was slaughtered by the release of bad high-profile games: *Pac-Man* (which doesn't look anything like the arcade original and suffers from crude flickering animated characters), and *ET: The Extra Terrestrial. ET* was programmed in just six weeks, and it showed. The sad truth was that the limited capabilities of the six year-old console were no match for the increasing complexity of early 1980s arcade games.

Still, the VCS sold over 25 million units before being discontinued in 1984. It was reintroduced for a short while as an ultra-cheap $50 budget console in the late 1980s. Even at a giveaway price, the unit couldn't compete with the sophistication of products from Nintendo and SEGA.

Atari Flashback 2: Return of the Atari 2600

The recent wave of emulated classic videogames makes me nervous – they're not the same as the originals. That's why I didn't bother to mention the original Atari Flashback, which 'emulated' twenty classic Atari games and featured a rather tacky case and controller design modeled on the ill-fated Atari 7800 (why?) Even with its flaws, they apparently sold over 500,000 of the little suckers.

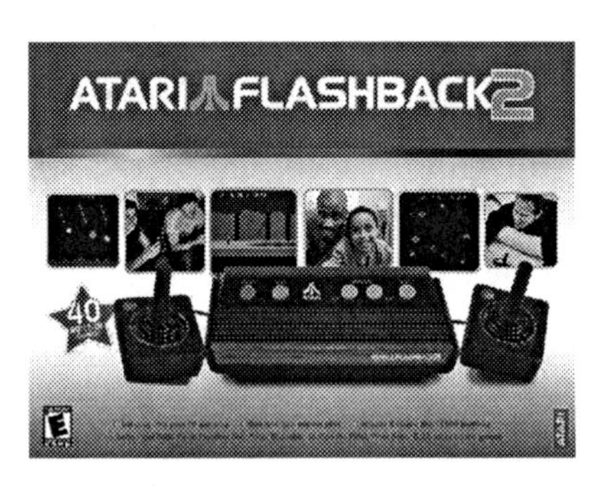

A 1982 magazine ad for Activision's smash-hit Pitfall! for the Atari VCS. It's included with the Flashback 2 retro console.

Now Atari is back with the $30 Flashback 2, and everything is different. The new unit features a single-chip recreation of the real 2600 hardware, so it runs exactly like the original. The controllers are full-sized modern versions of the old spasm-inducing 2600 joysticks, too. You can even attach real Atari paddles and other accessories.

The Flashback 2 includes 31 games drawn from the old Atari library, plus two Activision favorites (*River Raid* and *Pitfall*), along with seven brand new games. Classic titles include *Yar's Revenge, Missile Command,* and *Combat.* Rumor has it there are two paddle-based bonus Easter Egg games as well. The console design is a miniature faux-wood version of the original, except for round push-buttons that replace the original switches.

The truly awesome part? The Flashback 2 supports old (and new) Atari VCS cartridges. You'll notice it doesn't have a cartridge slot, but if you open the case (voiding the warranty), you'll discover the appropriate circuity already on the circuit board. Apparently, all you have to do is cut a couple of solder traces, wire in a suitable cartridge header, and add a switch to let you select between internal games or the cart. I won't be surprised to see Make Magazine run a how-to article in a future issue. Mark my words! [update: atarimuseum.com beat them to the punch – See their site for a step by step guide to the cartridge hack.]

The Atari press release mentions an "under $30" price tag, which I think is solid value. Still, one of my friends picked up an original 2600 VCS and a box of carts for a few bucks at a garage sale a couple of years ago. You may get lucky, too. [www.atari.com]

Other Atari Systems

Atari 5200

The VCS was the pinnacle of Atari's success in the videogame market. They realized that the old console was beginning to show its age in the early 1980s, and set about designing a replacement. The Atari 5200 was based on technology from the Atari 400 home computer, but it had two fatal flaws: Horrible controllers and incompatibility with their popular VCS titles. It flopped.

Atari 7800

Atari missed the opportunity to dominate the marketplace with the Atari 7800. This unit was affordable, compatible with the huge library of classic titles designed for the VCS, and offered sophisticated games. The system was announced in Spring 1984, just before the takeover of Atari by former Commodore boss Jack Tramiel. The system languished for several years before release, forcing it to compete with Nintendo's NES and its brilliant game titles.

Atari Jaguar

The 16-bit Jaguar was introduced in 1993. Atari's last console was designed to compete with the SEGA Genesis and Sony PlayStation. Although it was touted as a 64-bit system, the only 64-bit component was the bus design. Developers found the platform challenging to program, with less-than-complete developer tools that delayed releases and hampered quality. To their credit, Atari was able to line up a reasonable number of third-party developers, but the system failed to inspire public demand and faded into history.

Magnavox Odyssey 2 (1978)

As far as I know, the Magnavox Odyssey was the first home gaming console to offer a QWERTY keyboard. The keyboard was intended for use with educational programs, but since kids prefer games to dry educational packages it became an expensive and bulky way to select game settings and control on-screen characters.

The Odyssey 2 was based on the Intel 8048 microprocessor and its graphic resolution wasn't as high as the VCS or Intellivision. It included several standard sprite characters in its built-in ROM. These were re-used in many titles, which had the unfortunate side-effect of making many games look alike. A strange factoid about the Odyssey 2: One person, Ed Averett, wrote two-dozen titles for the system in the span of four years.

The Odyssey 2 sold approximately 1 million units between 1978 and 1983, good enough to rank as the third-place console of the early 1980s, following the Atari VCS and Mattel Intellivision. After Philips acquired Magnavox, the unit was marketed successfully in Europe as the Philips Videopac G7000. The Odyssey 2 was retired in 1983 to make way for the Odyssey 3. This system sold for a short time in Europe, but wasn't released in the USA.

Mattel Intellivision (1980)

The original Intellivision Master Component. Like the Atari VCS, this unit also had its share of fake wood trim.

Allow me to introduce The Mattel Intellivision – the world's first 16-bit game console. I was never a big fan of its awkward controllers and bank machine-like membrane keypads, but this console (and its descendants) remained on the market until the end of the 1980s. The Intellivision used an oddball GI 1600 microprocessor clocked at around 500KHz. The console itself included 7K of ROM and RAM and supported up to 64K cartridges. Graphic resolution was 192 x 160 pixels with up to 16 colors and 8 sprites for animated characters. The controllers were oddly futuristic-looking, including a membrane number pad and golden control disc instead of a joystick. I hated them, especially in comparison to the simple Atari joysticks.

The Intellivision was designed as a successor to the Atari VCS. It was first test-marketed in 1979 and a production run of 200,000 machines was sold throughout the United States in 1980, along with 12 cartridges. The unit was also available as the Sears Super Video Arcade and the Radio Shack Tandyvision One.

Mattel had a long history of announcing products that didn't quite make it to market. Initial plans called for a keyboard add-on to turn the Master Component into a full-fledged home computer. It didn't fare well in testing and was scrapped. A cosmetic redesign resulted in the release of the Intellivision II in 1982. Mattel went on to announce the Intellivision III but scrapped it too, folding many features into an 'Entertainment Computer System' add-on for the original. Most of its components never materialized.

Over 3 million Intellivisions were sold, but you get the feeling that had Mattel played their cards a bit differently things could have turned out even better.

Intellivision Lives! has introduced affordable libraries of Intellivision games for many popular platforms including Sony PlayStation 2, Windows and Macintosh.

Intellivision Lives!

I rarely get to hawk free stuff, so this is exciting – If you'd like to take a few Intellivision games for a spin, check out the free Mac & PC downloads from Intellivision Lives. They offer three free Intellipacks, featuring games like *Astrosmash, B-17 Bomber, Skiing,* and *Space Spartans.*

Their evil plan is to make you want more. To that end, they offer reasonably priced Intellivision (and Colecovision) game packs for PC, Mac, PlayStation 2, Xbox, Gamecube and mobile phones. [www.intellivisionlives.com]

Vectrex targeted game players who longed to bring the look and feel of vector-based games home.

Vectrex (1982)

If you're less than impressed by the Microsoft Xbox 360, how about considering something like the Vectrex game system that had brief success between 1982 and 1984?

The Vectrex included a built-in black & white vector graphics display, making it unique in the videogame world. Instead of pixels, Vectrex created images using razor-sharp white lines, just like the arcade version of *Asteroids.* Some games featured transparent color screen overlays in a dismal attempt at pseudo-color. Predictably, this ploy failed. Less than two dozen game cartridges were released and the system couldn't compete in the overcrowded mid-1980s market.

The original developer released the Vectrex games into the public domain in the mid-1990s and talented fans have released a handful of new titles. You can occasionally find used systems on eBay

– expect to pay around $100 for one in good condition. [Check out www.classicgamecreations.com for some clever new games for the Vectrex, Odyssey 2, and Colecovision.]

Colecovision (1982)

The Colecovision console took a few design cues from the Mattel Intellivision by including a numeric keypad on each controller. They replaced the control disc with a much easier to use stubby joystick.

Coleco returned to the videogame market with a vengeance in 1982. Their Colecovision was technically superior to any other console on the market and came packaged with an excellent port of the arcade hit *Donkey Kong*. Coleco followed up their initial success with a series of excellent arcade ports such as *Zaxxon* and *Donkey Kong Jr*.

Coleco went on to sell six million units in three years – a stunning achievement. They realized that home computers like the Commodore 64 were quickly overtaking consoles as the gaming platform of choice and introduced the Adam home computer add-on for their system. The Adam proved to be Coleco's undoing, with some reports claiming as many as 60% of the units were returned because of flaws. After losing tens of millions of dollars, Coleco retreated from the home console market in late 1984. Had they not embarked on the Adam project, it's quite likely that the Colecovision would have survived as the pre-eminent home console of the 1980s.

UK-based Telegames bought the rights to Coleco's titles and released a Colecovision clone called the Telegames Personal Arcade in the late 1980s. It sold for a mere $40 and included a single controller, but has been off the market for a while. There are other ways to get a Coleco fix, though – IntellivisionLives.com markets a collection of 30 Colecovision hits for Windows. They include many Activision and Coleco originals, but not licensed ports like *Donkey Kong* and *Zaxxon*. $29.95.

Nintendo Entertainment System / Famicom (1984)

The videogame industry crashed in 1984. Too many competitors found themselves fighting for too few customers who were increasingly disillusioned by the flood of low-quality game titles and the lack of progress in the industry. To make things worse, an increasingly sophisticated crop of home computers looked set to dominate the game market. Industry giants Atari, Mattel, and

Coleco collapsed almost simultaneously, leaving the market wide open.

Nintendo introduced the Famicom console to Japanese gamers in 1984, capitalizing on the success of their arcade titles. The system sold well, and they entered into negotiations with Atari to market the system in North America. Atari was going through major upheaval and Nintendo decided to enter the market on their own with a restyled console called the Nintendo Entertainment System.

The Nintendo Entertainment System included a pair of rather odd-looking controllers that worked extremely well. Unfortunately, the top-loading cartridge port didn't hold up to heavy use.

At first Nintendo found it difficult to convince retailers to stock their console, especially after the recent market crash. It took until early 1986 before the system was widely released in the USA. Nintendo initially agreed to buy back any unsold inventory to reduce risk for retailers. The system became a smash hit, driven by the popularity of the bundled *Mario Bros* game and subsequent high-quality releases.

Nintendo introduced a draconian licensing program in an effort to sidestep the quality problems that had plagued other manufacturers. Licensees were limited to two NES titles per year and couldn't release the same title for competing platforms. Game packs included a patented lockout chip, with Nintendo as the only legal manufacturer. These restrictions worked – Nintendo made piles of money and supported the NES until 1995. It sold over 60 million units, making it by far the most popular console of the 8-bit gaming epoch.

SEGA Master System (1986)

The SEGA Master System (SMS) was introduced to the USA in 1986. It was based on a mid-1980s Japanese system called the Mark III. The SMS was technically superior to the Nintendo NES, but SEGA just couldn't compete with Nintendo's top-calibre titles. To make things worse, Nintendo's restrictive licensing policies made it impossible for SEGA to offer desirable third-party titles. The system proved more popular in Europe, and a version of *Sonic the Hedgehog* was even available. In the end, SEGA retreated from the 8-bit gaming market, but the SMS design lived on as the foundation for SEGA's Game Gear handheld system.

The ill-fated SEGA Master System was technically superior to the NES but couldn't muster enough high-quality games to knock it from first place.

First Generation Handheld Consoles

By the end of the 1980s, several manufacturers were pursuing the holy grail of handheld cartridge-based systems. The most popular of these was the Nintendo Game Boy, but SEGA and Atari also fielded credible systems.

Here's a look at three early handheld units that defined the state-of-the-art. It's interesting that Nintendo's Game Boy system went on to dominate the industry, because their first offering was an underwhelming device with a torturous pea-green B&W reflective LCD display and sloth-like processor.

Atari Lynx (1989)

The Lynx was released in two case designs. This is the second, a slightly smaller version. It features a Nintendo-style + controller on the left.

The Lynx was the first handheld color game system. It resembles the modern Sony PSP, although with a much smaller 3.5-inch 160 x 102 pixel screen. The machine could display 4096 colors and included two 16-bit custom processors and 64K RAM. The system was originally developed by game company Epyx in 1987. It offered a color LCD display with backlighting, along with respectable ergonomics. Epyx eventually realized they didn't have the capital to bring the product to market and went shopping for a manufacturer. Atari signed on mid-1989, and small quantities of the unit (with Epyx software titles, of course) were available for the holiday season.

Unfortunately, Atari couldn't meet demand for the system and many people ended up purchasing the cheaper Nintendo Game Boy instead. Atari continued marketing the product through 1990, but its $200 price tag was almost double the Game Boy's and Nintendo had a much stronger selection of game titles – most ported from the NES. SEGA introduced the Game Gear in 1991, ending the Lynx's reign as the industry's leading color handheld. Atari withdrew the Lynx from the market in 1993, choosing to focus their efforts on the ill-fated Jaguar 16-bit console.

Nintendo Game Boy

Nintendo had several advantages in the late-1980s game market. They were the number one console maker, with about 90% of the market share. They also had a stranglehold on the world's hottest game titles.

The Game Boy was introduced in late 1989. It featured a low-power derivative of the Z80 processor, 8K RAM, up to 8 megabit games, and a 160 x 144 pixel display capable of showing 4 shades of grey. The fuel that drove it to dominate the handheld market can be summed up in a single word: *Tetris*. This addictive falling block game was bundled with the system, and proved the ideal way to addict a generation of gamers.

The Nintendo Game Boy was phenomenally successful, even though it was technically inferior to both the Atari Lynx and SEGA Game Gear.

The Game Boy competed head-to-head with Atari's Lynx. Interestingly, Elorg Software licensed Nintendo to produce home versions of *Tetris*, while arcade rights went to Atari Software. Nintendo's recipe for success was simplicity. The Game Boy was smaller and cost 40% less than the Lynx. Its design – offering an unimpressive 8-bit processor, minimal memory, and reflective monochrome LCD – was focused on battery longevity and low production cost. The result was a $119 device that offered the essence of console gaming for the masses.

The Game Boy is the most popular gaming unit in history. Nintendo reports that by the end of 2000, they had shipped over 110 million units, cornering an incredible 47% of the *entire* US gaming hardware market in the process.

SEGA Game Gear

SEGA introduced the Game Gear handheld in 1991. It was based on the ill-fated TV-based SEGA Master System that went head-to-head with the NES in the late 1980s. This meant that SEGA could port popular SMS titles to the new platform with little or no rework. The system featured a 3.58 MHz Zilog Z80 processor driving a 160 x 144 pixel color screen. It had 4-channel audio, along with 8K RAM. The star of the Game Gear lineup was *Sonic the Hedgehog*.

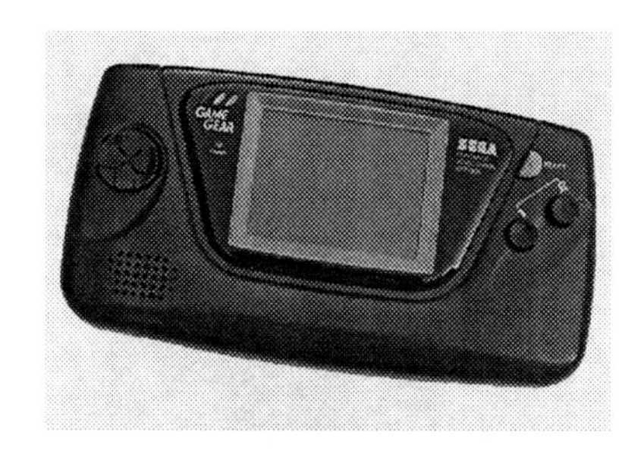

SEGA cleverly designed the Game Gear handheld to run their Master System titles. This reduced the cost of console development. The backlit screen ate far more batteries than the Nintendo's Game Boy, however.

Unlike the incredibly power-efficient Game Boy, the Game Gear's backlit display chewed through a set of batteries in a mere three to four hours. This, combined with a perceived lack of build quality and few hit titles, caused the system to struggle against the Game Boy. It lasted until 1997 although it was briefly revived by cut-price gear maker Majesco in the early 2000s.

LED Games

I had a paper route back in the early 1980s. When I wasn't slogging through the snow, I was cheerfully counting my hard-earned pennies and wondering what to buy. Regrettably, I didn't choose Microsoft stock.

Instead, I invested in an assortment of LED handheld games. For those who've never seen one, imagine a game of football or hockey played by glowing red or green rectangular dots. Your 'man' flickers, and your teammates glow brighter than the other guys. Sounds pathetic, doesn't it?

Mattel hit their stride with sports titles like Football, Hockey, Soccer and Basketball. This is a CGI model of Football by Peter Hirschberg.

In my 'hood, the most desirable games were made by Mattel, probably because of their reasonably compact size and studly titles like *Football, Hockey*, and *Soccer*. We quickly tired of dots, and companies like Coleco answered our despair with funky new VFD (vacuum fluorescent) displays that brought little glowing color icons to games such as *Alien Attack*. These tabletop units looked beautiful, but must have been insanely expensive to manufacture. As with most cool things, they were eventually crushed by an onslaught of drab monochrome LCD games from makers like Nintendo and Bandai. You can still buy used classics online, but expect to get fleeced.

Mattel Auto Race: The beginning of an era

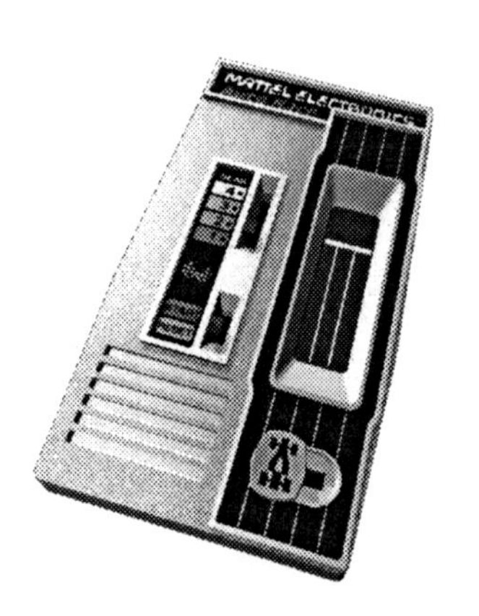

It's incredibly hard to find a good copy of Mattel's Auto Race for photos. This is a another rendering by Peter Hirschberg.

Mattel's 1976 *Auto Race* was the first all-electronic handheld game. I clearly remember checking this beauty out in the 1977 Sears Christmas Catalog. You needed a vivid imagination to play this one: the objective was to steer your car (red LED rectangle) left and right, to avoid other cars (more red LED rectangles). The entire game was coded to fit into a mere 512 bytes of memory.

Mattel followed *Auto Race* with *Missile Attack* (1977) *Football* (1977), *Soccer* (1978), *Hockey* (1978), and a host of others. Some of these titles were re-released in the early 2000s as handheld and pocket LCD versions. Sadly, they don't compare to the "I can even play in near darkness" coolness of the originals.

Vintage Mattel handhelds often show up on eBay but the good boxed ones fetch a premium from collectors.

Nintendo Game & Watch LCD handheld games

Nintendo started producing a line of pocket-sized handheld LCD games in 1980. Unlike Nintendo's later Game Boy system, each Game & Watch unit was dedicated to a single game. The characters were tiny little black LCD outlines that bleeped and blooped their way around the display. The earliest devices featured a single screen, but later models were housed in clamshell cases that opened to reveal dual play fields.

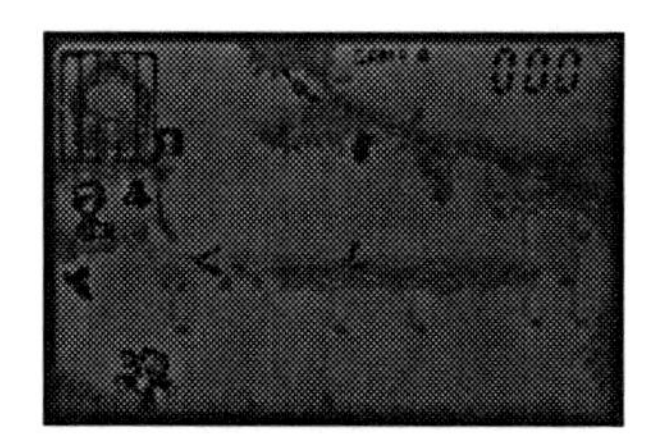

Game & Watch game play was incredibly simple, yet these tiny handhelds sold in the thousands. This is the widescreen version of Donkey Kong Jr.

www.gameandwatch.com includes a wonderful overview of dozens of these little games. They're planning to introduce a book based on the site, but I'm not sure when it will be published. Game & Watch titles were produced in stunning numbers and frequently show up at garage sales and on eBay. Prices vary – mint condition boxed units can be expensive, while unboxed "garden variety" titles often sell for next to nothing. These make great collector's items, but they're also tremendously fun to play.

Other Stuff: Arcade Emulators, Books and Re-releases

MAME: Bring the arcade experience home

This chapter has touched on many of the most popular home gaming consoles. I didn't spend much time on arcade machines because units in good condition tend to be extremely rare and expensive. Besides, there are less expensive ways to bring the arcade experience home.

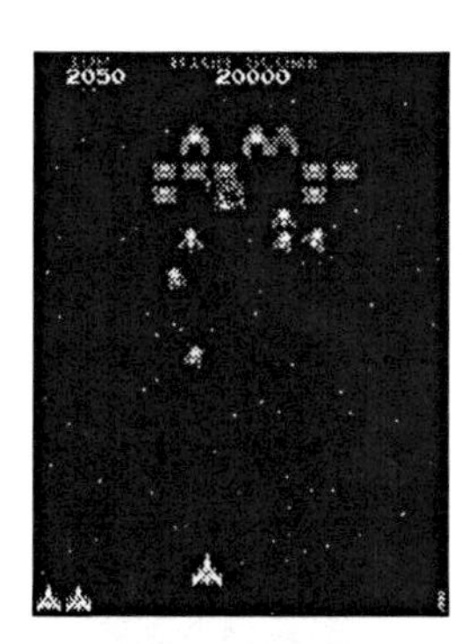

MAME may be the only way that many people will be able to experience an enormous array of arcade classics. This is a screenshot from Galaga, one of my all-time favorites.

MAME is PC-based arcade machine emulator. It started out in December 1996 as a series of separate hardware emulators written by Nicola Salmoria. He eventually merged them into a single program, naming it MAME (Multiple Arcade Machine Emulator). Development of the program continued as an open source project, eventually involving over 100 people.

The amazing thing about modern computer technology is that it's now fast enough to emulate vintage systems from the 1980s completely in software. The emulator pretends to be the old system, responding just like the original program expects and pretending to have the same video, audio, and input devices. You even pretend to insert coins for credits. Because it's a software imitation, things sometimes go slightly wrong. The most likely glitch is missing or not-quite-right sound, followed by strange character colors and video strangeness.

As of late 2005, MAME supports 3192 different games. It simulates popular arcade system hardware from the 1980s, right down to the graphic display engines and sound systems. Some games are better than others, but most of the most successful arcade platforms are well supported. The emulator runs electronic copies of the original game ROMs, which are subject to copyright. This can cause problems because finding legal copies of classic ROMs is a challenge.

Still, it is possible. StarROMs.com is a company set up to facilitate the download of classic ROM games. Their lineup currently includes Atari's entire family of arcade titles and I hope they license other manufacturers soon. Prices start at around $2 per game.

All in all, MAME makes a dandy core for an authentic PC-based Retro arcade system. [For more information or to download the software, visit www.mame.net]

Namco Museum 50th Anniversary Arcade Collection

The *Namco Museum 50th Anniversary Arcade Collection* was release several months ago for the PC, Xbox, PS2, Game Boy Advance and Gamecube. And somehow I didn't notice.

It offers up 14 classics from the 1980s: *Pac-Man, Ms. Pac-Man, Galaga, Galaxian, Dig Dug, Pole Position, Pole Position II, Rolling Thunder, Rally X, Bosconian, Dragon Spirit, Sky Kid, Xevious* and *Mappy*.

The word on the street is that these appear to be based on the original arcade code and that any embedded Easter Eggs (such as *Galaga's* 'hold enemy fire') work as you'd expect. Perfect for those who still have all of the old *Pac-Man* game patterns buried in their subconscious. Street price is around $20. [www.namco.com]

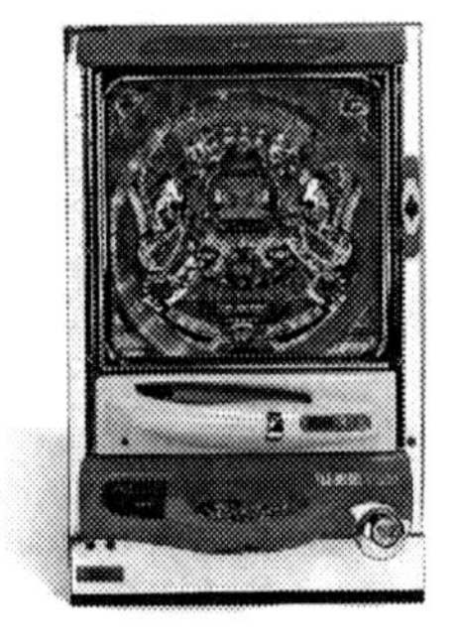

A shiny Y&O Model Pachinko machine. Be prepared for a lot of noise, fun and tiny steel ball bearings if you get your hands on one of these.

Pachinko

Hammacher Schlemmer is offering vintage Pachinko machines ($299) that apparently once lived in the world-famous Ginza in Tokyo. Pachinko is a demented upright variation of a pinball/slot machine that fires hundreds of tiny steel balls through a maze of spinning wheels, bumpers, and bonus traps.

Pachinko parlors first appeared in Japan shortly after WWII. Players purchase a large number of steel balls that are inserted into the machine. Because gambling for money isn't allowed under Japanese law, winnings (in the form of more balls) can be exchanged for prizes. Kinda like Las Vegas except powered by ball bearings. [www.hammacher.com]

Commodore DTV – $20 single-chip Commodore 64

At first glance this looks like yet another cheapo 30-games-in-1 retrogame knockoff. But it isn't.

In addition to thirty classic games, this unit contains a battery-powered single-chip recreation of the old Commodore 64. You can even attach a PC-compatible keyboard and Commodore 64 1541 disk drive – as long as you're not afraid of a little DIY tinkering.

The C-64 DTV is the brainchild of self-taught VLSI chip designer Jeri Ellsworth. She reverse-engineered the entire system so efficiently that the product can be sold profitably for a mere $20, including 30 classic Commodore 64 games. A stunning idea, and I can only hope that more classic systems are reproduced this way.

The Commodore 64 DTV (Direct to TV) joystick can function as a fully programmable imitation of the C-64.

Arcade Legends: SEGA Genesis reissued as a $30 retro-console

SEGA debuted their 16-bit Genesis system in 1989. The $189 system ran a 7.6 MHz Motorola 68000 and offered a reasonable screen resolution of 320 x 224 with a 512 color palette. SEGA managed to beat Nintendo to the 16-bit market by two years. Since the 8-bit Nintendo Entertainment System (NES) had crushed SEGA's offerings, Nintendo wasn't worried.

SEGA did everything right and knocked the NES out of first place that holiday season. The Genesis was fast and inexpensive, had good controllers, and came bundled with a respectable title – *Altered Beast.* When Nintendo finally released the 16-bit SNES in 1991, everyone thought Nintendo would regain the 16-bit crown. However, SEGA took full advantage of their system's significantly faster processor by releasing the dazzlingly fast *Sonic the Hedgehog.*

Radica Games has reintroduced the SEGA Genesis as a pair of miniature all-in-one consoles. Each features six games from the original Genesis library.

The result was a battle for market supremacy that resulted in a stream of top-quality titles throughout the early 1990s.

Radica now sells several inexpensive TV games based on the SEGA Genesis. *Arcade Legends: SEGA Genesis* includes *Sonic the Hedgehog, Golden Axe, Altered Beast, Kid Chameleon, Dr. Robotnik's Mean Bean Machine* and *Flicky.* It retails for about $25 and includes a pretty decent imitation of the original Genesis controller, along with a miniature console unit.

There's also a *Genesis Volume 2* unit that includes *Sonic 2, Ecco The Dolphin, Gain Ground, The Ooze, Columns,* and *Alex Kid & the Enchanted Castle.*

These are great games at a giveaway price. Isn't technological progress great? [More info at www.radicagames.com]

XgameStation is a brilliant way to learn the art of retro game programming. The system runs on a low cost Scenix SX52 microcontroller

XgameStation: A modern approach to vintage gaming

The XGameStation is a modern console development system that encourages coders to design old-school videogames. A brilliant idea, but definitely a niche market.

For $199, you get the XGameStation Micro Edition powered by an SX52 microcontroller along with documentation, software, cables, and what looks to be a vintage Atari joystick. The XGS software-controlled graphics system works in much the same way as the Atari 2600 and the Apple II, enabling the same strange chroma-shift effects. To create new games you'll need to get yourself up to speed on SX assembly language and classic coding techniques. Those without the background (or patience) can easily download numerous games and wicked-looking demos for the platform. [www.xgamestation.com]

Arcade controllers: X-Arcade

Vintage arcade consoles in good condition are becoming harder to find each year. Many were converted into less desirable games as the years passed, and others are sitting forgotten in the back of warehouses and basements. One option is to buy a new multi-game console, but that can be a multi-thousand dollar quest.

X-Arcade controllers offer the feel of genuine arcade-style controls at a fraction of the price of a dedicated console. Perfect for use with arcade emulators like MAME.

The best bang for the buck seems to be the X-Arcade series of game controllers along with MAME software (Multiple Arcade Machine Emulator). A single joystick model goes for $99.95, and the dual version fetches a reasonable $149.95. They include an adapter to connect to your PC, PlayStation 1/2, Dreamcast, or Xbox system. These units offer a bit more heft and playability than most plastic game controllers.

If $149.95 strikes you as a bit much, they have a limited number of refurbished dual joystick units on sale for $100, or you can purchase some affordable do-it-yourself kits to roll your own. [www.x-arcade.com]

Videogame Books

Supercade: A Visual History of the Videogame Age 1971-1984

Supercade is the 448 page brainchild of Van Burnham, a self-professed videogame junkie and contributor to WIRED magazine. This tribute to the golden age of videogaming is a couple of years old, but remains worthy of mention. It's crammed full of photos, screenshots, and snippets of information on hundreds of games. Burnham designed the book herself, making it a Herculean one-woman effort. Distributed by MIT Press, this is one videogame book no old-school gamer should be without.

As an aside, Burnham owns three NES consoles, two Colecovisions, arcade versions of *Robotron, Joust, Omega Race, Donkey Kong Junior* (my fave), the 1971 classic *Computer Space*, and dozens of others. She needs our support, lest she run out of quarters or electricity.

[ISBN 0262524201]

Electronic Plastic

Dutch interactive designer and author Jaro Gielens is one obsessed man. He spent over five years collecting more than five hundred electronic handheld games from the 1980s. Thankfully, he took the time to lay out his collection in printed form. The result? One hundred and seventy-six pages that capture the art and design of these strange little gamebots from the Eighties.

From the publisher: "Rare collector's items, retro-futuristic cases, bright logos, elaborate packaging and a generous helping of wistful nostalgia – in Electronic Plastic, a fascinating journey into the product design of the 80's, author Jaro Gielens presents more than 380 of the prettiest and craziest handhelds and tabletops from the Stone Age of consumer electronics..."

[ISBN 3931126447]

Videogames: In the Beginning

Ralph Baer is the father of modern videogaming. He created the Magnavox Odyssey console in 1972, although he had been experimenting with TV-based games throughout the 1960s. Baer wrote *Videogames – In the Beginning* to share his perspective on the early days of videogaming from before the creation of the Magnavox Odyssey, through his work with Coleco and beyond. It's an excellent retrospective written by someone who was in the thick of the action and had the good sense to keep meticulous notes.

[ISBN 0964384817]

Project Arcade: Build Your Own Arcade Machine

If you've ever yearned after your own *Pac-Man* or *Galaga* arcade machine, this is the book for you. John St. Clair's 501 page volume leads you through building a vintage-style arcade cabinet, constructing game controllers, and installing a PC-based game emulator inside. He even provides tips and examples for creating a graphic marquee for your new console. Includes a CD-ROM with MAME arcade emulation software and an evaluation copy of Paint Shop Pro. Personally, I think this would be ten times more satisfying than buying something pre-made. And ten times cheaper.

[ISBN 0764556169]

There are no substitutes for real knobs and the musical imperfections of old analog circuitry.

Electronic Musical Instruments

Synthesizers are fascinating electromechanical devices and it's no accident that synthesizer-heavy techno exploded onto the music scene with bands like Kraftwerk, the Human League, Depeche Mode and the Eurythmics in the early 1980s. Pop musicians responded with excitement to the arrival of microprocessor-based instruments – they no longer needed smelly drummers and pretentious long haired guitar gods to create desirable pop songs.

Modern computers are fast enough to simulate these classic instruments in software. As a result, there are hundreds of excellent softsynth recreations of in-demand vintage synthesizers like the Sequential Prophet 5, Minimoog, and ARP Odyssey. Most are excellent and substantially cheaper than the real thing. Just be warned that there are no substitutes for real knobs and the sonic imperfections of old circuitry. Besides, there is no guarantee that today's software will run properly on tomorrow's computers.

The Minimoog Voyager is proof that classics live on. This particular version was designed to commemorate the 50th anniversary of Bob Moog's first electronic instrument.

Bob Moog and the Early Days

Most early electronic instruments were huge modular systems that looked like telephone exchanges. A tangled web of patch cables connected huge racks of sound generators, filters and amplitude shapers to each other. Modulars were challenging to use and only the most popular musicians could afford to tour with these bewildering monstrosities.

As far as I'm concerned, the modern era of electronic music began in 1970, when Bob Moog crammed an entire synthesizer into a single compact box along with a keyboard. Moog, with a PhD in engineering physics, had a long history of designing and building ghostly-sounding electronic Theremins and complicated modular systems. As a result, he had an excellent sense of what modules were required to create a versatile synthesizer. Moog did away with patch cables by connecting the modules internally in a 'normalized' arrangement that became the template for nearly all instruments since.

Moog left Moog Music (then part of Norlin Industries) in 1978 but continued his work in the electronic music industry. He served as a Vice President of Kurzweil Music Systems in the mid to late 1980s, overseeing the development of some of the world's highest quality digital sampling instruments. He eventually won back the rights to the Moog Music name and offered brilliant Moog Theremins and electronic effect units in the late 1990s.

Meanwhile, electronic music had come full-circle. Moog's early instruments generated sound using discrete analog circuitry. This warm analog sound fell out of favour in the mid-1980s as musicians became fascinated with crisp digital sounds and sample playback. It took another decade or so before they rebelled against the harsh excesses of digital and started to seek out the warm and slightly unpredictable nature of analog instruments like the old Minimoog.

And so it was that Moog Music introduced the Minimoog Voyager in 2002 – it's a heavily updated version of the instrument that started the electronic craze in the early 1970s. It's quaint and expensive by today's standards, offering only a single voice driven by three analog oscillators. These instruments are built in the USA and designed to last a lifetime. Bob passed away after a brief illness in 2005, but his company lives on as the sole remaining Big Name synthesizer manufacturer in America. [See www.moogmusic.com – prices start at $3095.]

Some Interesting Vintage Synthesizers

Thousands of synthesizers have been manufactured in the past few decades. Much as I'd like to, I can't possibly list them all here – although others have attempted this feat. The most complete effort is Peter Forrest's two book series, *The A to Z of Analogue Synthesizers* [available from www.spheremusic.com]. This set includes information about hundreds of classics crammed into a few hundred densely packed pages. Peter also runs the prestigious VEMIA vintage synth auction site – one of the best places on the web to pick up a vintage instrument with a famous pedigree.

Anyway, back to the topic at hand. I've catalogued a variety of interesting retro synths over the next few pages. I paid particular attention to instruments that were produced in vast numbers, since they're often easier to find at affordable prices. Sadly, the time to purchase vintage synths was about ten years ago, before the emergence of eBay and before the widespread rediscovery of analog instruments and the resurgence of "organic" pop music. There are still deals to be had, but expect to search long and hard.

ARP Odyssey

It's a bit hard to make out the orange-on-black color scheme in this shot of the Odyssey. It was definitely a different style than Moog's early instruments.

ARP was Moog's main competition in the early 1970s. Their first success came with the massive semi-modular ARP 2600, but it was the all-in-one Odyssey that was to become their most popular instrument. The Odyssey was introduced in 1972 and rose to fame because of its duophonic (two note) capabilities. Its sound complimented the Minimoog well – the Moog was warm, while the Odyssey had a harsher tone. Odysseys are hard to find, but M-Audio offers a softsynth recreation – the Gforce Oddity. [Visit www.m-audio.com for details].

Moog Voyager

The Voyager is an updated version of the Minimoog, the instrument that started the electronic craze in the early 1970s. It's quaint and expensive by today's standards. The machine offers a single voice powered by three analog oscillators. The sound is classic warm Moog, as are its look and feel. These instruments are built in the USA and designed to last a lifetime. [www.moogmusic.com – prices start at $3095.]

Sequential Circuits Prophet 5

They don't get more famous than this. The Prophet 5 was a legend in its own time.

The Sequential Circuits Prophet 5 is one of the most famous musical synthesizers of all time. It was hard to find a pop record in the early 1980s that didn't feature a few Prophet sounds. It was also the first programmable polyphonic synthesizer, capable of playing a then-stunning five simultaneous notes. It pre-dated the MIDI communication standard by several years (adoption of the MIDI protocol was spearheaded by company founder Dave Smith in 1983). Later versions came equipped with MIDI jacks and a flourishing cottage industry sprang up to provide MIDI-mods for earlier models.

Sequential Circuits is a wonderful example of a Silicon Valley garage to riches story. Designer Dave Smith built the first prototype of the Prophet in his home. He and former Moog employee

John Bowen presented the Prophet 10 at the 1978 NAMM music show. It offered 10 note polyphony, but was notoriously unreliable because of the tremendous heat generated by the electronics. Smith solved the problem by cutting out half of the voice circuitry, and the Prophet 5 was born.

Less than 200 early 'home built' Prophet 5 Revision 1 keyboards were built, and few are still alive today. The redesigned Revision 2 became the "classic" P5 – it was more electronically robust than its fragile predecessor, but retained the same quirky SSM-built analog synthesis chips.

After selling just over 1000 of these $4595 instruments, Sequential introduced the Prophet 5 Revision 3 in 1980. SCI incorporated more reliable Curtis (CEM) chips into the new model, resulting in what some consider a much more sterile and generic sound.

Sequential went on to create a series of less expensive analog and digital synthesizers along with several digital sampling modules and the Studio 440 sampling drum sequencer. Sadly, their instruments fell out of fashion and couldn't compete with a flood of less expensive devices from Japan. The company was eventually purchased by Yamaha in 1987.

Founder Dave Smith stayed with Yamaha for a short while before moving on to found Seer Systems, a software company that released one of the earliest all-software synthesizers. If you're interested in purchasing a Sequential instrument, Wine Country Music was formed by ex-Sequential staff to repair and resell classic Prophets. [See www.winecountrysequential.com]

Fairlight Computer Music Instrument: A musical revolution

Music of the early 1980s was defined by computer technology. The world changed with the arrival of the revolutionary Linn LM-1 drum machine, along with digitally controlled synthesizers and effect units. But the most radical innovation was the Fairlight Computer Music Instrument (CMI).

Created in Australia by Kim Ryrie and Peter Vogel, the 1979 Fairlight was originally envisioned as a computer-based music synthesis system. But the Fairlight had other more influential tricks up its sleeve: it was the first digital sampling instrument, capable of recording snippets of real sound and playing them

An advert from Syco, the UK Fairlight distributor. The Fairlight CMI Series IIx featured a pair of gigantic 8-inch floppy drives and sold for about $32,000.

back at different speeds. This meant that incredibly complex and realistic tones could be captured and performed.

Only a few original Fairlights were sold to the likes of Stevie Wonder and Peter Gabriel. By 1982, an upgraded Fairlight Series II offered better sound and included a graphic sequencing program called Page R. It became possible for musicians and sound designers to quickly program complex musical pieces, and all of a sudden the Fairlight Sound was everywhere. The world would never be the same.

The Fairlight CMI Series II cost around $32,000 when new. It featured 8 voices of 8-bit lo-fi audio, and each sampling card had only 16K of Memory – enough for a fraction of a second of sound. Some features were light years ahead of their time: The main system was driven by twin 6800 microprocessors and featured an enormous (by 1982 standards) 64K of memory (upgraded to 256K in the subsequent Series IIx). The built-in video system featured a light pen for point and click control. Sequences could be played back directly from the twin 8-inch floppy disk drives, allowing incredibly long and complex performances.

The Fairlight soon had stiff competition. New England Digital introduced the stratospherically priced Synclavier (perhaps most famous for the chiming gong sound at the beginning of Michael Jackson's *Beat It*), and Emu Systems introduced the sub-$10,000 Emulator and Emulator II keyboards. Technology advanced so quickly that – by 1985 – the Ensoniq Mirage cost a mere $2000 and became known as the everyday musician's Fairlight.

Fairlight went on to introduce the CMI Series III in 1985. It offered pristine 16-bit sound, hard drive storage, tape backup, and a gigantic 14MB of sample memory. Unfortunately, stiff competition from manufacturers such as Sequential Circuits, Roland and Akai forced the company out of business by the late 1980s.

[Update: Fairlights show up occasionally on eBay. Decent Series III instruments are usually around $5000-$10000, depending on configuration and condition. Horizontal Productions offers serviced Series IIIs and upgrades to 32MB memory. Series IIx (with MIDI/timecode sync) also show up sometimes, but spare parts for the IIx are almost impossible to find. See www.ghservices.com/hz/ for details.]

Yamaha DX7

The Yamaha DX7 (introduced in 1983) was the first affordable instrument based on digital Frequency Modulation synthesis (FM). The instrument was notoriously difficult to program because of the unfamiliar synthesis system based on cryptically named operators and algorithms. To make things worse, the sparse user interface relied heavily on a series of membrane keys, a data slider, and a tiny LCD display. Still, the DX7 became a bestseller because of its incredibly clean and modern sound. The DX7 tine piano sound was overused to the point of agony in mid-1980s ballads and the instrument eventually fell out of favour. Native Instruments now offers FM7, a powerful soft synth that extends the DX7 architecture. [www.nativeinstruments.de]

The Yamaha DX7 combined an incomprehensible user interface with an equally confusing synthesis technique. Luckily, it sounded unique.

PPG Wave

The German PPG (Palm Products Germany) Wave synthesizers shaped the sound of many albums in the 1980s. The PPG Wave used extremely short single-cycle wavetables to generate sound. Traditional analog filters and amplitude generators then modified the digital tones. By playing a series of wavetables in a sequence, the instrument could produce shifting and shimmering soundscapes. Thomas Dolby often paired his PPG synthesizer with a Fairlight CMI sampler to create an even broader sound palette. Steinberg introduced a softsynth version of the PPG Wave several years ago [www.steinberg.de].

The Waldorf Wave was the ultimate extension of Wolfgang Palm's Wavescanning synthesis system, first introduced in the PPG Wave synthesizers.

Waldorf Wave

This is my all-time favorite synthesizer – the Waldorf Wave – introduced by German manufacturer Waldorf GmbH in 1993. It is a direct descendant of Wolfgang Palm's incredibly popular PPG Wave digital synthesizers from the early 1980s (Palm actually designed the Waldorf ASIC sound synthesis chip, although he wasn't a Waldorf employee).

The Wave was the ultimate extension of Palm's digital wavetable scanning concept, in which various different sound waveforms could be played back in sequence. The effect was an unmistakable burble of sound. Old-fashioned analog filters were used to process the sound because digital audio still lacked warmth in the early 1990s.

Most functions had a corresponding physical knob and there was a huge (for the time) 480 x 64 pixel display. The instrument could be expanded from 16 to 32 or 48 voices and offered a 3.5-inch disk drive for sound storage. Three stereo outputs were provided to give you the freedom to mix and mangle the Wave's output as needed. Alas, Waldorf disappeared into the mists of time before I had a chance to get my hands on one.

Roland Juno-106

Here's a look at the clean and simple Juno-106 front panel. Good 106's fetch around $500, thanks to their continuing popularity.

The Juno-106 was introduced in 1984 as an entry-level synthesizer. It became incredibly popular because of its slider-based user interface and simplified design. Each of the Juno-106's six voices featured a single digital oscillator and only one modulation envelope. This is my choice as the perfect beginner's synth. It has a classic sound and its controls are a delight to tinker with.

Akai AX-60

The AX-60 (introduced in 1985) was Akai's answer to the Juno-106. Like the Roland Juno-106, it offered a front panel full of sliders, along with a surprisingly full sound for a single oscillator instrument. It had only six voices, but offered a bi-timbral mode that lets you play two different sounds simultaneously. The AX-60 usually sells for less than the Juno-106, mainly because Akai is an unfamiliar brand.

Ensoniq Mirage & ESQ-1

This is a late-model Ensoniq Mirage DSK. The programming interface was incredibly spartan, with a 2-digit LED display that required you to count in hexadecimal.

The Ensoniq Mirage (1985) was the first affordable digital sampling keyboard. It was based on a chipset developed by Bob Yannes, who is best known for creating the SID sound chip in the Commodore 64 computer. Ensoniq also designed the incredibly successful ESQ-1 digital synthesizer (1986) around the same chip, throwing in a quite capable 8-track music sequencer as icing on the cake.

By creating their own eight voice custom sound playback chip, Ensoniq was able to offer incredible performance at an extremely low price. The Mirage was initially priced at $1995 – about a quarter of the cost of any other digital sampling keyboard. Even though its sound quality is dismal by today's standards, it offered up sonic realism that had previously been the realm of extremely wealthy musicians. The synthesizer version was popular, too. Over 50,000 ESQ-1 synths were sold with a list price of $1395.

Kawai K5

The Kawai K5 was introduced in the late 1980s as one of the first (and only) synthesizers designed around additive synthesis technology. Sounds were built by summing together sine waves at different frequencies. The result was a bright and brittle sound that layered extremely well with analog synthesizers. The K5 featured a huge graphic LCD display in an effort to simplify the complicated programming interface.

Korg Wavestation

The Sequential Circuits design team created the Korg Wavestation following the collapse of Sequential in the late 1980s. It was based on sample playback technology and offered the ability to play wavetable sequences, much like the earlier PPG Wave. The instrument also had excellent digital effects (for the day) and it was possible to synchronize wavetable sequences to an external clock source (a computer-based music sequencer, for example). The result was a fun and powerful instrument that is still much sought after. In fact, Korg recently reintroduced it as a software synthesizer in their *Legacy Collection.* [See www.korg.com]

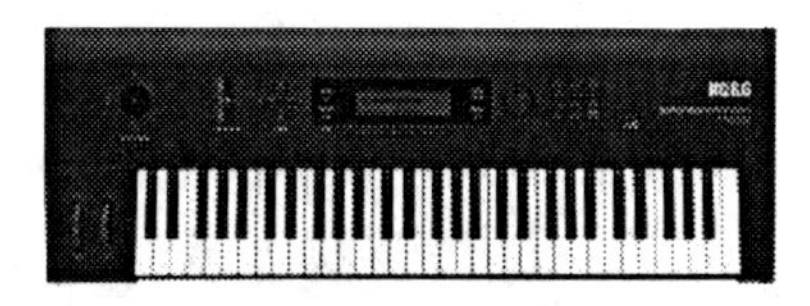

The Wavestation has a decidedly modern appearance, but it was created by the same gang who brought you many of Sequential Circuits' classics.

Modern Retro Synthesizers

There are still a few affordable hardware synthesizers being made. It is extremely difficult to compete with the low cost and flexibility of software, yet some companies continue to thrive because of the incredible ease-of-use and stability of hardware-based instruments. Here are a few modern instruments with decidedly retro features and sound.

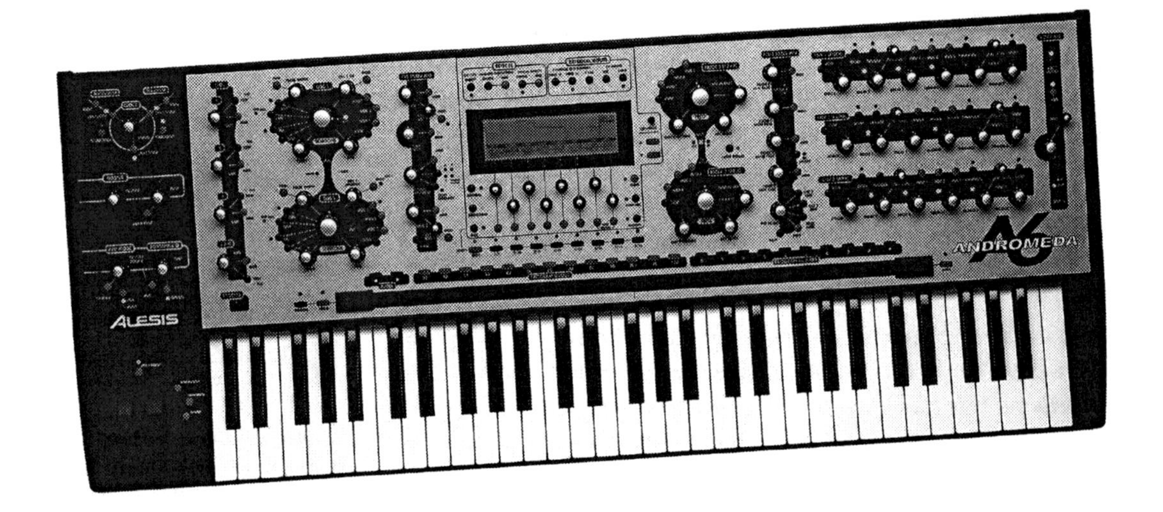

The A6 offers sixteen voices of genuine analog synthesis, along with the convenience of a large LCD display with multi-use rotary controllers.

Alesis Andromeda A6

Alesis surprised the world by introducing a high-end analog synthesizer in 2000. This instrument features 16 voices of analog sound under the direction of a Motorola Coldfire processor. Andromeda offers a front panel slathered with knobs, rotary controllers, buttons, and a nice large graphic LCD. It lists for $3499. [www.alesis.com]

The Nord Lead offered a metal case, with wooden pitch-bend lever and a stone(!) modulation wheel.

Clavia Nord Lead

Swedish company Clavia became famous because of their electronic drum sets. Their powerful and elegant synthesizers have overshadowed that fame. The Clavia Nord Lead was introduced in 1995. This 'virtual analog' instrument faithfully recreated the sound of classic analog synthesizers using complex digital signal processing (DSP), rather than sampled waveforms. I bought one in 1996, and it remains my favorite instrument to this day.

Clavia extended the analog illusion by including a beautifully designed front panel full of knobs, switches, and LEDs. The Nord Lead was followed by several more advanced models and a series of brilliantly flexible 'virtual modular' systems. [www.clavia.se]

The Minimax ASB is the first in a series of virtual analog modules modelled on classic synths.

Creamware Minimax ASB

Creamware is now shipping the Minimax ASB virtual analog synthesizer they announced early in 2005. It's always a relief to see products move beyond the vaporous 'development stage' and into production. The $899 desktop unit features a front panel design heavily inspired by the classic Minimoog. Unlike the original Minimoog, this little sucker offers 6-voice polyphony, USB and MIDI connections, and 128 digital memories.

The software inside the box is based on the Minimax plug-in for Creamware's Scope DSP sound cards. If you can do without the nifty knobs and switches, you're probably better off buying their $799 Scope Project card instead. It offers a modular DSP synth with multi-channel I/O, plus 10 more synths and a decent array of DSP effects.

Creamware also released an emulation of the Sequential Circuits Prophet 5 late in 2005. [www.creamware.de]

Dave Smith Instruments: The next generation

Back in 1985, every keyboard player had a stack of synthesizer keyboards and modules connected by a rat's nest of MIDI and audio cables. Something new and exciting was introduced every six months. Fast-forward twenty years and the average electronic music studio looks more like a computer shop, dotted with flat panel monitors and a PowerMac or two. Sounds are mostly simulated in software these days, and it's getting hard to find real physical instruments.

That's why I was excited when veteran synth designer Dave Smith (of Sequential Circuits fame) added a genuine keyboard synth to his company's lineup. The Poly Evolver is based on a little synth module he released several years ago. It has 4 voices (each with analog and digital sound generation circuitry) and sounds amazing. But – best of all – it offers 77 knobs, 59 buttons, lots of blinky lights, and weighs a cool 23 lbs (9.5 kg). A rack-mount version is available if you don't want knobs (hah!).

They're not cheap at $2,699.00, but they'll last a few decades and run without a computer. Try that with a soft synth. [See www.davesmithinstruments.com for details]

Former Sequential Circuits boss Dave Smith is back with a vengeance. This is the four-voice keyboard version of his massively successful $499 Evolver monosynth.

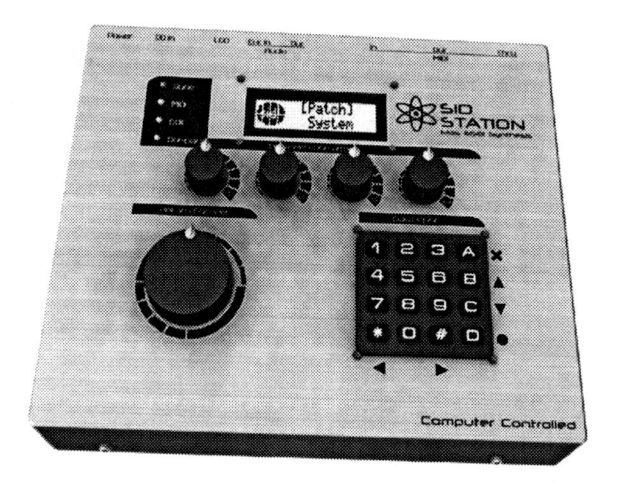

Don't let the modern design fool you. The Sidstation contains the musical heart of a vintage Commodore 64 computer.

Elektron Sidstation: Old meets new

The Commodore 64 was a landmark in personal computing history. It was well known for its capable 3-voice sound synthesis system (remember, this was back before the availability of CD-quality computer audio).

The C-64 generated sound using the Sound Interface Device (SID), a 3-voice digitally controlled analog synthesizer on a chip. Its capabilities were astounding, especially since they were crammed into a $595 home computer. It didn't take long for enterprising programmers to write innovative game soundtracks and music composition programs to mine its potential.

Twenty-two years after its introduction, people still make stunning music with the Commodore SID chip. Many use emulator programs, but you can also buy music synthesizers built around the old chips. The most famous of these is the Elektron Sidstation. It was introduced in 1999 as a $950 standalone MIDI synth. SID chips are getting hard to find, so the current batch of Sidstations will be the last.

Elektron also manufactures several other brilliant (and expensive) instruments. The Monomachine is a 6-voice synthesizer that offers six different monophonic sound generators in a single unit. The result is a machine with an enormous sonic palette. Their Machinedrum is a stand-alone programmable drum machine that is well known for its flexibility and ease of use. [For more information, visit www.elektron.se]

The Novation X-Station is also available in 49 and 61 key versions.

Novation: Another British invasion

British manufacturer Novation rose to fame by producing an analog bass synthesizer module in the mid-1990s. They followed up with an increasingly impressive selection of virtual analog synthesizers and MIDI-based controller keyboards. Novation offers good bang for the buck, but my favorite piece of Novation gear is the amazing X-Station ($799), which combines a virtual analog synthesizer with a MIDI controller keyboard and audio input/output to communicate with your computer via USB. Add a laptop and you have an incredibly versatile 2-piece portable recording studio. [See www.novationmusic.com]

Technosaurus: Pocket-sized analog synths & modern modulars

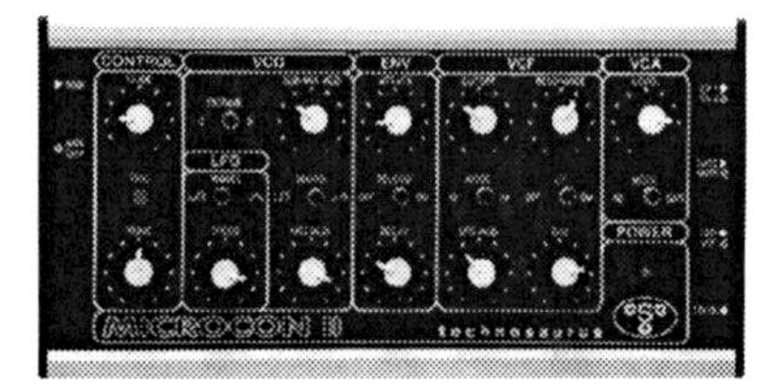

The Microcon II is an updated version of the original with MIDI input. Handy if you don't have an analog controller lying around.

Mention Switzerland and people think of handmade watches, yodeling, and exorbitant property prices. Think again. Swiss company Technosaurus manufactures a line of top-quality analog music synthesizers. Their equipment uses nothing but analog circuitry to generate sound – no digital waveforms or DSP algorithms allowed.

The Microcon II is their smallest – and least expensive – instrument, barely larger than a VHS tape (for any who remember that archaic format). It plays one note at a time, has no program memories (zip, nada, none) and a distinct absence of LCD touchscreens and fancy gimmickry. What it *does* offer is top-notch analog sound and an organic feel that can only be attained by reaching out and flipping a few switches. Priced at 359 euros for the MIDI version. Plan on plugging in a separate MIDI keyboard, since it don't 'ave one.

If you've just signed a contract with a major label, consider their incredibly complex modular synths which look like someone plugged a few bowls of spaghetti into a telephone exchange. Prices start at around 2500 euros and escalate rapidly. [www.technosaurus.ch for more details.]

Resonator Neuronium

Veteran music synth designer Juergen Michaelis has unleashed the fabulously strange 2499 euro Resonator Neuronium. As the name suggests (ahem), this little monster uses six interconnected analog neurons to generate music. How does it sound? Addictively odd, but comfortingly analogish. Imagine a robot ant playing the best of Tangerine Dream through your starship's hyperspace drive. It offers a huge low end but has no problem generating ripping, squealing melody lines and percussion. You definitely won't find a General MIDI soundset lurking in this machine.

Michaelis is in the process of developing a line of less expensive devices based on this technology.

The primary programming interface is a series of six touch-sensitive rotary controllers that allow you to build complex summing and FM networks. Neurons can self-resonate, and the unit features two external audio inputs that can be used to excite the network. Neuron envelopes can be triggered by MIDI, and the output from the six nodes can be mixed down to familiar stereo outputs. For anyone interested in burning a few brain cells, the user's manual is available online.

If you're a wealthy technostar, this thing should be all over your next album. You'll be in rare company – so far Michaelis has delivered 20 units, with orders for five more. [More information at www.jayemsonic.de]

Suzuki Omnichord

Suzuki introduced the Omnichord in the early 1980s as an instrument targeted at beginners. At its simplest, making music required no more than pressing a chord key and strumming the little touch-sensitive pad.

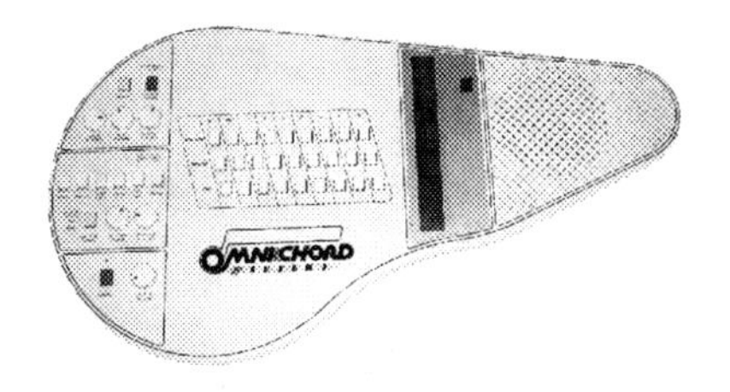

The original Suzuki Omnichord. It was also available in Grey.

But something strange happened. Professional musicians everywhere started picking up this odd little electronic gadget. Robbie Williams, David Bowie, Dave Stewart of the Eurythmics, Bjork, and even Ringo Starr have recorded with them. What makes them incredible is that it's possible to pick one up and make decent music within a few minutes. Try that with a trumpet!

These days, Suzuki offers the sleek QChord – a replacement for the original series of instruments. The QChord features MIDI in/out ports (for interfacing with computer recording systems), a cartridge-based song system, and runs on 8 C batteries. Visit the QChord network for some example recordings – and ignore the cheesy photos of Grandpa wielding his QChord like a weapon. [www.suzukimusic.com/qchord/]

Yes, The Soviets Made Synthesizers Too

Polyvoks analog synthesizer

There was an episode of the original *Star Trek* series in which Kirk found himself trapped in an alternate universe populated by a most unfriendly version of his crew – the evil version of Spock sported a fantastic looking goatee. I get the same strange feeling (minus the facial hair) when exploring the world of Soviet-era electronics.

The Polyvoks is actually surprisingly attractive. I'd love a chance to put one of these through its paces.

Many vintage Russian synthesizers end up on eBay, like this early 1980s Polyvoks analog synthesizer. Built in 1982 by the Formanta electronic factory, it offers two analog oscillators, an aggressive filter, and tons of twiddly knobs. What excites me most is the idea of struggling with a front panel full of controls labeled in abbreviated Russian. Non-Russian users will be forced to experiment and fumble around, ensuring the production of fantastic-sounding accidental bleeps and squawks. [Visit the Museum of Soviet Synths online at www.ruskeys.net/eng/synths.php]

It makes sense to learn photography the old-fashioned way – with a manual film camera.

Cameras and Optical Gadgets

Photography is a fascinating blend of art and science. Modern cameras are beautiful examples of precision manufacturing and miniaturization, but without a talented artist behind the lens the result will be disappointing.

Photographers traditionally have to learn a great deal about light to truly excel. Sadly, the operator of a modern digicam doesn't have to be a skilled technician to produce acceptable results – the camera takes care of annoying details like lens aperture, shutter speed and focus. The trouble with this approach is that the quality of the picture relies on computer algorithms rather than common sense, and everything takes on a 'snapshot' feel.

It makes sense to learn photography with a manual film camera. You'll be forced to experiment and truly understand the interrelationship between lens aperture, shutter speed, and chemical film. This hard-won knowledge will help you to become a better photographer in the digital realm as well.

The first permanent photograph is usually attributed to Frenchman Joseph Nicéphore Niépce in 1826. It took over 8 hours to expose – hardly suitable for portraits! Until the beginning of the 20th Century, photography remained largely the messy domain of professionals and dedicated amateurs. That changed with the introduction of Eastman Kodak's Brownie box camera in 1901. This simple device cost only a dollar and could capture 8 exposures on a roll of 120 medium format film. Photography had become a hobby for the masses.

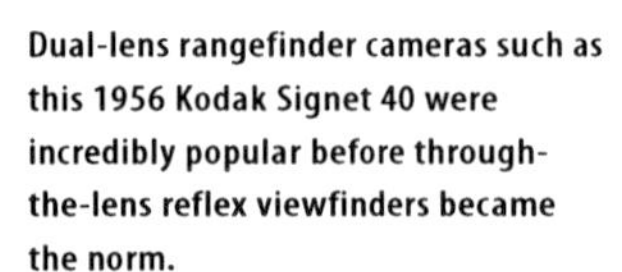

Dual-lens rangefinder cameras such as this 1956 Kodak Signet 40 were incredibly popular before through-the-lens reflex viewfinders became the norm.

35 MM MANUAL CAMERAS

Believe it or not, 35 mm cameras owe their existence to motion picture film. The first prototypes were built by the Ernst Leitz Company in Wetzlar, Germany in 1913. Thirty-five millimetre motion picture film was chosen as the basis for the format, presumably because it was easy to obtain. The Leica I was released in 1925 – the first of many successful Leica models. You can still buy brand new Leica film and digital cameras today. They're famed for their top-notch German optics and equally top-notch price tags. [Visit Leica Camera AG at www.leica-camera.com]

Pentax K1000 and some modern replacements

Over the past 30 years, thousands of photography instructors have recommended the Pentax K1000 manual 35 mm SLR to their students. It was first introduced in 1976 and remained in production for an astonishing 21 years. Production of the K1000 was shifted from Japan to China late in the model's lifespan and several design changes were made to reduce costs. If you're shopping for a K1000, I suggest picking up one of the earlier bodies (distinguished by their metal top and bottom plates). Good K1000s often show up in used camera shops and on eBay for less than $100. I think they're an excellent way to get into "serious" photography on a limited budget.

A classic Pentax K1000 35 mm SLR camera. This one is an early model with metal top and bottom plates.

A pair of modern manual SLRs

There are several affordable substitutes for the K1000 still in production, most notably the Pentax ZX-M and Vivitar V3800N. The ZX-M is the only manual-focus member of the Pentax ZX family. It isn't built with the same rugged tank-like feel as the old K1000, but it will last many years if handled carefully. Expect to pay about $160 for the body alone, or around $230 bundled with a 35 - 80 mm zoom lens.

The Vivitar V3800N is an extremely affordable alternative. You can get a complete kit including body, 28 - 70 mm zoom lens and flash for less than $180. The trade-off is a bit more plastic than I'd like to see on a camera body, but it'll certainly be as durable as most point-and-shoot digicams, but with 35 mm film quality.

Zenit Russian 35 mm cameras

Sooner or later, digital camera manufacturers are going to run out of Megapixels. They'll open up the warehouse to discover nothing but a few crushed pix lying in the corner. And it'll be completely their own fault, for wantonly cramming millions more of the little things into each new model.

The Russian Zenit km. Don't be put off by the cheap plastic case, it's a respectable entry-level 35 mm SLR.

Avoiding digital obsolescence is easy – go against the flow and buy a shiny new film camera. I especially like the new Zenit km 35 mm SLR from Zenit "Krasnogorsky Zavod" in jolly old Russia [www.zenit-foto.ru/English]. It features manual focus, auto/manual exposure, power film advance, and a 50 mm f/2.0 Pentax K-Mount compatible Russian lens. The price? A very respectable $135 from rugift. They have dozens of other cameras and lenses to choose from as well, starting well under $100. Don't forget the best part: Film has better resolution than all but the best Capitalist digicams, and it lasts for decades. [Visit rugift at www.rugift.com]

Venerable Voigtlander cameras: Under $100

The Voigtlander Bessa L is a strikingly affordable 35 mm rangefinder. Note the top-mounted viewfinder.

On October 9th, 1959, my grandfather walked into a camera shop on New Bond Street in London and picked up a shiny new Voigtlander Vitomatic II. He took good care of it, and it was passed on to me about a decade ago. I admired it and fiddled, but without instructions I couldn't even make the shutter fire. Zeiss/Voigtlander had stopped making cameras in 1972 and I was unable to find a manual. Luckily, I recently found an excellent free source for old manuals and brought the Vitomatic back to life [see tinyurl.com/b8rym for more].

The Voigtlander name was eventually licensed by Cosina and reintroduced in the late 1990s. The Voigtlander Bessa L was the least expensive model in the line-up; it has been discontinued and you can pick them up for as little as $100 (without lens). These cameras don't include a built-in eyepiece; they're designed to accept Leica mount wide-angle lenses which include detachable viewfinders. This simple design has its advantages; the optics are simpler, the cameras are smaller, and the film is closer to the lens (for sharper images). A brilliant way to get into wide-angle photography. [Explore www.cameraquest.com for great deals on Voigtlanders]

Canon Camera Museum

The Canon Camera Museum is a virtual showcase of Canon's film and video past. The museum is divided into four sections: Cameras, Design, Technology, and History.

If you've ever wondered about a particular model, this is your opportunity to find out when it was made and what its specifications were. Sadly, the pictures are a tad on the small side – I was hoping that Canon would make decent hi-rez images available for viewing. They are an imaging company, after all. It appears that their first magazine advertisements included photos of a wooden prototype because the famed Kwanon wasn't ready in production form. It soon became a profitable reality thanks to a little optical help from the company that later became Nikon. [The museum is open 24 hours a day at www.canon.com/camera-museum]

Medium Format Photography

Kodak's immensely successful Brownie box cameras introduced amateur photographers everywhere to the joys of medium format photography. They introduced 120 film for their Brownie No. 2 camera in 1901. It is a fantastic way to shoot awe-inspiring portraits and landscapes on a negative almost four times the size of regular 35 mm film. You'll capture amazing detail, and enlargements will stay crisp and clear. Medium format's popularity was eventually eclipsed by compact and affordable 35 mm cameras, but it remains a fabulous way to capture high-quality images.

Believe it or not, there are several affordable ways to get into the world of medium format without robbing a bank.

Seagull TLR cameras offer a fascinating and affordable introduction to the world of medium format photography. And they look cool, too.

Seagull medium format TLR

Most people are kept away from the wonderful world of medium format by the lack of affordable cameras – a professional Hasselblad 555ELD will set you back over $3,500.

Essential Retro to the rescue! Be sure to check out the inexpensive Seagull line of medium format TLR (twin lens reflex) cameras. These Chinese-made devices produce respectable images and are priced from an incredibly affordable $140. The viewfinder is a nifty top-down Fresnel lens that's much more entertaining than a boring old digicam display. Beware, though: shutter speed, aperture, and film winding are all manual. You'll need more than a glimmer of photographic skill to take a decent picture. [Available from www.adorama.com]

The Holga 120 CFM includes a built-in flash with color wheel. Medium format doesn't get less expensive than this.

Holga: Dirt cheap medium format fun

If the Seagull's price tag still seems a bit high, give the $15 Holga 120S a try. This plastic camera is definitely low-end, but it's a great way to dabble with medium format film. The Holga is also available with a Polaroid back, enabling instant feedback. A slightly more expensive model includes a built-in flash with color wheel, too. [Search the Holga range at www.adorama.com]

Kiev 88CM

Top-mounted viewfinder and old-school styling make the Kiev 88CM an attention-getter.

The Kiev 88 is a clone of the prehistoric Hasselblad 1000F medium format camera, which shoots high-resolution negatives that are approximately four times the size of regular 35 mm film. It's manufactured in the Ukraine by Zavod Arsenal and sold in a variety of configurations.

If you're worried about the quality of Ukrainian manufacturing, I suggest visiting Mike Fourman's Kiev Camera site. Fourman offers carefully inspected and tweaked versions of the brand new Kiev 88CM model featuring interchangeable lenses, a new film cartridge loading design, a new cloth focal plane shutter, and a modernized metering system attached to a TTL viewfinder.

Kiev Camera sells Kiev 88CM packages starting at $599 for a kit featuring the respectable Arsat 80 mm f/2.8 lens. That's a decent price for pro-quality equipment.
[I recommend www.kievcamera.com or www.kievusa.com if you're hunting for a top-quality Russian camera in the USA.]

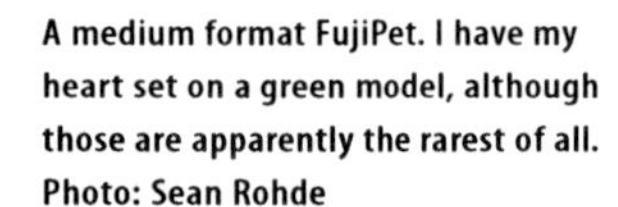
A medium format FujiPet. I have my heart set on a green model, although those are apparently the rarest of all. Photo: Sean Rohde

FujiPet (and FujiPet 35)

The FujiPet was marketed as a simple point-and-shoot camera and wasn't exported out of Japan. It was originally released in 1957 to shoot medium format (6 x 6 cm negative) film, but the rising popularity of 35 mm encouraged Fuji to introduce the FujiPet 35 in 1959. The series went on to sell almost 1 million units. To keep things interesting, Fuji manufactured this plastic and aluminium camera in three colors: red, black, and green (my fave).

According to the disastrously worded FujiPet page at Mediajoy [tinyurl.com/7tde6] "it had such a simple mechanism and function that even children and women could easily make use of it." No way I'm touching that delightful comment without a hundred foot pole and a flack jacket. FujiPets show up occasionally on eBay, but they usually command high prices. I suggest e-mailing Tak Kohyama at Retro Enterprises in Japan. He specializes in Single-8 movie cameras but might come across the occasional FujiPet [e-mail: mail@retro8.com]

Unusual Photographic Formats

Polaroid Land cameras

Modern Polaroid cameras are decidedly more attractive than their 30 year-old cousins.

Most of us think in terms of instant photography these days. Digital cameras are everywhere and it's getting difficult to buy a mobile phone that can't snap a few pics.

Back in the late 20th Century, instant photography still seemed like magic and the Polaroid Corporation was home to the master sorcerers. Edwin Land's company got its start selling polarized sunglasses and moved into the instant camera market in 1948. They competed head-to-head with Kodak for many years, and even managed to develop Polavision – an ill-fated instant movie system that cost the company millions.

Alas, they were late entering the digital camera market and filed for bankruptcy in 2001. The company is now owned by Petters

Group Worldwide and markets a variety of affordable digital cameras, video equipment and instant cameras.

In recent years, Polaroids have become an incredibly popular artistic medium. Perhaps the most beautiful example of this is Sia's *Breathe Me* music video featuring thousands of animated Polaroid shots [Sia's official site is www.siamusic.net].

Polaroid instant film cameras start at about $35 and are available all over the place. Drop by www.polaroid.com if you're interested in a bit of window-shopping.

Pinhole Cameras

Pinhole cameras have no lens. They're simple lightproof boxes with a tiny pinhole-sized opening on one side and a film holder on the other. The hole acts like a crude lens, casting an image on the film behind. Early cameras used this incredibly simple approach to capture pictures on film. It's slightly unpredictable and decidedly different.

Dirkon DIY pinhole camera

As a child, I once covered all ten digits of both hands with dribbles of glue while attempting to put together a model aircraft. Things didn't get much better with age, so my desire to glue together a working camera from stiff paper will remain nothing more than an unfulfilled dream.

A free paper camera. What more could one possibly want from life?

The Dirkon paper camera was originally published as a set of plans in Communist Czechoslovakia, presumably as an evil plan to encourage teenagers to glue themselves to tables instead of rising up in rebellion. Recently, someone took the time to make the original instructions available on the web in Adobe Acrobat format. This little pinhole camera accepts 35 mm film and takes dreamy pictures that will look suitably pretentious in art galleries everywhere. [Plans for the Dirkon can be downloaded from www.pinhole.cz/en]

Polaroid pinhole cameras

The best thing about Polaroids is the instant physical reminder of the moment. The 11,000 Yen Polaroid Pinhole 80 Camera takes the fun of Polaroid art to a new level. One never really knows exactly what a pinhole camera is about to capture, making the idea of a pinhole Polaroid irresistible – if you don't like the image, shoot it again or try something slightly different. The result will be dreamy, soft-focused and addictive. [See tinyurl.com/bkm79 for product information. The Japanese site has been automatically translated to English, so expect to be confused.]

A pair of Polaroid Pinhole 80 cameras. As of late 2005, no one was importing these into North America.

Lomography.com: Weird and Wonderful Cameras

I love the Lomography.com site. It showcases several dozen unusual cameras that are hard to find anywhere else. The best thing about it is the stunning variety of user-submitted photographs that adorn every corner of the site and online shop. It's one thing to understand technically how a camera works, but quite another to actually see it in real-world use. Two of my favorite cameras from their site are the LOMO and Colorsplash. Here's the low-down.

A LOMO Compact Automat. They are now discontinued, but reconditioned cameras are still available from lomography.com

LOMO cameras

LOMO PLC is the largest optical manufacturer in Russia. The abbreviation stands for Leningradskoye Optiko Mechanichesckoye Obyedinenie. Try saying that three times fast. The organization was formed in 1914 and went on to became the largest supplier of optics to the Red Army.

The LOMO LC-A (Compact Automat) is a quirky 35 mm camera that quickly became a favorite friend of experimental photographers everywhere. Unfortunately, LOMO announced in early 2005 that they could no longer produce this little gem.

Their distributor – Lomography.com – stepped up to the plate and is doing a booming business refurbishing lightly used LOMOs. They offer two year warranties and several nifty add-ons like the Colorsplash Flash and Tunnel Vision lens. Prices start at around $200 for a complete package (camera, flash, batteries, how-to book and film).

It's sad to see the production of old-fashioned film cameras slowly winding down. Be warned – they're going to become increasingly hard to find. [www.lomography.com]

The cute and cuddly colorsplash takes unforgettably cool pictures, especially at night.

Colorsplash cameras

Colorsplash. The word sounds like something Kodak or Polaroid should have trademarked in the 1970s. What's colorsplashing? Well, imagine a camera that lets you dial-in colored filters to cover the flash. Then imagine that this camera has two shutter modes. In Instant Exposure mode, you press the button and the picture gets taken (with flash, of course). The result is a color-shifted image – like a defective Polaroid.

Things get more interesting when you choose the Long Exposure setting. Now, the shutter stays open long as you hold the button and the flash goes off when you release – moments before the shutter closes. Et voila... Brilliant arty pictures that make you look like you know what you're doing.

Oh, and check out the $85 Colorsplash Ice Bear Edition – the perfect faux fur covered hybrid of retro technology and pointless marketing. [www.lomography.com]

Toycamera.com site and book

It's time to introduce you to the crazy folk at toycamera.com. While most serious photographers dismiss cheap plastic cameras as useless junk, the toycamera.com brigade embrace them as an opportunity to produce affordable and unpredictable art. The site was founded by two people with a love of toy cameras, but quickly grew to showcase the work of dozens.

They did what any merry band of lunatics would do – collaborated to produce an elegant $38 coffee table book. Twenty-six photographers from seven countries contributed to the *Toycam Handbook*, a collection of 104 images captured with their 'toys.' This well-designed compilation includes biographies, pictures of the cameras and an informal 'tongue-in-cheek' interview with the co-founders. The site itself is worth a long visit. It presents dozens of stunning pictures in the gallery section as well as an intriguing tech section for do-it-yourself gear manglers.

Once you see these pictures, you might have to pick up a 'toy' camera for yourself. [www.toycamera.com]

The Toycam Handbook from toycamera.com. If you're looking for inspiration, get your hands on this book.

Alfred Klomp's fabulous camera page

The unfortunately-named Alfred Klomp has compiled all sorts of weird and wonderful Russian cameras, Yashicas, Nippons, Zeiss Ikons, and even a page explaining the history behind most of the famous Russian camera logos. After a few minutes cruising this stuff, you too will know titillating factoids like the full name of LOMO (*Leningradskoye Optiko-Mechanicheshkoye Obyedinenie*). Check out cameras.alfredklomp.com for dozens of beautiful camera pics.

Three Dimensional Fun

Spatial Imaging holographic portraits

Hungarian physicist Dennis Gabor invented holography in 1948. It didn't become a commercially viable technology until the introduction of the laser in 1960. Lasers enabled holographers to capture the phase of light along with its amplitude and wavelength.

This additional information enables viewers to see holographic pictures as three-dimensional images.

Spatial Imaging Portraits near London is one of the leading studios specializing in holographic portraits. Their archive includes Queen Elizabeth II, pop group Oasis, and technology whiz Clive Sinclair. These three-dimensional pictures should be hung on a wall and illuminated from above for best effect. I suspect you'll have to fork out quite a bit for their top-notch work. [www.portraits.co.uk]

Litiholo Hologram Kit

The $139 hologram kit from Litiholo includes everything you need to make holograms of small inanimate objects.

If your budget is smaller, several companies make affordable do-it-yourself hologram sets such as the $139 Litiholo Hologram Kit, which includes a small laser diode, twenty pieces of "instant" hologram film, plate holder, LED darkroom light and everything else needed to create your own small images. [Available direct from www.litiholo.com]

Miscellaneous Optical Gadgets

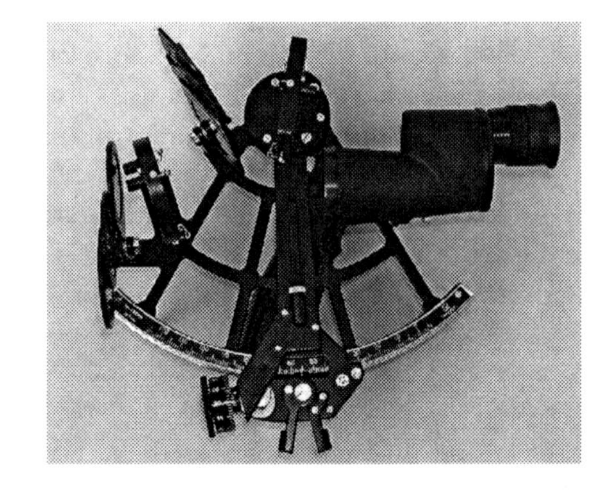

You probably won't see a Tamaya sextant if you live inland, but they're quite common among serious amateur sailors.

Sextants - Tamaya Jupiter

Once upon a pre-digital time, seafaring explorers had to rely on the sun and stars for navigation. They used Sextants to measure the angle of celestial bodies (sun, stars or geostationary space stations) above the horizon. The angle and time it was taken could be used to compute a position line on a navigational chart. Of course, this didn't do a lot of good for intrepid explorers traveling with incomplete, incorrect, or non-existent maps.

The Tamaya Jupiter is a beautifully modern sextant. It weighs almost 4 lbs (1.8 kg) and includes a molded plastic carrying case. After that, I admit to not having a clue. Here's what the product page says:

"It has many of the features of more expensive sextants yet still has impressive +/- 12 arcsecond accuracy. The large 57 x 42 mm index mirror and 57 mm diameter horizon offer a bright view. The inclined handle provides a natural and comfortable grip. Built to rigid specifications and engineered for quality, the Jupiter professional marine sextant is the most popular selling sextant Tamaya offers. The Tamaya Jupiter Sextant offers full illumination on both the arc and drum. Interchangeable 4 x 40 or 7 x 35 monocular scopes are available."

[Mental note: Add "Learn to use a sextant" to my list of things to do before I'm relegated to Shady Acres Retirement Village. Visit www.stanleylondon.com/TamayaJupiter.htm for product details.]

Russian night vision equipment

Near as I can tell, the best thing about the breakup of the Soviet Union is the amazing amount of pseudo-military technology that is now manufactured for export. Take night vision scopes, for instance. In the real world these things have limited uses. Rugift lists military, law enforcement, hunting, and 'entertainment.' I'll leave their last suggestion to your imagination.

A pair of BNV Viking Pro night vision binoculars. These use passive infra-red technology and retail for under $500.

Prices range from $159 for a Generation 1 model (passive infra-red), all the way up to several thousand bucks for a state-of-the-art Generation 2+ unit (improved resolution and sensitivity). The best of these scopes enable you to see a person standing over 180 m (200 yd.) away on an overcast moonless night. Now, if only the Russians would perfect X-Ray goggles. [www.rugift.com]

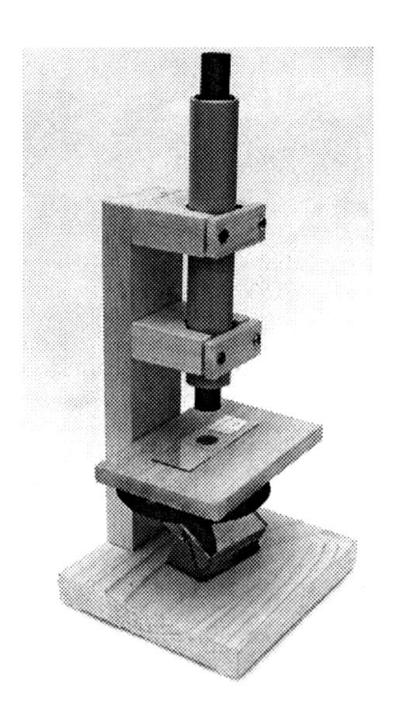

All you need is a little woodworking skill and four disposable camera lenses.

Make your own compound microscope

Everyone should have a microscope, especially if you can get your hands on one for practically nothing. With that in mind, I offer you this link to Giorgio Carboni's do-it-yourself compound microscope. It's capable of 75X magnification and even offers fine focusing. To keep expenses low, he salvaged four lenses from disposable cameras. [Details on the web at tinyurl.com/9wvgp]

Makes me wonder why cheap plastic 'toy' microscopes cost so much in comparison.

Microscopes first appeared around 1600. Some attribute the invention to Galileo Galilei, but Wikipedia.org says "Anton van Leeuwenhoek (1632-1723) is generally credited with bringing the microscope to the attention of biologists, even though simple magnifying lenses were already being produced in the 1500s, and the magnifying principle of water-filled glass bowls had been described by the Romans."

Super 8 film has outlasted its contemporaries because of its unique look and simplicity.

Shooting Movies On Super 8

Kodak introduced the revolutionary cartridge-based *Super 8 mm* movie format in April, 1965. It was designed for simplicity – insert a cartridge, point and shoot. At the height of Super 8's popularity in 1979, Kodak sold over 18 million film cartridges each year.

The arrival of cheap video in the early 1980s decimated the home movie industry almost overnight. Twenty years after the onslaught of video, a few thousand film-makers still shoot Super 8 because nothing beats the magical look of real film. And, even though no new cameras have been produced for almost two decades, the last few years have seen a dramatic rediscovery of Super 8 filmmaking.

The Canon Auto Zoom 814 Electronic dates from 1972. They were made in large numbers and often sell for under $100 on eBay.

Super 8: Movies for the Masses

It has been forty years since the introduction of Super 8. Although technology has progressed dramatically since then, Super 8 lives on. When the format burst onto the moviemaking scene in 1965, it was a breath of fresh air. It was designed to be as easy to use as possible – click a cartridge into the camera, point and shoot. The world had never seen anything like it, and the Super 8 revolution influenced several generations of filmmakers and home movie buffs. The simplicity of the technology helped to assure its continued success and the affordability of the format still encourages filmmakers to experiment and dream. Some might say it makes magic.

Ironically, advances in technology saved Super 8 from obscurity. Once upon a time, filmmakers huddled in their caves with only the fire for warmth and light, nervously editing film by cutting and gluing little strips into a final masterpiece. It's a useful skill to learn, but manual editing is as relevant to current filmmaking as typewriters are to the modern novelist – interesting but impractical.

Enter the personal computer. Reputable PCs can be purchased for well under $1000 these days with huge hard drives, lots or memory, and lightning quick processors. With the addition of some relatively low-cost software, they make excellent platforms for editing digitized film. There are several inexpensive ways to capture your movies on digital videotape, allowing you to manipulate film just like you'd edit home videos. Respectable computer-based video editing packages can be purchased for under $100 and Apple even includes a free copy of their *iMovie* video editing program with every new computer they sell.

The Internet has helped to strengthen the filmmaking community as well. Equipment is available from eBay and various online retailers at quite reasonable prices, and thousands of people hang out on Internet forums that specialize in small format filmmaking. Finding documentation and repair for old equipment was a daunting task ten years ago, but these days it's relatively easy to track down professional service by e-mail or through online recommendations.

Why Super 8 is special

Mention filmmaking in casual conversation and people immediately think of bulky professional cameras, complicated controls, and awkward reels of film. Kodak designed the Super 8 format to avoid all that.

Super 8 film cartridges (officially termed "Kodapak" cartridges) cram two side-by-side film reels into a tiny space – one feed reel and one take-up reel. You don't have to worry about threading film or accidentally exposing it to light – simply take it out of the box and foil-lined bag and click it into the camera's film chamber. A series of small notches on the front edge of the cartridge tell the camera whether the film is for daylight or indoor use and what the film speed is. Nearly all Super 8 cameras include built-in automatic exposure as well. All you have to worry about is focusing and shooting.

Simplicity. That's what has kept Super 8 alive for over 40 years, but that's not the end of the Super 8 story. While it's a great introduction to filmmaking for students and amateurs alike, Super 8 can also be used to create stunningly beautiful professional films. Cameras such as the Beaulieu 4008 and Leicina Special series accept professional quality removable lenses and offer fully manual exposure controls that are perfectly suited to a professional environment. And even high-end equipment rarely costs more than a few hundred dollars these days.

Overview of a Typical Super 8 Camera

Super 8 cameras are basically lightproof boxes with a door in the side for inserting a film cartridge and a lens mounted on the front for recording images. Most of them share the following features:

Film trigger

Squeeze the trigger to start shooting. Just be sure to focus the lens first – only a few late-model Super 8 cameras offer camcorder-like autofocus.

Electric zoom buttons

That's right, push-button zoom control. Some more expensive cameras offer a two-speed zoom. Press lightly for a slow zoom or harder to zoom faster. Many cameras can also be zoomed manually, and this is my preferred method.

Manual focusing ring

Most Super 8 cameras require you to focus the lens. Note that the viewfinder eyepiece usually has an adjustment knob or lever so you can set it to match your vision. Before shooting, take the time to configure the eyepiece while viewing a distant object through the viewfinder. Manual focus is like driving a standard transmission car; it becomes automatic with practice.

Indoor / daylight switch

Nearly all Super 8 film is color balanced to look correct under indoor (tungsten) light. When you put a cartridge of Ektachrome 64T into the film chamber, most cameras sense that they are loaded with "indoor" film. If you're shooting outdoors with this film, you must activate a color correction filter (known as an "85 filter"). Many cameras have a two-way switch marked sun/light bulb. Select the sun icon for outdoor shooting, and the light bulb for indoor shots. A few cameras use filter keys – little flat pieces of metal that are inserted to remove the filter when shooting with daylight balanced film.

Speed control

The more, the merrier. Look for a camera that can shoot 24 fps, but also offers single frame and 9 fps, along with maybe 36 fps and even 54 fps (both slow motion). Cameras often offer an intervalometer that allows you to take time-lapse shots.

Manual / automatic exposure control

Look for cameras that let you override their built-in exposure metering. This will give you more artistic control and ensures that the camera can be used with future film types.

Kodak's Super 8 film lineup as of late 2006. Two B&W films, two color negatives, and one color reversal for projection.

All about Super 8 film

All Super 8 film comes loaded into 50 ft (15 m) cartridges. Magnetically striped sound film was available until 1998, when it was discontinued by Kodak. This isn't as much of a limitation as you might think because most Super 8 cameras are quite noisy and the quality of the recorded sound is anything but high fidelity. Many modern Super 8 filmmakers capture sound using minidisc or hard drive digital recorders. The soundtrack is synchronized with the image during editing, using a process similar to the one professional cinematographers use.

Surprisingly, there are more types of Super 8 film available now than there were five years ago. And no matter what anyone else might tell you, Kodak is currently the only manufacturer of Super 8 film.

In addition to Kodak's offerings, Pro 8 mm in Burbank, California [www.pro8mm.com] remanufactures a wide array of Kodak and Fuji 35 mm motion picture film and loads it into Super 8 cartridges. This gives you an incredible range of choices, but at $35/ roll for film and processing it's an expensive way to get into Super 8. Wittner Kinotechnik of Hamburg, Germany also markets several types of Kodak-made film under their own Wittnerchrome brand. These include a 100 ASA medium-speed daylight color reversal film, and their own house-branded version of Kodak's famous Kodachrome K-40 [www.wittner-kinotechnik.de]

Sadly, Kodak discontinued the sale and processing of Kodachrome K-40 Super 8 movie film in 2005. For a short while, Kodachrome was the only color projection film offered by Kodak. It's a very slow film stock, which means that it required lots of light but captured a relatively grain-free image. When people talk about the saturated colors of home movies, they're actually referring to the vibrant and somewhat old-fashioned look of Kodachrome.

The loss of Kodachrome is a huge blow for three reasons. Foremost, it was extremely cost effective. Until recently, it was possible to buy process-prepaid K-40 film for as little as $12 per roll. Secondly, Kodachrome exhibits excellent archival properties – it is extremely resistant to fading and discoloration with age.

The most important reason to morn the loss of Kodachrome is that all Super 8 cameras were equipped to handle it. Many inexpensive Super 8 cameras were designed to accept a limited number of film speeds. Most common were cameras that supported 40 or 160 ASA films.

Kodak replaced Kodachrome with a new Ektachrome 64T stock. Unfortunately, this film speed cannot be read properly by 40/160 compatible cameras, resulting in overexposure. If you own a 40/160 ASA camera, your only options are to shoot B&W film or to purchase Wittnerchrome 40T by mail-order from Germany.

So, before you buy a Super 8 camera, verify that it can correctly read the exposure notch on Ektachrome 64 film carts. Most knowledgeable online retailers and eBay sellers will include this information in their product listings. If they don't, the answer is only a quick e-mail away. When purchasing cameras from swap meets, garage sales, and camera shops, you might have to do a little more research. Pop open the film chamber door; you'll often find a list of supported film speeds. If not, scribble down the model number and run a Google search for details. If you still come up empty handed, I suggest dropping by the Super 8 forums at Filmshooting.com and Cinematography.com – chances are that someone can give you the answer off the top of their head.

The length of time you can shoot with a 50 foot cartridge depends on how many frame per second (fps) you shoot. Traditional "home movie" Super 8 was shot at 18 fps, giving a shooting time of 3 minutes & 20 seconds per roll. Quite a few low-end cameras support only this speed. The results are acceptable for projection, but not so great when converted to video.

The films you watch in a theater are usually captured at 24 fps (European TV films are often shot at 25 fps to match the frame rate of the European PAL TV format). Twenty-four frames gives smoother motion, but it chews through film 1/3 faster: a roll will last a mere 2 minutes & 30 seconds.

The result of these abbreviated shooting times is that you find yourself becoming more selective about what you film and shots tend to be more planned than they would be if you had the luxury of waving a video camera around for an hour at a time. The final product will be much easier to edit, I guarantee.

Projection and Negative Film

Super 8 film comes in two main types: reversal and negative. Reversal is the stuff that's run through projectors. Each frame looks like a tiny photographic slide, with correct coloration. This is the easiest film for amateurs to use, since it can be screened with a projector or desktop film viewer. It's also the cheapest to convert to video, since the conversion process can be performed with a modified film projector.

Negative film looks like the stuff that comes back from the film lab when you send in a roll of 35 mm still camera film. The film stock has a strong orange tint, and the color shading is the opposite of what we're used to – darks are lights and lights are darks. This is the stuff used by professionals who are planning to either convert it to digital or manufacture projection copies. Why do they use it? Because it captures a better image than reversal film – the range of contrast and color saturation tends to be far broader on negative, which helps to ensure that filmmakers capture the fine nuances of each scene. Negative film is expensive to convert to video because special color correction is required.

I suggest starting your Super 8 career with a color or black & white reversal film. It'll be less expensive than shooting and transferring negative. Once you've learned the ropes, consider switching to negative film to give you a bit more quality and control.

The Super 8 Film stock List

This list includes every Super 8 film stock that was in production as of late 2005.

Eastman Kodak

Kodak [www.kodak.com] remains the ten-thousand pound gorilla of the film industry. Their current Super 8 film line-up includes a little bit of everything. Note that Ektachrome 64T is Kodak's only color projection film, intended to replace Kodachrome K-40. Many low-end cameras cannot read the 64 ASA speed notch correctly, leading to incorrect exposure.

Kodak Ektachrome 64T (64 ASA indoor balanced color reversal film)
Kodak Plus-X (100/80 ASA B&W Reversal)
Kodak Tri-X (200/160 ASA B&W Reversal)
Kodak 500T (500 ASA indoor balanced color negative)
Kodak 200T (200 ASA indoor balanced color negative)

What happened to Kodachrome?

Kodak isn't having a good year. With sales of traditional film dropping about 15% annually, they awkwardly chose the 40th anniversary of Super 8 in 2005 to discontinue Kodachrome 40.

For those who've been under a rock since 1971, K-40 is the classic Super 8 movie film. At the height of its popularity, Kodak sold over 18 million cartridges each year. These days, they sell a mere 100,000 annually, but there is a vibrant and dedicated small-gauge film community built around this stuff. A hopefully-good-enough replacement (Ektachrome 64T) was released in October 2005, but it doesn't include prepaid processing.

The Kodachrome cancellation notice first appeared on the Kodak UK site, but quickly spread across the rest of the world. Rumor has it that Kodak will process Super 8 Kodachrome at their Swiss lab until the end of 2006. Dwayne's Photo in Kansas (USA) has indicated they will continue to process the film as long as it remains available from Kodak in 16 mm and 35 mm formats.

KAHL

KAHL is a German film company that offers processing-included pricing on all film. Be warned that you have to get your film processed within 12 months of purchase. Prices range from 27 to 36 euros per roll.

KAHL 21 (100 ASA B&W negative)
KAHL 24 (200 ASA B&W reversal)
KAHL 27 (400 ASA B&W negative)
KAHL 320T (320 ASA indoor balanced color negative)
KAHL 500T (500 ASA indoor balanced color negative)
KAHL 800T (800 ASA indoor balanced color negative)
KAHL UT18 (50 ASA daylight color reversal)

Pro 8 mm

Pro 8 mm of Burbank, California offers a broad variety of Super 8 film manufactured from Kodak and Fuji 35 mm motion picture film. They charge $35 per roll, including in-house processing.

Pro 8/05 (250 ASA daylight balanced Kodak Vision color negative)
Pro 8/12 (100 ASA tungsten balanced color negative)
Pro 8/85 (100 ASA daylight balanced color reversal)
Pro 8/17 (200 ASA tungsten balanced color negative)
Pro 8/18 (500 ASA tungsten balanced color negative)
Pro 8/73 (500 ASA Fuji Eterna tungsten balanced color negative)
Pro 8/92 (500 ASA Fuji Reala daylight balanced color negative)
Pro 8/45 (50 ASA daylight balanced color negative)
Pro 8/48 (100 ASA tungsten balanced color negative)
Pro 8/77 (320 ASA tungsten balanced color negative)
Pro 8/79 (500 ASA tungsten balanced color negative)
Pro 8 Hi-Con (10 ASA B&W reversal)

This last film is an ultra-low grain film that requires tons of light. It was originally marketed for surveillance shooting.

Kodachrome 40 film was discontinued in mid-2005, but Wittner Kinotechnik in Hamburg, Germany plans to market their own version as Wittnerchrome 40T.

Wittnerchrome: A new name for a classic film.
Wittner Kinotechnik in Hamburg recently announced that they'll be marketing Wittnerchrome 40T, a house-branded version of the classic Kodak stock. Wittner estimates they have enough to meet worldwide demand for at least a year. From pictures, it looks like it will be loaded in genuine Kodak cartridges. There are plans to offer Kodak's Ektachrome 100D film in a similar format. I suspect their Wittnerchrome 40T version of Kodachrome will be incredibly successful.

Wittnerchrome 40T (40 ASA indoor balanced color reversal)
Wittnerchrome 100D (100 ASA daylight balanced color reversal)

Film Processing

Unlike video, film is useless until it has been chemically processed. Kodak used to include the cost of processing with every roll of Kodachrome, but that's no longer the case. These days, you have to send your exposed film to a third-party lab. I've listed a number of North American and European labs below. Prices vary quite a bit between countries, and don't forget that international postage can make a huge difference to the final price.

My recommendation? If you're just starting out, shoot Ektachrome 64T color reversal film. The film costs about $13 per roll, direct from Kodak. Use Dwayne's Photo in Parsons, Kansas for the processing: they charge $9 per roll, plus $4 shipping for the first roll, and 50 cents for each additional. If you live in the USA and there's a Wal-Mart nearby, consider dropping off your film there for processing. They'll send your Ektachrome (or old Kodachrome, if you still have some) to Dwayne's at a cost of only $5.88 per roll, with no shipping charges.

North American and European Super 8 film labs

This list is by no means comprehensive; labs frequently change their processing capabilities based on workload and anticipated market conditions. I recommend checking a film site such as www.onSuper.org for up-to-date information. You might get lucky and discover an affordable lab just around the corner.

Andec Filmtechnik (www.andecfilm.de – Berlin, Germany)

Andec was slated to begin processing of Ektachrome 64T film in early 2006. They also process Kodak negative film and offer a negative to positive printing service.

Dwayne's Photo (www.dwaynesphoto.com – Kansas, USA)

Dwayne's processes Kodachrome K-40 and Ektachrome 64T color reversal film from Kodak. Express courier is offered as an option if you require faster turnaround.

Forde Labs (www.fordelabs.com – Seattle, USA)

Forde offers processing and Telecine preparation for Kodak negative film, B&W reversal, and may offer Eltachrome 64T in the near future.

Kodak (Lausanne, Switzerland)

Kodak's Kodachrome facility near Lausanne is scheduled for closure some time in 2006. If you still have Kodachrome prepaid film, this is the only place in the world where it's processed. For fastest service, send your film to the Swiss address listed on the little yellow mail-in envelope in the film package.

Pro 8 mm (www.pro8mm.com – Burbank, USA)

Pro8mm sells its film with processing included. Their processing facility handles Kodak and Fuji negative as well as reversal film.

Yale Film And Video (www.yalefilmandvideo.com – North Hollywood, USA)

Yale processes B&W reversal and Kodak negative Super 8 film stock.

Interesting Super 8 Cameras (plus a couple of Single-8 models)

The Bauer S 207 XL is a medium quality camera with low light shooting capability produced in the late 1970s. I purchased this one on the German eBay site for about $35 in late 2004.

Bauer: Super 8 workhorses

I'm a big fan of late-model Bauer Super 8 cameras because they're cheap and plentiful – perfect starter cameras. I've owned several, both made in Malaysia. The cases are made from curvy plastic and the controls are elegantly laid out. The C 107 XL is a low-light capable camera that shoots at 18 fps. They seem incredibly common and regularly sell on the German eBay site [www.ebay.de] for less than 10 euros. For a tad more money, you can get your hands on the C 207 XL which includes 24 fps 'professional speed' shooting.

NOTE: these cameras accept only 40/160 speed film and are not compatible with Kodak Ektachrome 64T. Be sure you have a good supply of Kodachrome, Wittnerchrome, or are willing to shoot B&W before purchasing.

The Beaulieu 4008 ZMII is a beautiful and versatile camera. The lens is a removable C-Mount, in this case a Schneider Kreuznach F1.8/ 6 - 66 mm zoom.

Beaulieu 4008 ZM II: Form and function

Every grown-up should have a ray gun. This was a core belief of my college years. Regrettably, my vision of the future hasn't come to pass. I still lust after ray guns, a desire that virtually ensured I'd buy a Super 8 movie camera the moment I stumbled across one on eBay. And the Beaulieu 4008 is one of the most beautiful Super 8 cameras ever made.

The 4008 series are desirable because of the flexibility of the removable C-mount lens system and also because they are fully manual. Unlike most Super 8 cameras, you set the film speed control by hand. This makes them compatible with all film stocks on the market.

Beaulieu was an early adopter of rechargeable battery technology. All 4008s use a rechargeable NiCd battery pack that screws into the side of the body. These packs are now 30 years old and are either dead or have been re-celled with new batteries. Be sure to check before purchasing.

Wittner Kinotechnik in Hamburg purchased the entire inventory of Beaulieu parts in 2004. They still offer brand new "professional" Beaulieu cameras along with the occasional refurbished 4008.

Repair is also available from several reputable technicians. Search the www.filmshooting.com forum for the latest information. Expect to pay around $400 for a Beaulieu 4008 in good working condition with re-celled batteries. [www.beaulieu.de]

A Canon 814 XL-S. The lens isn't as massive as it seems; I left the rubber sun shade on for this photo. The handle folds up for storage and tripod use.

Canon 1014 XL-S: They saved the best for last

Many consider the Canon 1014 XL-S and 814 XL-S to be among the best Super 8 cameras ever made. Introduced in 1979, these were the final top-end cameras offered by Canon before the market shifted to video in the early 1980s. Both models were similar, differing only in maximum zoom (10x for the 1014 and 8x on the 814) and a few extraneous bells and whistles. They can record sound, although Kodak discontinued Super 8 sound cartridges in 1998.

Both cameras use a digital timing circuit that ensures that they run quite close to the indicated filming speed (although they're not crystal synchronized cameras). This is a departure from traditional designs that offered not-so-perfect electro-mechanical timing. The lenses are sharp and fast (f/1.4 in both cases) and the viewfinder features excellent split-image focusing like you'd expect to find in a vintage SLR still camera.

The 1014 XL-S typically sells for $100-$200 more than its little brother, but I actually prefer the 814. The smaller lens weighs a bit less and it's not missing any absolutely necessary features.

Fujica ZC 1000: Top of the line Single-8

The Fujica ZC 1000 was Fuji's top-of-the-line movie camera. It uses Fuji Single-8 film cartridges which are incompatible with Kodak's Super 8 format. Film is still available from Andec Filmtechnik (www.andecfilm.de) in Germany and Single 8 Film (www.single8.com) in the USA.

The ZC 1000 offers a removable C-Mount lens system and a wide range of shooting speeds. The Single-8 film cartridge is often touted as superior to Kodak's technology because it takes advantage of a high-quality metal film pressure plate built into the camera, rather than a disposable plastic plate in the cartridge. Single-8 carts also allow rewinding.

The Fujica AX100 is an incredibly simple and small Single-8 camera. It also has an incredibly fast f/1.1 lens and XL shutter for low light shooting.
Photo: Juergen Lossau

Fujica AX100: Zen simplicity in Single-8

Thanks to computer-based editing, filmmaking is more popular today than it was ten years ago. To get you started, how about The Fujica AX100? It's a tiny Single-8 movie camera produced by Fuji in the early 1970s. It's easy to use, with an extremely fast F/1.1 lens for low-light shooting and one button point-and-shoot filming. The AX100 uses Fuji Single-8 film cartridges, which are still available for $16 plus processing (see above).

If you're really lucky, you might find one with the Fujica MarinePack 8 underwater housing. It has a targeting sight, weird plastic fins, and suspicious looking lens holes. This is definitely not something to toss into your carry-on luggage. See members8.tsukaeru.net/muddy/single8/single8_e/AX100_e.htm for a look at Single-8 cameras.

Leicina Special: Don't let the simple shape fool you

The Ernst Leitz Company is well known for its Leica cameras. The Leicina line of 8 mm and Super 8 mm cameras aren't as well known, but they're beautiful examples of German craftsmanship. My favorite is the Leicina Special. This boxy looking camera with peculiarly positioned low-angle eyepiece captures great footage. Like the Beaulieu 4008, film speed is set manually. It accepts interchangeable M-Bayonet mount lenses, although most examples I've seen come with the same Schneider Optivaron f/1.8 6 - 66 mm zoom. These occasionally show up used for a few hundred dollars. Maintain it well and it should last a lifetime.

The Leicina Special accepts removable M-mount lenses, offering extreme flexibility and excellent image quality.
Photo: Benjamin Dietze

Nikon 8X Super Zooms occasionally sell on eBay for well under $50. They make a great first Super 8 camera. This one's shown with the hand grip folded up. Photo: Rick Palidwor

Nikon 8X Super Zoom: Solid design at a bargain price

Nikon made several beautiful Super 8 cameras. Their R8 and R10 models are highly recommended workhorses (the Super 8 feature film *Sleep Always* was shot with an R10 as the 'A' camera).

Since the R10 usually sells for a pretty penny, I'm going to introduce you to a different Nikon – the 8X Zoom. These little beauties often sell on eBay for under $50, making them a great bargain. Some people don't like the boxy styling, but I happen to find it quite easy on the eye. They're simple to use and feature good optics, too.

The 8X Super Zoom is compatible with Kodak's new Ektachrome 64T film stock, making it an excellent option as an everyday low-cost shooter.

The Nizo 801 Macro is not a small camera. Photo: Giles Perkins

Nizo 801: Classically styled and well equipped

I was dying to include one of the compact Nizo models on this list, but they can't automatically read Kodak Ektachrome 64T film. Their bigger brother, the Nizo 801, can. It's a high quality camera that typically sells for a few hundred dollars. It's big and bulky but capable of capturing sharp footage. Its somewhat small and gloomy viewfinder offers a nice split-image focusing system. A word of warning: the light meter uses a couple of oddball PX-13 button cell batteries. You can find modern replacements, but it won't be cheap.

A Russian Quarz 1x8 S-2 Kinoflex, with wind-up key visible on the side. Photo: Michal Jonca

Quarz 1x8 S-2: The Kinoflex

The Russian-made Quarz 1x8 S-2 (known in the USA as the Kinoflex) is the only clockwork Super 8 camera. It has a big fold-down silver winding key on one side. Quarz cameras often show up used at bargain basement prices. They offer versatile manual exposure control, too.

Make sure not to pay too much for one of these because their quality was notoriously variable. Some are great, some not so great. If you can find a good one for only a few bucks, snap it up – it should last forever.

Zeiss Ikon Moviflex MS 8:

Carl Zeiss optics make this a top-notch performer

I'm a huge fan of Zeiss lenses. I'm also a huge fan of their chunky little Super 8 cameras. Manufactured between 1970 and 1972, the MS includes a nice Zeiss Vario-Sonnar f1.9 / 9 – 36 mm zoom lens and supports 24 fps. The MS 8 features manual/automatic exposure control. You may find one of these selling cheaply simply because people are unfamiliar with the Zeiss brand in the 21st Century.

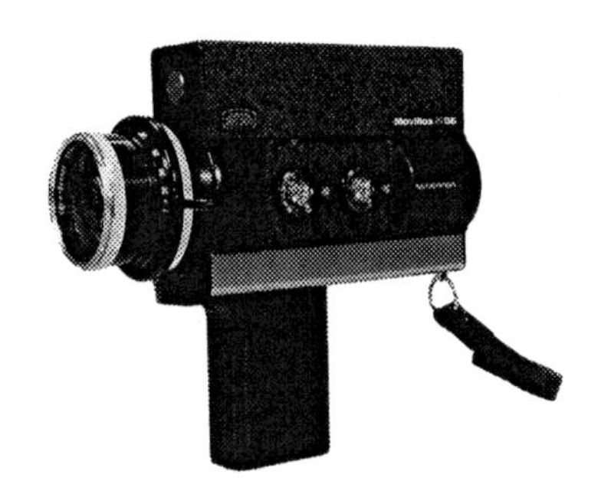

Zeiss Moviflex MS8. You can sometimes pick these up at bargain prices because of their boxy styling. Photo: Juergen Lossau.

Quick Start Guide To Filming

Most people have spent some time fiddling with a camcorder. The result is often a half hour of shaky home video peppered with eye-popping zooms and head-spinning back-and-forth 'swish' pans.

Luckily, Super 8 film doesn't give you the time to make many mistakes. A standard 15 m (50 foot) roll lasts 3 minutes and 20 seconds at 18 frames per second (fps), and two and a half minutes at 24 fps. It's important to make every second count. Here's a ten point guide to the basics:

1. Maintain & clean your camera

Before every shoot, make sure that your batteries are good and that the camera is fully functional. It's also a good idea to clean the film compartment and film gate (the metal window behind the lens). Be careful not to clean with anything that will leave a residue or particles of cloth behind.

2. Use a tripod

This is probably the most important secret to capturing good footage. Shaky hand-held shots are a dead giveaway that you're an amateur. It's useful to watch a film or two in the same style that you'll be shooting, paying special attention to how the shots are framed. Watch how the camera moves, follows the action and uses selective focus to control our eyes. If your shoot involves a great deal of action, borrow or rent a camera stabilizer. These devices support the camera while you're moving, giving you enormous flexibility. Be sure to practice.

3. Careful with the zoom lens

The trick to a good zoom? Don't do it. Here's a worthwhile exercise: Grab one of your favorite movies and some popcorn and spend half an hour or so watching it with the sound turned down. Pay attention to how the camera moves. You'll discover pretty quickly that most shots have very little movement. If the camera does move, it tends to slide back and forth quite gracefully using a wheeled dolly. How many times did the camera zoom in and out quickly? Unless you're watching a music video or kung-fu film, it probably didn't.

4. Plan your shots

It may sound obvious, but your films will benefit from consciously deciding what you're trying to achieve. We're often so swept up in the excitement of filming that we neglect to tell ourselves what the goal of the shot is.

5. Vary your shots

Film and television are close-up mediums. It makes sense to capture a few wide "establishing shots," but because of its relatively low resolution, Super 8 isn't good for panoramic, sweeping vistas.

6. Frame your images

Notice where the subject is in relation to others and check your backgrounds. There's nothing worse than shooting "the perfect take," only to discover later that there's a lamppost sticking out of an actor's head. Watch a few of your favorite movies and notice how the cinematographers frame shots: in a close-up, the actor's eyes usually fall about 1/3 of the way down the screen. Be careful not to leave empty space between an actor's head and the top of the screen. It's called headspace, and leaving too much is a sure sign of an amateur.

7. Use interesting camera angles and perspectives

Nothing is more boring than a static shot taken from eye-level. Try shooting from ground level, or from above or below to add emotional impact. Be careful not to impart unintended meaning to your shots.

8. Celebrate variety

Include interesting scenes and transitions that involve movement and action. They can be difficult to block out and film, but they can have a big effect on your audience. Make sure that the effects support the script rather than detracting from it, though.

9. Pace your film

Make sure each shot is long enough, but not too long. You can always edit a scene later. If you shoot too long, you'll simply waste film.

10. Focus, focus and re-focus

We've been spoiled by auto-focus camcorders and digital camera. In the old days, everything had to be done by hand. The best way to learn? Practice framing and focusing without actually shooting film. Spend a few minutes trying to capture the action at a local soccer game, or shooting cars driving by. Filmmaking is a learned ability, and the more shooting the better.

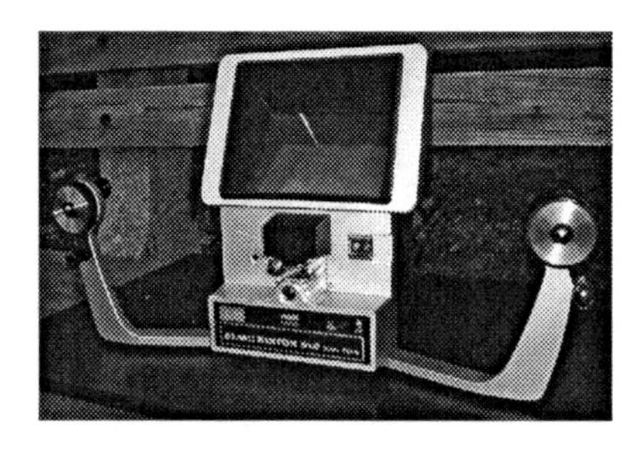

The Elmo Editor 912 is an excellent Super 8 film viewer and editor.

Super 8 Film Viewers

Film projectors require considerable space for setup and projection. If you're looking for a quick and easy way to view your film, consider purchasing a desktop film viewer. These little systems have a small backlit screen that's perfect for reviewing and editing your reversal (projection) footage after you get it back from the lab.

I own a sturdy little Elmo 912 viewer, but Goko and Minette also made excellent examples. They're usually inexpensive – well under $100 – and often appear on the used market in good condition. They can be a tad hard to find on the garage sale/pawnshop circuit, though.

Super 8 Projectors

I don't project my film. It's shot with the intention of transferring to video and editing electronically. I'll admit that I don't know much about Super 8 projectors, but here are a couple of words of advice.

1. Try to stay clear of dual-format Regular 8 mm/Super 8 mm projectors unless you really need the ability to project the old Regular 8 format as well. A projection path capable of handling both formats may not be as reliable as a well-built machine designed to handle only Super 8.

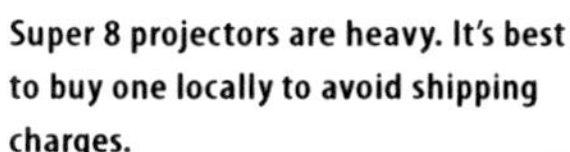

Super 8 projectors are heavy. It's best to buy one locally to avoid shipping charges.

2. Make sure you can get spare projection bulbs because they have a tendency to burn out at the most inopportune times.

3. Projectors are great big heavy things. Rather than shopping on eBay, check Craigslist [www.craigslist.org] or the classifieds. If you're not picky about make or model, you'll probably be able to pick up a decent projector at a bargain basement price. And you'll save a small fortune on shipping.

4. If you're planning to transfer your film to video, do it before projecting it. Projecting your film is guaranteed to add a few scratches and some dust. It's also possible for the film to slip, damaging a few sprocket holes.

Super 8 Odds & Ends

Muplet Projector – Toy Super 8

The Muplet is a tiny hand-cranked battery powered Super 8 projector from the 1970s. Brilliantly low-end.

The Muplet was an incredibly cheap (in every sense of the word) battery-powered Super 8 film projector. An Italian company produced them in the early 1970s. In an attempt to keep the price as low as possible, they used a plastic hand crank for advancing the film. Muplets were infamous for accidentally scratching your film, and the projected image was neither bright nor clear. But forget those minor annoyances – they're awesome fun.

Retro Enterprises in Japan received a shipment of 22 Muplets in late 2005. They're asking 9,800 Yen ($85) for units in excellent condition. Projectors in slightly damaged packaging cost 7,800 Yen ($70), but condition cannot be guaranteed. Packages of five replacement projection bulbs are available for 1,200 Yen – just over $10. [film.club.ne.jp/english/englishindex.html]

Telecine: Converting film to video

Telecine is the process of converting film to video. Professional Telecine is performed using expensive high-resolution digital scanning equipment and can cost upwards of $300 per hour. I don't recommend this type of service for amateurs and beginning filmmakers. If you shoot reversal (projection) film, you can make do with less expensive transfers using a computer and modified projector, such as the Moviestuff Workprinter (below). Workprinter transfers to miniDV (digital camcorder) tapes typically cost around $10 per 50 foot reel. Once you have your footage converted to miniDV, it can be edited using any popular digital video editing program on your PC or Macintosh.

See www.onSuper8.org for an up-to-date list of Telecine and film transfer services.

Moviestuff Workprinter

Super 8 moviemaking is fun and the end result can be spectacular. As an added bonus, you're guaranteed to turn heads wherever you shoot.

The Moviestuff Video Workprinter XP is an excellent way to convert Super 8 film to digital video.

There is a dark side, though. After getting your film processed, you're faced with the choice of cutting and splicing film by hand (ugh) or transferring it to digital video so you can edit it on a computer. Professional film-to-video conversion is expensive – expect to pay a few hundred dollars for each hour of film you transfer.

Moviestuff in Houston, Texas has a solution – the Video Workprinter. The Workprinter is a film projector that has been modified to offer frame-by-frame digital capture. Instead of simply projecting film on a screen and videotaping the result, Moviestuff equipment digitizes each movie frame sequentially using a digital camcorder connected to a Windows or Macintosh computer.

Almost 2000 units have been shipped, with prices starting at $1295 for a 'Jr.' model (capable of processing one frame per second) or $1395 for a faster XP unit (6 frames per second). [www.moviestuff.tv]

Amazing movie camera books

As a kid, I was amazed by the amount of information crammed into each volume of the encyclopedia (boy, do I sound like a geek). I get the same feeling when admiring Juergen Lossau's *Complete Catalog of Movie Cameras* ($49.95). It includes over 1,500 color photos and lists about 4,000 different vintage camera models across 480 pages. Each of the major manufacturers is given their own chapter loaded with history and fascinating anecdotes. The tome measures a reasonably compact 8.3" x 6.3", so you can read it almost anywhere.

This is the second movie camera guide written by Lossau – the first was released about 30 months before this volume. He's also written similar volumes detailing projectors and film splicers. If

A pair of excellent movie camera books from Juergen Lossau. He's also written volumes on projectors and splicers.

you're a die-hard collector, I'd suggest picking up the other books as well. They're not cheap, but they're beautiful.

Lossau's books are printed in German and English. The translation is awkward at times, but it's easy to overlook such a minor fault when faced with so many amazing pictures and stories. I couldn't find either book at the large on-line retailers, but you can order direct from the publisher – international shipping is included in the price.

The Complete Catalog of Movie Cameras - $49.95 incl. shipping [Atoll Medien, Hamburg – www.atollmedien.de]

Small Format Magazine

Film is an endangered species; it's estimated there are only 20,000 serious Super 8 shooters left. To raise the profile of the format and keep it alive, a German publisher is introducing *small format*, an English version of their 50 year-old German moviemaking magazine. To be successful, they apparently need 1000 subscribers. That's a lot of people for such a small community.

If you're interested in filmmaking or think you might be, buy a copy of the magazine for $10. And if you like it, subscribe. [Visit www.smallformat.de for subscription details]

[Disclosure: I recently joined the editorial staff of small format. I decided that the best thing I could do to support the magazine was participate in its production. So far, so good!]

16 mm Motion Picture Cameras

I tried to restrict the scope of this chapter to Super 8 mm film, but it looks like a handful of beautiful 16 mm and Single-8 cameras snuck in.

Even though they tend to be a bit more expensive and challenging than their Super 8 brothers, 16 mm cameras capture beautiful high-resolution images. I decided to include a handful in this book as a reminder that film can compete quite effectively with modern High Definition video.

Amateur motion picture cameras have been around since the 1920s, when Kodak introduced the 16 mm *Cine Kodak* camera and Kodascope projector. Back then, filmmaking was the domain of the wealthy: the original Kodak package came bundled with a tripod at a price of $335 – about the same cost as a Ford Model-T automobile.

Eventually, other more economical film formats followed. The most popular was double-run Regular 8/Standard 8 film which captured images on half of a 16 mm roll of film. The film was then flipped and reloaded into the camera to expose the other half. This format required filmmakers to handle and thread little light-sensitive reels of film.

Bolex: Clockwork cameras in the 21st Century

Swiss manufacturer Bolex is one of the last remaining makers of 16 mm film cameras. They occupy only a small portion of the old Bolex building, and these days they produce a mere few dozen cameras per year. In fact, most of their business comes from the repair of vintage Bolex and Eumig equipment.

The Bolex H-16 came in many slightly different styles. This is an RX-3 model with three lens turret from the mid 1960s.

Bolex was founded in 1927. The company gained international attention with the introduction of the Bolex H-16 self-threading 16 mm movie camera in 1935. They went on to produce cameras for several film formats, but failed to make a dent in the enormous amateur Super 8 market that emerged in the late 1960s. Austrian giant Eumig purchased the company in 1968 and used the historic Bolex logo to re-brand their own equipment. All the while, the Bolex division quietly continued production of H-16 cameras.

After the collapse of Eumig in 1981, Bolex once more became a self-sufficient enterprise focused entirely on the production and repair of 16 mm cameras. Most modern Bolex H-16's are electrically-powered EL units, but it's still possible to buy a brand new spring-operated SBM model – expect to get around 20 seconds of shooting time from each wind.

Prices start at about 5,460 Swiss Francs ($4,250) for the H-16 SBM mechanical body, lens not included. Several companies offer Super 16 widescreen modifications for a broad range of H-16s produced from the early 1960s onwards. When modified to shoot Super 16, these elegant old workhorses become wonderful tools for shooting modern music videos, outdoor films, animation and high-quality shorts.

H-16 cameras were produced in quite large numbers over a long period. As a result, it's quite easy to find nice examples of older mechanical H-16s at extremely good prices. Keep your eye on photo swap meets, estate sales, and garage sales in established communities and you might find yourself the lucky owner of one of these beauties. [www.bolex.ch]

Ikonoskop A-Cam SP-16: Camcorder-sized filmmaking

The Ikonoskop A-Cam SP-16 is just about the smallest Super 16 camera possible.

Professional movie cameras are extremely expensive precision gadgets. It's not uncommon for them to cost more than a nice luxury car. Amateur and independent filmmakers often have to rent forty year-old Arriflex, Bolex or Eclair 16 mm cameras while making their breakout films on a shoestring budget. Shooting Super 16 (wide-screen) usually isn't an option.

Swedish newcomers Ikonoskop decided to tackle the problem head-on by producing the smallest, lightest, least expensive Super 16 camera possible. They did away with luxuries such as a through-the-lens reflex viewfinder and built-in video tap. The result was the diminutive A-Cam, priced at 4,950 euros ($6,250).

The A-Cam is designed to be hand-held and accepts industry-standard 100 foot (30 m) daylight film spools. To keep costs down, it accepts standard interchangeable C-Mount lenses. This little camera isn't quiet enough to shoot synchronized sound, but thanks to built-in crystal timing it can easily be used to shoot music videos, commercials, and experimental films. The picture quality is well matched to the demands of HD television. Be sure to check out the DVD-quality sample footage on the Ikonoskop site.

Hopefully, camera rental houses will make these available to budding young filmmakers at decent prices. Just remember me when you're famous. [www.ikonoskop.se]

Aaton A-Minima: Chasing perfection

I know perfection is subjective, but the Aaton A-Minima is a brilliant little moviemaking device. It weighs a mere 5 lbs, somehow appears classic and bleeding-edge at the same time, and shoots top-notch Super 16 images. Of course, perfection has its price – a basic A-Minima costs around $15,000. If you find the price tag shocking, consider that most other professional motion picture cameras run $50,000 plus. Very few indie filmmakers actually own equipment like this; it would be financial suicide. Instead, they rent the best gear they can afford and shoot quickly.

The Aaton A-Minima is an extremely portable professional Super 16 camera. While it's a tad noisy for close-up sound shooting, it works very well in documentary and 'B' camera settings.

The A-Minima accepts 200 ft (60 m) spools, giving just over 5 and one half minutes of shooting time per roll. It's almost quiet enough to capture synchronized sound, and light enough for a lone cinematographer to handle without a crew. This makes it a popular choice for documentaries and hand-held shorts.

Just in case you're wondering why you'd go to the trouble of shooting film instead of HD video: It looks absolutely stunning in comparison. Super 16 transfers extremely well to digital (for editing), and offers considerably wider exposure latitude than video. Besides, it already has the "film look" that videographers are always trying to imitate. By the way, if you're feeling generous, I'd love one for Christmas.

Krasnogorsk 3: 16 mm filmmaking on a budget

Soviet manufacturers had a certain knack for making incredibly rugged mechanical things. The incredibly affordable Krasnogorsk 3 is a great example of rugged Soviet simplicity. This spring-powered 16 mm camera was manufactured until the early 1990s. It accepts standard Kodak 100 ft 'daylight load' film spools (which can be loaded in subdued lighting) and includes a built-in electric exposure meter and through-the-lens viewfinder.

Most K-3s in North America and Europe have a Pentax M-42 lens mount, but you occasionally see the older Russian bayonet mount, too. As far as I'm aware, the bayonet is not compatible with any Western lens system, so check before you buy.

A full wind of the hand-cranked clockwork motor will give you about 25 seconds of shooting time – more than enough for most scenes. It should come as no surprise that something that looks like a tank sounds like one, too. The K-3 in action reminds me of a shoulder-mounted sewing machine. Don't expect to go unnoticed as you shoot with this beastie.

Many film schools in the USA purchased K-3s for student use in the early 1990s because of their low cost and utter simplicity. Now that video has become omnipresent, it's getting harder to find these devices in an academic setting.

A shot of the Krasnogorsk 3 16 mm movie camera showing the film feed path. Many filmmakers remove the film guides and load the film manually for more reliable operation.

There always seem to be one or two K-3 kits for sale on eBay in the $100 range. Many are sold direct from Russia, and it is impossible to assess the mechanical and optical condition of the camera before you part with your money. Also, be warned that shipping from Russia is an expensive and unpredictable process. To make things even more of a crap-shoot, late model K-3s often exhibited a surprising lack of quality control. It's not uncommon to discover mis-calibrated film transports, rough edges, and small imperfections in the glass.

If you're seriously considering the purchase of a K-3, my recommendation is to buy a serviced and calibrated example from a reputable dealer in your country. Expect to pay around $750 in the USA for a 'new-old-stock' K-3 kit – including Pentax-mount f/1.9 17 - 69 mm zoom lens, shoulder stock, lens filters, and cable release – in ready-to-film condition.

Kiev USA (www.kievusa.com – 203-531-0900) offers new-old-stock K-3 'plus' cameras in North America, along with a fabulous collection of other Russian photography equipment. These have been looked over by a camera technician and carry a warranty.

An esoteric selection of strangely appealing household essentials and gadgetry.

Household Retro Stuff

I'm not a huge style and furniture buff, so this section is mercifully short. It includes a few of the more entertaining household items that have appeared on *retrothing.com*. I'm a huge fan of Mathmos Lava Lamps, so their new Space Projector has me enthralled. The same goes for the stunning chrome Tix toaster, and I'm even strangely attracted to the weird and whacky world of British Teasmade automatic alarm clock/tea makers.

Let's start with a household appliance that helped to define the latter half of the 20th Century – the lowly telephone. I'll take mine with rotary dialling and a bell ringer, please.

Telephones

The invention of the telephone ushered in the age of instant communication. Until its arrival, the fastest way to communicate was Morse telegraph, which was cumbersome and expensive. If you wanted more personal communication, letters were your only real option. These days, nearly everyone has a mobile phone stuffed in a back pocket in addition to a home line, and I suspect more and more people will give up traditional hard-wired service as the price of mobile communication continues to fall.

Until the 1970s, only the telephone company was allowed to install handsets in your house. You were tethered to the wall by the phone cable, and ring tones were limited to the sound of a piercing bell at various volumes. It's quite easy to pick up refurbished (or even new) phones from the 1950s and 1960s, and it's not that hard to install a modern modular plug. I guarantee that a vintage set will turn heads.

Western Electric Model 500

Remember these? The Western Electric Model 500 phone vanished with the arrival of do-it-yourself phone installation.

My new mobile phone arrived with a bunch of iffy ring tones preinstalled. The one that puzzled me the most sounds like an old-fashioned telephone ringer played through an AM radio. I heard it recently on the train and noticed how my seat-mates jumped. Perhaps it subconsciously reminded them of the days before the Internet, texting and voice mail – when we actually had to talk to callers.

If you're hunting for a classic phone set, check out www.oldphones.com. They have some brand new military surplus Western Electric Model 500s. The Model 500 was introduced in the 1950s and millions were made in a multitude of colors before being supplanted by the touch-tone Model 2500. These $65 desk phones have been rewired with modular line cords and come in shades of white, black, beige, or brown that are guaranteed to clash with every bit of furniture purchased in this century.

It's a shame that more pseudo-organic devices like this haven't been built. They last for ages and recycle easily.

Gfeller Trub

Here are a few words from Retro Thing contributor Giles Perkins about his beautiful wooden phone: "It's a Swiss design classic from the 1970s made entirely from Rosewood by Gfeller, the communicator of choice for tree huggers everywhere. From its perfectly balanced handset to the sturdy and functional base, Trub is a truly organic piece of technology. Its wooden construction breathes and changes according to the seasons, its distinctive grain becoming more tactile and prominent in damp weather.

Even after thirty years, with an occasional polish Trub looks as good as the day it was hewn from its parent tree trunk. Without a doubt, Trub is the King of telephones, but if you want one you'll be in for a long and patient wait. Long discontinued, the Trub is highly sought after, its fate being sealed after celebrity enthusiasm in the UK saw the final few evaporate into eager collector's hands."

Art Thang: Restored telephone classics from Argentina

Art Thang founder Russell Johnson has a simple philosophy for finding timeless treasures. He travels to "countries that were prosperous at the beginning of the last century." His travels took him to Argentina, where he dug up a treasure trove of Swedish-made Ericsson Bakelite telephones.

These have been carefully restored with up-to-date wiring and a new microphone capsule. They not cheap – $385 – but they are the real thing. Art Thang offers a variety of other models from the 1920s through the 1960s. See www.artthang.com for a sinful collection of ringing things.

Nortel Classics

The Nortel Contempra phone set included either a rotary or touch-tone dial in the handset. These were once as common as snowballs in Canada.

Nortel is 100 years old, founded in 1895 as Northern Electric and Manufacturing. The company was involved in many technological breakthroughs of the Telephony Era – the first dial system built in Canada, a 1950s electromechanical switch that allowed push-button dialing, and even the first all-digital system. These days they produce a variety of behind-the-scenes equipment and are best known to the public for their incredibly complicated office telephone systems – the type that allow you to accidentally blast conference call attendees into hyperspace at a touch of the wrong button.

Nortel (then Northern Telecom) created the first dial-in-hand telephone set – the Contempra – in 1968. Prior to this, the dialing mechanism was built into a desk or wall-mount set and phones tended to be regarded as dull appliances rather than fashion statements. They went on to sell 3.4 million of these indestructible phones and forever changed telephone design. One striking thing about the Contempra line was their distinctive rainbow of bright colors, driven by advances in manufacturing and lower plastic costs.

Contempra sets are still quite common – they show up regularly at garage sales and chances are that someone you know has one lurking in the basement or tucked away in a dusty attic. They're easy enough to clean up and put back into service, and there were nine colors to choose from, ranging from fire-engine red to garish mauve.

Mathmos – Lava Lamps to Space Projectors

Mathmos invented the Lava Lamp in 1963. The idea came from watching an egg timer in which a glob of oil rose to the top when sufficiently warm. These days, Mathmos Lighting UK produces an astounding variety of odd lamps.

The Mathmos Space Projector is a device that belongs in the sci-fi classic *Barbarella*. It conjures "constantly moving chaotic images" on walls and ceilings by shining a 20 W spot lamp through a color wheel filled with oil. They're available in violet/red, violet/green, and blue/red combinations to suit the mood of the party.

If you drop by their site, be sure to check out the five current Lava Lamp designs, along with their selection of strange squeezable rubber Bubble lamps. Never thought I'd find myself writing about squeezable rubber. Sigh. [Visit www.mathmos.co.uk for tons more psychedelic craziness.]

The Mathmos Space Projector uses oil-filled color wheels to project psychedelic mayhem on any convenient flat surface.

Incandescent light bulbs and the future

The incandescent light bulb is usually attributed to Thomas Alva Edison. This is probably because he was the first to successfully market them through his wee startup company, General Electric. Reality is not that simple; dozens of inventors produced (and patented) incandescent light bulbs in the 1800s, and Heinrich Goebel created the first modern carbon-filament bulb in 1854. Somehow, this little fact is omitted from most American history books.

Incandescent bulbs are simple to make but they waste a lot of energy as heat. White LEDs (light emitting diodes) are being hailed as a potential successor – they're tiny, robust, and extremely efficient. The C. Crane Company now offers a range of ultra-efficient VIVID LED light bulbs which use a small fraction of the power required by their incandescent cousins. They're also really expensive, starting at $34.95. Such is the price of progress. [www.ccrane.com]

C. Crane's LED light bulbs are expensive, but they're much more efficient and long-lasting than traditional incandescents.

Furniture

So Happy Chair

I am a fashion fraud. My entire knowledge of interior decorating can be summed up in two words: IKEA Catalog. That won't stop me from bleating about the pseudo-retro So Happy Chair from Italy's Max Design. It's available in a rainbow of colors, but my

The So Happy Chair is guaranteed to bring a smile to even the grumpiest of friends.

humble opinion is that happy faces were meant to be yellow. To prove my taste must have some merit, this little bum pod won the Chicago Anthaneum *Good Design Award.* They're approved for outdoor use and are stackable if you're thinking of buying a dozen for your phone booth sized loft.

The modern smiley face was popularized by two brothers – Bernard and Murray Spain – in the fall of 1970. Bernard drew the cheerful little guy, and his brother helpfully added the dippy 'have a happy day' tagline. It's guesstimated that over 50 million buttons, cards and trinkets were churned out before the smiley fad died in 1972. [Available from www.gordoninternational.com]

Gerbol Beanbags

A couple of things attract me to Gerbol's beanbags: They're enormous and they come in a multitude of coverings such as faux Cheetah, rabbit, porcupine, alligator and even boring old denim blue. I think the pictured design is Brown Italian Wolf, but it could be Lonely Lama, too (I'm obviously not an experienced predator). I'm saving my pennies for Baby Snow Leopard. They feature 20" zippers – apparently a good feature – and are washable, because accidents do happen.

A Gerbol beanbag would go perfectly with an evening of yakking on your Northern Telecom Contempra phone, don't you think?

Gerbol has been known to offer free shipping in the UK and 50% off worldwide shipping. Stuffing not included (North Americans: Wal-Mart sells huge bags of stuffing at almost unbeatable prices). They also mutter something about getting a "free Gerbol Pouf" with the really large bags. I'll leave that to your imagination.

Gerbol beanbags are available on the web at www.gerbol.co.uk or at Camden Lock Market, Camden Town, London every Saturday & Sunday.

Foof Chairs

Beanbags ran rogue across the planet in the 1970s and 1980s. Fast-forward a couple of decades and their kids are set to reconquer the Earth.

Foof chairs look like beanbags, but they're not. Traditional beanbags are filled with lumpy foam peanuts that compress over time, lowering you uncomfortably to the floor. Not so with Foofs. They're filled with a patented urethane foam that doesn't break down over time and can be "re-foofed" as required. The result is what they claim "may just be the most comfortable chair on Earth."

It may look like a beanbag, but it's actually a Foof. A completely different soft furniture species, y'see.

Their line offers a truly astounding variety of squishy furniture: basic beanbags, cubes, stars, pillows for watching TV, massive multi-person foofs and even soft fruit. If you're looking for compressible furniture, this is the place to be. [www.comfortresearch.com]

Appliances – Toasters and Other Fun Stuff

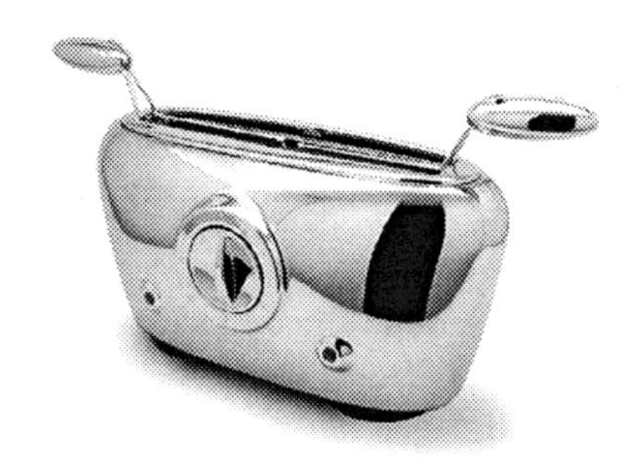

It's hard to believe that such a beautiful device could be designed to burn bread.

Tix Toaster

The Tix Toaster by Italian designer Luca Trazzi is absolutely stunning. So stunning, in fact, that I'd probably starve to death staring at it instead of making lunch. According to Marianne Rohrlich of The New York Times, "It grills sandwiches to perfection, with two hinged baskets that slightly squeeze everything together for a result that's somewhere between the usual grilled cheese and a panini...Of course, the machine also makes perfect toast."

What more could a man want? Well, except for a billion dollars and a personal chef to do the toasting. [www.viceversa.com]

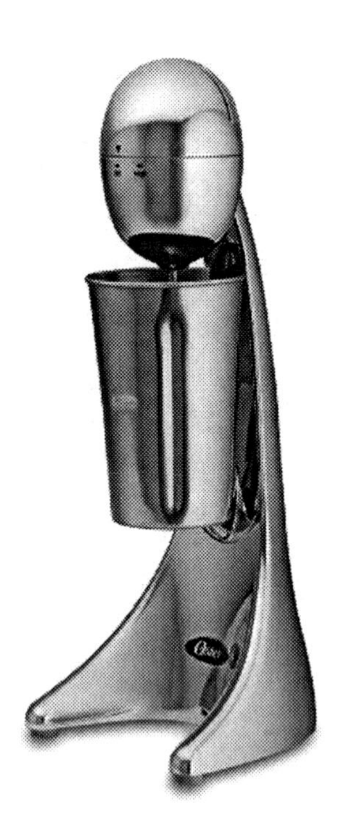

This Oster milkshake machine is so beautiful that it would be a shame to actually use it.

Oster Milkshake Machine

I have a three year-old who loves milkshakes. Strawberry flavored, to be precise.

His sweet tooth started me wondering about milkshake mixing machines. I remember watching chromed mixers whirring away on the back counter of the local family restaurant back in the late 1970s.

Oster makes a really nice looking $60 two-speed chromed mixer. It features a 28 oz. mixing cup and a whirry little 100 Watt motor. I know I could just use a blender, but this will be much more exciting for a kid. [www.oster.com]

Straight Blade Razors

I've always been fascinated by straight razors. I occasionally nick myself with a safety razor (albeit one with three blades), so I'm not sure I have the manual dexterity to reliably guide a sharpened bar of teflon-coated stainless steel across my face. I'm willing to try, though.

DOVO of Solingen, Germany manufactures some of the most beautiful straight razors I've ever seen. Their site is a bit light on comprehensible content (even in the "English" version), but there are some great pictures in the Shaving and thinning instruments section. A basic stainless steel model starts at about $75, but exotic models are available in the $400 range. The perfect gift for the surgeon in your life. [www.dovo.com]

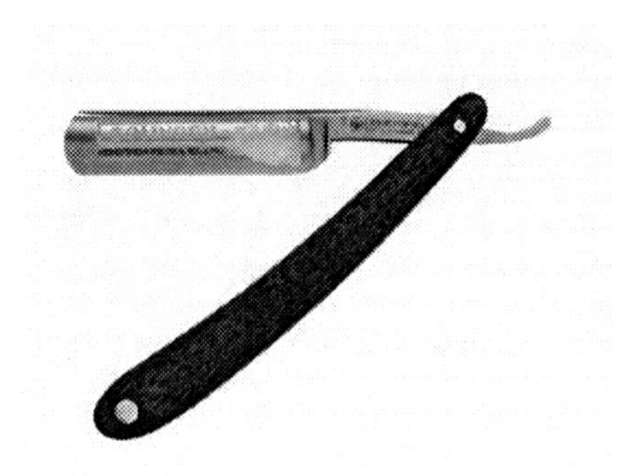

Terrific Teasmades

Making tea has always been an art form for the British. My dad used to let his tea bag soak in milk and sugar for a few minutes before steeping a cupful. Sadly, I gravitate toward coffee or fizzy sugar water instead.

The Teasmade is an automatic teamaker/alarm clock, designed to cheerfully ensure that you have a cup or two of scalding brown water available as soon as it wakes you. They typically feature tacky analog clock faces built into the side of a kettleish thing. And – to my great delight – their designers were completely stark raving mad; metal spouts emerge at crazy angles from the back, electric alarm clocks are grafted awkwardly to the front and a lamp shade usually balances on top of it all.

It goes without saying that there are hundreds of rabid Teasmade collectors out there who snap up vintage Goblins, Pifcos and even the occasional Ecko Hostess at the drop of a tea bag. Find out more than any sane individual would ever want to know about these odd little things at www.teasmade.com/models.htm.

Vintage toys offer the chance to escape from daily life into a wonderful childhood world of discovery and imagination.

Classic Toys for Modern Fun

Vintage toys cast a spell over me like none other. Perhaps it's because they offer the opportunity to escape from daily life into the wonderful childhood world of discovery and imagination. Whatever the reason, I often find myself wandering the back streets of the Internet, enthralled by specialist toy shops and the online museums of die-hard collectors.

Some of today's injection molded plastic toys are ingenious, but they can't hold a candle to the simple elegance of a classic wind-up tin train or robot, nor can clever computerization match the elegant aerodynamics of a well-made kite. The next few pages chronicle a few of my favorite toys – tin robots, model rockets, LEGO and even a mischievously modern slingshot.

An affordable Schylling reproduction of the famed Japanese Lilliput robot.

Tin Robots & Model Kits

In the 1950s, shortly before Japan became a technological powerhouse, they made toys. Robots, to be more precise. Companies such as the Yoshiya Toy Company and Nomura Company pumped out gazillions of cheap windup tin robots which were eagerly bashed and dented to smithereens by children everywhere. These days, the precious few that remain are expensive collector's items that fetch hundreds or thousands of dollars.

The $95 wind-up walking Hex Head Robot from Metal House Toys is one of a new breed of well-made Japanese tin robots. It's an original design, but you can also find reproductions of classic robots – such as a $159 limited edition of Nomura's original 1955 Radar Robot on their site [www.neatstuff.net/space-robots]. These little guys are great fun, fantastic collector's items, and a wicked way to terrify the dog.

Schylling tin toys

Schylling was founded 30 years ago in Rowley, Massachusetts. They offer a mix of retro-styled classic toys and brand new inventions. By far my favorite Schylling products are their stunning line of tin toys. This is the place to come if you're seeking a reproduction of the Lilliput tin robot, believed to be the first tin robot made in Japan.

The real thing would fetch tens of thousands at auction, but the reproduction is a mere $15.99 through their online store. If you're more into cars, they offer tin recreations of the Blue Bird and Sunbeam land speed record cars, too. They even come in retro-style boxes. See www.tintoys.com for details.

Airfix model kits

I built dozens of Airfix plastic models as a child. They marketed a line of small kits that were always just out of reach to a child with limited pocket money. The company was founded in 1939 to produce inflatable rubber toys. They entered the world of plastic model manufacturing almost by accident. In 1948, Airfix was asked to build a scale model of a Ferguson tractor. Faced with a limited budget, they offered it as a do-it-yourself kit molded from acetate. Their next kit, a model of Sir Francis Drake's ship *The Golden Hind*, was released in 1952. They followed this success with the release of a scale Supermarine Spitfire fighter plane that solidified their place as Britain's top model maker. Airfix was sold to hobby manufacturer Humbrol in 1986 and continues to market plastic model kits today. Visit www.airfix.com to view their current lineup.

A Wallace & Grommit Airfix model. A far cry from their roots as a maker of plastic ships and aircraft.

Space Guns: Mark Bergin Toys

I'm a vintage kid hiding in an adult body. Maybe that explains why I was visibly tingling with nostalgic excitement after discovering Mark Bergin Toys. His site displays more vintage space guns than I ever thought I'd find in one place. The collection includes a Dan Dare Cosmic Raygun, Atomic Orbiter-X sets, Ultra Man (ahh... it's sold!) and Rex Mars space pistols, along with literally dozens of other Atomic Age space weapons. There are no prices posted and most of the items are in their original packaging, which means I probably can't afford any of 'em. That won't stop

Oh, how I wish I could visit a toy store in the early 1960s. This is a cool little Rex Mars Planet Patrol Atomic Pistol.

me from dreaming about the Atomic Space Pistol, though. [Hide your credit card before visiting www.bergintoys.com]

Pedal cars & Ride-on toys

LIKEaBIKE harkens back to the days before battery-powered devices stole our children's attention. I would have loved one of these as a kid.

LIKEaBIKE

The little LIKEaBIKE traces its roots to the Draisienne (hobby horse) invented by Baron Karl von Drais in the early 19th Century. The hobby horse was a primitive wooden bicycle with two in-line wheels, handlebars, and a saddle. It lacked pedals, though – you had to scamper along energetically with both feet. The LIKEaBIKE site suggests the Baron used it to traverse the royal gardens, but other sources suggest he rode it while collecting taxes from tenants. I bet they did their best to camouflage potholes when he was due for a visit.

Let's fast-forward a couple of centuries. In 1997, a father in southern Germany came up with the idea of building miniature Draisiennes for his kids, and the LIKEaBIKE was born. It was love at first sight for parents (and children) everywhere, and the Mertens family formed a company to manufacture the clever almost-bike. They're made from beech or birch plywood with a hard wax coating. Some are equipped with air-filled pneumatic tires, while others have solid rubber tires that won't mark interior floors. The saddle is adjustable to suit kids up to six years old. Safety is carefully engineered into the design – the steering is damped with felt strips that keep munchkins from crushing inquisitive fingers between the fork and frame.

If you pick one of these up for a little person, remember to buy a helmet. [www.likeabikeusa.com]

Pedal planes

I'm always disheartened by the number of not quite good enough cheap plastic toys in shops. My little guy has a beaten up twenty year-old metal tricycle and loves it. Regrettably, not many of today's toys will survive that long.

The all-metal Red Baron pedal plane. Just remember that you need two for a good backyard dogfight.

Airflow Collectibles is trying to change that. Their all-metal pedal toys aren't cheap, but they look built to last. This $529 Red Baron pedal plane is 45" long, with a padded pilot's seat and a propeller that spins when you pedal. As a kid, I would have gladly surrendered my entire marble collection for one of these. [www.airflowinc.net]

Creative Toys

LEGO's 50th anniversary

LEGO crawled out of the primordial ooze a half century ago. The studded plastic block was created in 1949, but it wasn't until the 1950s that the familiar stud-and-tube coupling system we all know and love was developed. Before that, the blocks were apparently prone to catastrophic collapse without warning.

Here are some official LEGO stats for your amusement:

>> More than 400,000,000 children (and adults) will play with LEGO this year, spending five billion hours at their play.

>> On average, every person on Earth has 52 LEGO bricks.

>> The LEGO Group is the world's largest tire producer, with an annual production of 306,000,000.

>> You'd need a column of approximately 40,000,000,000 LEGO bricks to reach the moon.

>> The first LEGO wheel arrived in 1961, predating the evolution of LEGO people by 13 years.

>> LEGO MINDSTORM robotic products were a joint venture between the MIT Media Lab and LEGO.

>> LEGO structures are not waterproof. I learned this the hard way as a 10 year-old home aqueduct builder.

Visit www.lego.com to check out their latest releases.

Meccano sets

This modern 30-In-One Meccano set offers the same thrill that the original did 100 years ago.

Meccano-like mechanical toys first appeared in Liverpool in the late 19th Century. Inventor Frank Hornby patented his metal nut & bolt assembly kits and started marketing Meccano in 1907. His toy construction sets became extremely popular and additional factories were opened in Germany and France. Ownership of the company changed hands a few times over the decades – it was even owned by cereal maker General Mills for a few short years in the early 1980s. These days, Meccano is part of the Japanese Nikko group. And, almost 100 years after their humble beginning in Liverpool, they still manufacture metal construction sets, along with modernized plastic versions. [www.meccano.com]

Slot Cars & Train Sets

Scalextric slot cars

This Renault is just one of Scalextric's popular Formula One offerings.

Scalextric slot cars were introduced at a British toy fair in 1957. They became an instant sensation and the manufacturer was unable to keep up with demand. After changing hands several times, the Scalextric brand is still going strong 50 years later. They had a tough time in the late 1980s, but recovered nicely with a huge range of cars and track systems.

For the uninitiated – slot cars race in pairs along snap-together polyethylene tracks which have a couple of parallel grooves to provide electricity, offering wicked speed in a tiny package. Prices start at around £50.00 for a complete set (my eye is on the Porsche vs. Audi package). Available in specialty toy stores. [www.scalextric.com]

Lionel electric trains

Electric train sets remain popular, but they had a hard time competing in the age of videogames. Part of the difficulty is that precision-made trains sets are expensive to manufacture, resulting in stratospheric prices that only adult collectors can afford.

Three Norfolk & Western J-Class engines were put into service in 1950. They were the last 4-8-4's built in America, until Lionel introduced this O-Gauge reproduction.

One of the most famous toy train names is Lionel. Joshua Lionel Cowen founded the company around 1900. The rise and fall of his company mirrors the emergence of suburbia in North America. Lionel enjoyed considerable success throughout the first half of the 20th Century, until the advent of suburbanization and the rise of the transcontinental trucking industry. As trains faded from public view, so did their mystique. Modern diesel-electrics were no match for the romance of 1940s vintage steam flyers.

Lionel fell on hard times in the 1960s, but has staged a comeback in recent years. Complete O-Gauge sets are available starting at $199.99, including an engine, rolling stock, power transformer and rails. Be warned that this is an expensive pastime – it's not unusual to pay $150 for a reproduction engine – but it can develop into a satisfying lifelong hobby. [www.lionel.com]

Paya tin trains & cars

Clockwork toy trains were immensely popular before the introduction of electrically powered sets. Spanish tinsmith Rafael Paya created his first tin toys in 1902 and his sons built the first toy factory in Spain four years later. In 1985, Lino Paya made the decision to reintroduce limited editions of their classic toys. This is a re-issue of a 1930 wind-up car that I find immensely alluring. Perhaps it's the draw of a finicky old-fashioned clockwork motor that attracts me.

Paya made a brilliant selection of toy cars, like this 1986 reissue of their Model 970 that was originally released in 1930.

Paya is now defunct, but their toys are widely available from specialists and collectors worldwide. Visit www.toytent.com for a selection of vintage Paya toys like the Model 970 pictured on the right.

Lynxmotion Robot Kits

The Lynxmotion Hexapod 3-R robot includes 18 servo motors and, thanks to its round shape, can walk in any direction with ease.

Every evil Empress needs an army of drones to do her bidding. I learned that early in my dating career. These days, the neighborhood royalty will most likely build a mechanized force to dominate their suburban enclave. Lynxmotion.com offers a mind-boggling array of robot kits, parts, and software to facilitate the construction of the cyber-army of your dreams.

I was originally browsing their site in search of a cool robot arm (don't ask), but was quickly distracted by the humanoid biped you see here. Apparently, he's built from odds-and-sods available in their servo erector set. They have dozens of cool kits: bipeds, quadrapods, and hexapods. No tripods, though.

Flying Toys

The Estes Alpha III Starter Set is a fantastic introduction to model rocketry at an incredibly affordable price.

Model Rocketry: Estes solid propellant fuels a fad

Rocketry has been around in one form or another for thousands of years, but modern model rocketry became a craze in 1958, when Estes introduced solid-propellant model rocket engines. These offered safe and consistent propulsion and Estes began selling complete rocket kits in 1960. The company still exists today, although model rocketry has fallen in popularity since its heyday during the 1960s Space Race.

I got my start in rocketry fifteen years ago with an Estes kit that included the rocket, launch pad, launch control, and a couple of engines and igniters. They still manufacture it – the Alpha III, available for less than $20. [On the web: www.estesrockets.com]

Quest Tomahawk model rocket

Apogee offers a rather impressive and affordable model of the Tomahawk Cruise Missile. Agents from the Department of Homestyle Security should be tromping through my door in mere moments. Before they get here, check it out.

The affordable $14.82 Quest Tomahawk SLC kit is available from Apogee Components. They stock a full range of model rocket kits, software, engines and other mysterious gizmos. Don't forget to pick up a launch pad and some rocket motors, too. A Quest C6-5 motor should propel this beast about 590 ft (180 m) high.

If you're more interested in designing your own rocket vehicle, Apogee offers RockSim design and simulation software to test your ideas for stability and performance. It's free for the first 30 days, $99.95 after that. [www.apogeerockets.com]

The Quest Tomahawk SLC is capable of climbing almost 600 ft. No guarantees about how easy it will be to retrieve, though.

Stunt kites

Flying things are fantastic. Flying things that don't require fuel or electricity are even more amazing. Kites have existed in one form or another for thousands of years – the earliest written records refer to bird-like designs created in China around 400 B.C.

Modern kites come in many shapes and sizes. Most people remember playing with diamond-shaped single line models when they were young, but there are literally dozens of designs available – box shaped, soft airfoils, and multi-line sport and fighting kites.

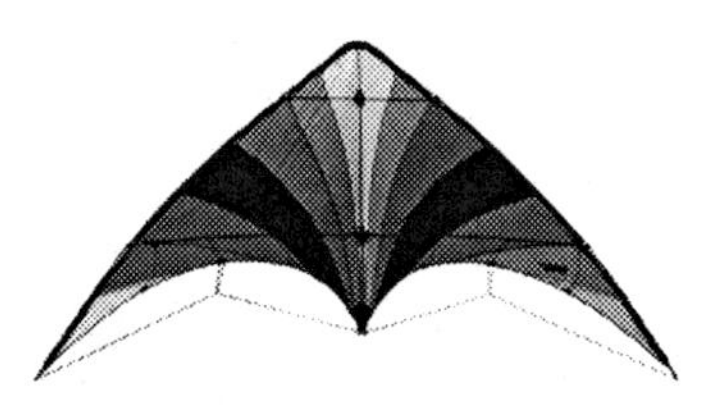

The New Tech New Jam is a $79 stunt kite based on the Jam Session, one of the most popular freestyle kites ever made.

Stunt (sport) kites interest me most. Unlike old-fashioned single-line designs that go wherever the wind takes them, sport kites include up to four control lines and can be flown with incredible precision. They're normally made from extremely light-weight nylon with durable but featherweight carbon fibre spars.

Wind Power Sports Kite Store (www.windpowersports.com) sells hundreds of different kite models. Expect to pay around $50 for a good beginner's stunt kite, plus another $25 to $50 for flying line and a winder. These will help you to explore the basics of the sport – turns, controlled landings, crashes and unassisted ground launches.

Radio controlled blimps

The Mach IIIz America radio controlled helium blimp includes three directional thrusters for excellent indoor control.

As far as I know, no one makes personal blimps. I've been anxiously waiting for a couple of guys in Amherst to get one off the ground, but they're still sewing away on the prototype. These things have a way of becoming either a runaway success or the lead story on CNN.

In the meantime, I'll keep myself entertained with the more reasonable indoor variety. My favorite flying toys come from Canada's Draganfly, located in Saskatoon – about 1500 miles east of Vancouver. Their Mach IIIz helium blimp is available in several neat designs, although I haven't a clue why a Canadian company is pimping the American flag. Shouldn't it be a giant grinning beaver?

The Mach IIIz uses a three channel radio remote to control three thrusters, theoretically allowing you to avoid ceilings, walls, and the occasional shotgun blast. It's available in silver, yellow, the Goodyear logo, or an American flag. They're currently on sale for a mere $77.95. I think I'm going to e-mail them about the grinning beaver right now. [www.draganfly.com]

Bladerunner indoor electric helicopter

This is a great way to try out radio controlled flight without investing hundreds of dollars in a fragile and hard-to-fly aircraft.

I struggled while trying to come up with a Retro excuse for including this little helicopter. Rest assured that flying toys have existed for thousands of years and even Galileo toyed with helicopter designs.

Maybe it's just me, but the Bladerunner R/C helicopter looks like the perfect way to while away dreary winter evenings. It weighs a mere 50 g (1.7 oz.) and the main rotor measures 29 cm (11.5ish inches) in diameter. *Radio Control Helicopter Magazine* picked it as their Best Beginner aircraft in the Winter 2006 issue.

What makes this gnat of an aircraft so easy to fly is its unique dual counter-rotating rotor system, controlled by a full 3-axis R/C transmitter. The electric motor is powered by a tiny rechargeable LiPo battery pack. All that's required to power the transmitter is a single 9 V battery.

Here's the lowdown from the Bladerunner FAQ: "The controls are similar to high-end model helicopters so the Bladerunner is great for learning to operate those horrendously expensive models without making a huge dollar commitment. The Bladerunner is built to withstand minor crashes such as bumping into walls and furniture. The tail rotor is intentionally very small in order to keep the forward / backward speed low - thus making the helicopter easy to fly and to give you lots of time to react. The ring around the small tail propeller is a safety feature, but it also slows down the speed of the tail propeller to keep the forward / backward speed low." [www.interactivetoy.com]

To tempt you even more, Draganfly [www.draganfly.com] has the original Bladerunner Mark I for a mere $69.95 (there's apparently a new model in the works), and refurbished units are available for under $40. I bet Harrison Ford would love one for Christmas *[update: Harrison Ford owns one. Ali Jafri of Interactive Toys tells me they were on the set of his upcoming movie Firewall. He apparently got to take one home. Lucky Movie Star!]*

Laser-sighted slingshots

I purchased my first slingshot at the tender age of ten. I remember promising the shopkeeper that I wouldn't use it in town – an easy commitment to keep, since I lived half an hour down the road. Back then, the idea of a cheap battery powered laser was the stuff of science fiction. Everything is laser equipped in 2005; laser-sighted carpentry tools are everywhere and annoying little laser pointer keychains are available for next to nothing.

The PS-52 slingshot features an open sight, just like a gun. It offers elevation and horizontal adjustment to assure precision accuracy.

The time was obviously right to equip slingshots with laser sights. Precision Shots offers the $49.95 PS-52 – apparently accurate enough to hit a pencil from 20 feet (not that 20 ft is particularly far). Twenty dollars more gets you the PS-55, which adds a red-dot sight to make targeting even more accurate. Just remember: never shoot anything at your sister. I did, and she won't let me forget it. [www.catsdomain.com]

EBay Tips and Tricks

eBay is a fantastic resource for discovering, researching, and buying vintage gear. I often while away an hour or two browsing through vintage cameras and synthesizers. I even make a purchase every once in a while, although my wife gets really nervous when I start paying too much attention to old gizmos online.

All is not gold in Paradise, however. Buying and selling vintage equipment involves a great deal of trust. None of this stuff is on-warranty anymore, and if it arrives broken, chances are you'll have a hard time finding someone to fix it at a reasonable price. Unscrupulous sellers occasionally "forget" to mention defects or missing parts, so make sure you read descriptions carefully and ask lots of questions along the line of "Does it work perfectly?"

Here are a few hints to improve your eBay experience:

1. There's no point in bidding until the end of an auction. It drives up prices and gets you involved emotionally.

2. Use "swiping" software. See www.snipeswipe.com – it allows you to choose the maximum price you'd bid for an item, and then places your bid when there are only a few seconds left in the auction. It works exactly the same way as if you were to sit waiting until the last second to bid, without requiring you to waste your time.

3. If possible, find a couple of the same item to bid on. This helps you to avoid a "I must have it at any price" bidding frenzy.

4. Ask questions. If you don't get answers or you don't like the tone of the answers, don't bid.

5. Bid on items offered by sellers with a decent amount of strong positive feedback. Avoid sellers with single digit feedback or more than one or two negatives. Be careful with sellers with 1000+ feedback – they're probably brokers who are shovelling merchandise through the door without really knowing what they're selling.

6. Bid on items by people who seem to know what they're talking about, and who have tested the item. The excuse "Untested because I don't know how this works" is sometimes a cover-up for selling broken items.

7. If a deal seems too good to be true, it probably is.

8. Items with large pictures are helpful. They allow you to see scratches, missing or chipped parts, and other possible problems. A tiny photo can hide a lot of imperfections.

9. Start small. Better to learn the ropes with a few $20 items than blow hundreds on a bad learning experience. Look for bargains. They are there if you look hard and get lucky.

10. Items listed as "available internationally" do not always show up on the various national sites, because the organization of the sale categories are sometimes different. For example, movie cameras on eBay.com are categorized differently than on eBay.de, where they are split out by film format. If you're willing to pay higher shipping charges, it makes sense to check out the various international eBay sites.

11. Check shipping costs. Some shippers are very fair and charge exact postage, while others pad the price with handling fees or really high international fees. A good seller will estimate the cost to ship to you if you're serious about bidding.

Good luck and happy bidding!

Conclusion: Why old stuff is sometimes the best stuff

Even though we rarely notice, the products we use are created by skilled industrial designers. Their job is to make impossible ideas real. At the same time, they have to come up with designs that look good and can be manufactured profitably. Sadly, the rush to outpace the competition and provide 'better' products causes nothing but headaches for these folks.

This is a far cry from the past, when technological limitations often prevented inventors from taking shortcuts that would have made a great product merely ho-hum. Manufacturers also had a simpler range of materials to play with back then. These days, it's out of the question to churn out hand-made wooden cases for everyday things, but that was the norm 100 years ago; early Kodak Brownie cameras were built around simple wooden boxes, as were RCA Victrola gramophones.

Examples of almost-good-enough modern design are everywhere:

My DVD player shipped with a 44 button remote, yet many important buttons are arranged in a grid of almost identical rubber dots. Oh, and the large buttons arranged like navigation buttons aren't actually for navigation. Cheap to make, does everything, but impossible to use.

My mobile phone has more computing power than most micro-computers did 20 years ago. It e-mails, photographs, browses the web, and plays games. Is it easier to use than my last one? Not a chance.

It's hard to find modern machines that do one thing and do it well. Which is surprising, since such gadgets often thrive in the marketplace. A case in point: the ubiquitous iPod. Even a child can figure out (and enjoy) the clickwheel interface. Its design is the antithesis of most electronic devices; sparse and simple. And it works.

And let's design in some good controls. I spend significant time filming with 30 year-old movie cameras. Even though they require manual focusing and zooming, they're easier to use than modern point-and-shoot camcorders. Why? Because they offer immediate physical feedback – I twist the lens to zoom, rather than pressing a button that sends a signal to a microcontroller that activates a motor that moves the lens. Physical immediacy equals mental immediacy.

My plea to designers is this: Look back on the past to rediscover what made some devices such classics. Oh, I know there were a few clunkers along the way, but there were also some amazing gems. And if you want to be really successful, streamline your products. Create single-use appliances that help us to work quickly. Design in tactile feedback rather than touchscreens and menus – we love real knobs, levers, and switches, especially if they're made out of something other than cheap plastic. And say no to the marketing department's endless list of gee-whiz features that look great on specification sheets, but languish unused.

Simple is good. It reminds us of the way things were.

Acknowledgements

A book like this relies on the wisdom, advice and support of many people. I had the desire to write *Essential Retro* several years before I actually put pen to paper, but I was initially blinded by the sheer quantity of vintage technology. It took a long time to realize that the secret of this book was to draw from personal experience. The result is decidedly quirky and eclectic, but I hope that's part of its charm.

To keep myself motivated while penning *Essential Retro*, I created *retrothing.com*, a web site that highlighted hundreds of the gadgets you see here. Bohus Blahut deserves mention for his dedicated work as co-author of the site, and special thanks to A-list bloggers Peter Kirn and Tom Whitwell for welcoming *retrothing.com* onto the Internet – your support helped to get the word out about my Retro quest far better than I could have managed alone.

Thanks to Karen Kemppainen for pointing out that I'd forgotten 8-Tracks entirely, Henning Mortensen for convincing me that pinball should be in the next edition, Zack Vex for responding to my queries almost instantaneously, and Dr. Steve Reyer for letting me use photos of the Regency TR-1 radio from his personal collection. Last moment thanks to Peter Hirschberg, Rick Palidwor, Michal Jonca and small format editor Juergen Lossau for their pictures. And Giles Perkins earns my sincere thanks for shooting a much-needed photo mere hours before the final deadline. Some images in this book came from my collection or the archives of iStock International in Calgary, but dozens of manufacturers and collectors contributed as well. Thank you all.

About the author

James Grahame is CEO of Reflex ASI, a consumer electronics company. His obsession with classic gizmos led him to start *retrothing.com*, a successful web site dedicated to vintage gadgetry. He is also on the editorial staff of *small format*, a European magazine focused on small format moviemaking. James lives in Western Canada with his wife and young son.

He encourages you to visit *retrothing.com* for a glimpse of even more classic gadgetry and vintage technology.

Index

Symbols

A

B

C

M

N

O

P

R

S

T

U

V

W

X

Y

Z

Lightning Source UK Ltd.
Milton Keynes UK
UKOW01f0751260914

239227UK00005B/105/P